Organ Preludes

Supplement

by

Jean Slater Edson

The Scarecrow Press, Inc.
Metuchen, N.J.   1974

This present work constitutes a supplement to Edson's Organ
Preludes: An Index to Compositions on Hymn Tunes, Chorales,
Plainsong Melodies, Gregorian Tunes and Carols; Volume I--
Composer Index; Volume II--Tune Name Index; Scarecrow Press,
1970 (L. C. card number 73-8960; ISBN 0-8108-0287-2).

Library of Congress Cataloging in Publication Data

Edson, Jean Slater.
   Organ-preludes; an index to compositions on hymn
tunes, chorales, plainsong melodies, Gregorian tunes
and carols.

    CONTENTS.--v.1. Composer index--v.2. Tune name index.
-- ---Supplement.
    1. Organ music--Bibliography. 2. Organ music--
Thematic catalogs. I. Title.
ML128.06E4 Suppl.   016.7868'3'52   73-8960
ISBN 0-8108-0287-2
ISBN 0-8108-0663-0 (Suppl.)

To

GRELLET COLLINS SIMPSON

good friend and wise counsellor

TABLE OF CONTENTS

PREFACE

As I wrote in the "Preface" to Organ Preludes: "This work is not a finished product, but a beginning, a foundation for further research. It presents only a picture of work in progress and a plea for corrections and additions." This Supplement is an attempt to continue the work, fill in some of the gaps and correct any mistakes that have been brought to my attention.

One point that I should like to re-emphasize is that in compiling the Index I did not intend to include all editions of a composer's works. The purpose is to find out which tunes a composer has used in his compositions, not how many publishers have printed the compositions.

Two areas of concentration in the Supplement have been the French Noëls and Scandinavian music. A great help for the former was Rouher's book of 450 Noëls; the Swedish Music Information Center (STIM) supplied a great deal of information on the latter. Where I have been in doubt about a Scandinavian tune, I have entered those that are in the Swedish, Norwegian or Danish Hymnals. I have not put in cross-indexings for the slight differences in spelling in these languages--use your imagination!

The same format, abbreviations, etc., are used as in the original two-volume Index. Where a tune is already in the Index, I have placed an asterisk in the right-hand column rather than reprinting the incipit. There are six exceptions to this: for the tunes Albano and Intercessor I have given the corrected versions. For Glaed dig, du Kristi Brud, the variant was so different from the original tune that I have entered the variant. For three others: Heilige Namen, Puer Natus Est Nobis and Salve Regina, the only way of identifying which of the tunes in the Index was referred to was to reprint the tune.

When I use the word "Index" I refer to the original two-volume edition of Organ Preludes (Scarecrow, 1970). When I use the word "Supplement" I refer to this present volume.

The lists of additional information and corrections to the Index which appear in an Appendix at the end of this volume are, I hope, self-explanatory.

I have put them in several different categories for ease of reference.

Once again I want to thank the staff of the Music Division of the Library of Congress for their patience with my many requests and their help in locating music. I want also to thank Richard Rancourt, Claude Duvall and DeWitt Wasson for their help with recently published compositions. A special note of thanks goes to Per Olaf Lundahl of the Swedish Music Information Center in Stockholm for his valuable assistance with Swedish music, and to Jane and Paul Pfeiffer for their careful and patient proof-reading.

As a background to the whole work, I want to thank Karl Halvorson, Minister in Music at All Souls Church, for the inspiration which his musical scholarship and his ability to produce truly creative worship music have given me.

ORGAN PRELUDES SUPPLEMENT

COMPOSER INDEX

Aahlen, Waldemar   Swedish   1894-

Postludier (ed. Runbaeck and Aahlen)-------------------------Nordiska
 Vol. 1:
  "Vilken kaerlek oss bevisad"
 Vol. 2:
  "I denna ljuva sommartid"
  "Paa dig jag hoppas, Herre kaer"
  "Vaken upp! en staemma bjuder"
 Vol. 3:
  "Jag gaar mot doeden var jag gaar"
  "Jag lyfter mina haender"
  "Nu tystne de klagande ljuden"
Introitus Preludier (ed. Runbaeck and Aahlen)------------------ Nordiska
 Vol. 1:
  "Av himlens hoejd"
  "Bereden vaeg foer Herran"
  "Dig, min Jesu, nu jag skaader"
  "Du kom till oss av himlen ned"
  "Glaed dig du Kristi brud"
  "Jag lyfter mina haender"
  "Med pelarstoder tolv"
  "Nu segrar alla trognas hopp"
  "O Gud, det aer en hjaertans troest"
  "O Jesu Krist, du naadens brunn"
  "Om Kristus doeljes nu foer dig"
  "Till haerlighetens land igen"
 Vol. 2:
  "Allt maenskoslaektet"
  "En gaang doe och sedan domen"
  "Gud aer haer tillstaedes"
  "Hoer, Gud aennu sin naad"
  "Min sjael, ditt hopp till Herran"
  "Min synd, O Gud"
  "Mitt vittne vare Gud"
  "Naer vaerldens hopp"
  "O maenniska, glaed dig och prisa din Gud"
  "Oss kristna boer tro och besinna"
  "Si Herrens ord aer rent"
  "Tiden flyr: naer vill du boerja"

Aahlen, Waldemar (cont.)

> "Till dig jag ropar, Herre Krist"
> "Vad gott kan jag dock goera"
> "Vak upp, bed Gud om kraft och mod"
> "Vi bedje dig, sann Gud och man"

Aamodt, Thorleif

> 3 Koralpreludier -- Lyche
> (melodies by L. M. Lindeman)
>   "Kirken den er et"
>   "Som torstige hjoert (Lindeman)"
>   "Min sjel, min sjel, lov Herren (Lindeman)"

Aekerberg, Herman   Swedish

> 50 Koralpreludier (out of print) ----------------------------- Nordiska

Ahlberg, Verner   Swedish   1896-1967

> Koralfoerspel "Haerlig aer jorden" ------------------------mss. STIM'S

Ahrens, Josef   German   1904-

> Cantiones Gregorianae pro Organo --------------------------- Ed. Schott
> Vol. 1:
>   "Agnus Dei"
>   "Credo In Unum Deo"
>   "Et Incarnatus Est"
>   "Gloria in Excelsis Deo (Mode 8)"
>   "Ite Missa Est (Gregorian)"
>   "Sanctus"

Alain, Jehan   French   1911-1940

> Variations on "Lucis Creator (Mode 8)" ------------------------- Leduc

Alberti, Johann Friedrich   German   1642-1710

> 80 Chorale Preludes by German Masters of the 17th and
>   18th Centuries (ed. Keller) -------------------------------- Peters
>   "Herzlich lieb hab' ich dich"

Albrecht, Moonyeen Brown

> Consoliere: Vol. 1, #6 ---------------------------------------WLSM
>   Let All Mortal Flesh ("Picardy")

Albrechtsberger, Johann Georg   Austrian   1736-1809

> 4 Fugen (ed. Biba)---Doblinger
>   "Christus ist erstanden"
>   "Komm heiliger Geist mit deiner Gnad"

Albright, William

> Chorale Partita "Wer nur den lieben Gott" ------------------Elkan-Vogel

Allgen, Claude L.   Swedish   1920-

Chorale Preludes--mss. STIM'S
   "In Dulci Jubilo" (2)   "Vaar blick mot heliga berget gaar"
   "Jag hoeja vill till Gud"   "Veni Sancte Spiritus (Old Church)" (2)
   "O Haupt voll Blut"

Alnaes, Eyvind   Norwegian   1872-1932

Orgelbearbeidelse -- Norsk
   "Den store hvite flokk (Norwegian)"

Altman, Ludwig   American   contemporary

Consoliere, Vol. 3, #3------------------------------------- WLSM
   Meditation Song ("Wach auf, wach auf, du deutsches Land")

Andersson, Reinhold   Swedish   1894-1960

Introitus Preludier (ed. Runbaeck and Aahlen)----------------- Nordiska
   Vol. I:
       "Det gaar ett tyst och taaligt lamm"
       "O du, som gav ditt liv foer faaren"
       "Vad ljus oever griften" ("Hvad lyus oefver graeften")
   Vol. II:
       "Ack, laatom oss lova och bedja vaar Gud"
       "Aat dig, O Gud, som allt foermaar"
       "Fader, jag i detta namn"
       "I dag om Herrens roest du hoer"
       "Min sjael, ditt hopp till Herran"
Koralfoerspel (ed. Andersson and Norrman)------------------- Nordiska
   "Ack bliv hos oss"
   "Bereden vaeg foer Herran"
   "Dig, Helge Ande, bedja vi"
   "Dig skall min sjael sitt offer"
   "Dig vare lov och pris, O Krist"
   "Din klara sol gaar aater opp"
   "Din spira Jesu straeckes ut"
   "Ditt namn, O Gud, vill jag lova" (2)
   "Ditt verk aer stort"
   "Fader, jag i detta namn"
   "Foerlossningen aer vinnen"
   "Helige Ande, lat nu ske"
   "Herre signe du och raade"
   "Hur froejdar sig i templets famn"
   "I denna ljuva sommartid"
   "I himmelen (Swedish)"
   "I hoppet sig min fraelsa"
   "I moerker sjoenko lycho droemmens"
   "Jag vet paa vem jag tror" ("Jeg ved paa hvem")
   "Jesu, djupa saaren dina"
   "Min synd, O Gud"
   "O Gud, ditt rike ingen ser"
   "Si Jesus aer ett troestrikt namn"
   "Sion klagar med stor smaerta"
   "Tig dig allena"

Andersson, R. (cont.)

 "Till dig jag ropar" ("Til dig jeg raaber")
 "Upp Psaltare och harpa"
 "Vaar Gud aer oss en vaeldig borg"
 "Vad ljus oever griften (Jesperson)"
 "Vad min Gud vill"
 "Var haelsad skoena morgonstund"
 "Vi tacke dig, O Jesu god (Swedish)"
Postludier (ed. Runbaeck and Aahlen) ------------------------Nordiska
 "Herre signe du och raade"
 "O Jesu, naer jag haedan skall"
 "Som den gylne (Schop)"

Andriessen, Hendrik   Dutch   1892-

 6 Communion Pieces by 6 Dutch Composers--------------------- WLSM
 Meditation on "O Lord with Wondrous Mystery"
  (in this Great)

Anjou, Hjalmar   Swedish   1882-1965

 Introitus Preludier (ed. Runbaeck and Aahlen)-----------------Nordiska
 Vol. 1: Koralpreludium "Jesus, aer min haegnad"

Anonymous (Buxheimer Liederbuch) (15th Century)

 Cantantibus Organis, Vol. 8--------------------------------------- Pustet
 "Christ ist erstanden (Folk)"
 Liber Organi VIII ---------------------------------B. Schotts Soehne
 "Christ ist erstanden (Folk)"

Anonymous (Sweelinck School)

 Sweelinck: Opera Omnia, Vol. 1, Fascicle II --- Ver. voor Nederlandse
 "Psalm 60 (Dutch)"   Musiekgeschiedenis

Archer, J. Stewart   English   1866-

 Christmas Album--- Paxton
 Variations on a Noël

Armsdorff, Andreas   Austrian   1670-1699

 80 Chorale Preludes by German Masters of the 17th and
  18th Centuries (ed. Keller) ----------------------------- Peters
 "Komm, Heiliger Geist, Herre Gott"

Arnatt, Ronald K.   English-American   1930-

 Preludes for Hymns in the Worship Supplement (ed. Thomas)--Concordia
 "Westminster Carol"
 3 Plainsong Preludes---------------------------------------H. W. Gray
 "Divinum Mysterium"
 "Victimae Paschali"
 Variations on a Theme by Sowerby----------------------H. W. Gray
 "Palisades"

Asma, Feike   Dutch   1912-

Muziek voor Kerk en Huis------------------------------------ Basart
   "Heer, ik hoor" ("Even Me -Bradbury")
   "Roept uit aan alle Stranden"
   "Song 83 (Dutch)" ("Kommt Seelen")
   "Song 107 (Dutch-Bach)"
Orgelbok van de Enige Gezangen---------------------R. R. Ganzevoort
   "Avondlied" ("Die Tugend wird durch's -Halle")
   "Berijming van de 12 Artikelen"
   "Eere zij God"
   "Hemelvaartslied"
   "Het Kruis"
   "Old 100th" (Veni Creator Spiritus)
   "Psalm 118 (Geneva)" (De hoop der Zaligheid)
   "Slotzang" ("Song 297--Dutch")
   "Song A (Dutch)" (Tien Geboden)
   "Song B (Dutch)" (Lofzang van Maria)
   "Song C (Dutch)" (Lofzang van Zacharias)
   "Song D (Dutch)" (Lofzang van Simeon)
   "Song E (Dutch)" (Vater Unser)
   "Song H (Dutch)" (Voor de Predikatie)
   "Song I (Dutch)" (Morgenzang)
   "Song L (Dutch)" (Avondzang)
   "Song 1 (Dutch)"
   "Song 32 (Dutch)"⎫
   "Song 43 (Dutch)"⎬ (Goede Vrijdag)
   "Song 50 (Dutch)" (Het sterven)
   "Song 62 (Dutch)" (2) (De Opstanding)
   "Song 76 (Dutch)" (Pinksteren)
   "Song 89 (Dutch)" (Halleluja)
   "Song 96 (Dutch)" (Ein feste Burg)
   "Song 132 (Dutch)" (Te Deum)
   "Song 153 (Dutch-Huet)"
   "Song 173 (Dutch)"
   "U heilig Godslam"

Asola, Matteo   ?-1609

Cantantibus Organis, Vol. 8----------------------------------Pustet
   "Victimae Paschali"

Bach, Johann Christoph   German   1642-1703

Orgue et Liturgie, #24, Notre Père------------------Schola Cantorum
   "Vater Unser"
80 Chorale Preludes by German Masters of the 17th and
   18th Centuries (ed. Keller)------------------------------Peters
   "Aus meines Herzens"
   "In dich hab' ich (Leipzig)"
   "Mit Fried und Freud"
   "Wenn wir in hoechsten"
   "Wie schoen leuchtet"

Bach, J. Michael   German   1648-1695

80 Chorale Preludes by German Masters of the 17th and
   18th Centuries (ed. Keller) ------------------------------Peters

Bach, J. M. (cont.)

   "Wenn mein Stuendlein"

Baden, Conrad   Norwegian   1908-

   Partita over "Den Herre Krist i doedens baand"----------- private pub.
   29 Koralforspill av Norske Organister (ed. Sandvold)-------------Norsk
   "Hjerte loeft din (Steenberg)"
   "Jeg ser dig, O Guds Lam (Norsk Folk)"
   "Korset vil jeg aldrig (Folk Tune)"

Balbastre, Claude   French   1727-1799

   L'Organiste Liturgique----------------Ed. Mus. de la Schola Cantorum
   Vol. 55-56: Livre de Noël III
      "Noël - A minuit fut fait (Lorrain)"
      "Noël - Comment tu oses petite Rose"
      "Noël - Divine Princesse"
      "Noël - Fanne coraige, le diale â mor"
      "Noël - Il n'est rien de plus tendre"
      "Noël - Je rends graces à mon Dieu"
      "Noël - Laissez paître vos bêtes"
      "Noël - Noei vén, j'aivon criai"
      "Noël - O jour ton divin flambeau"
      "Noël - Or nous dites Marie" ("Chartres")
      "Noël - Qué tu grô jan, quei folie"
      "Noël - Quel désordre dans la nature"
      "Noël - Qui a ce peu machuret"
      "Noël - Si c'est pour ôter la vie"
      "Noël - Vé noei Blaizôte"

Balderston, Mahlon   American

   Noël Symphonique---J. Fischer
   "Adeste Fideles"
   "First Nowell"
   "Stille Nacht"
   "Three Kings"

Bangert, Emilius   Danish   1883-

   95 Forspil till Salmemelodier-------------------------------Boesens
   "Aldrig er jeg uden vaade (Horn)"
   "Alene Gud i himmerik"
   "Av dypest noed (Phrygian)"
   "Av hoeiheten oprunnen er"
   "Bryt frem, mit hjertes (Zinck)"
   "Den signede dag (Weyse)"
   "Den tro som Jesum"
   "Fra Himlen hoit" ("Vom Himmel hoch")
   "Fryd dig du Kristi Brud (Regnart)"
   "Frykt mit barn" ("Da Christus geboren")
   "Gjoer doeren hoei" ("Old 100th")
   "Gud skal all ting (Crueger)"
   "Guds soenn er kommet" ("Es ist das Heil")
   "Her ser jeg da et lam (Strassburg)"
   "Hvad kan oss komme (Klug)"

Bangert, E. (cont.)

"Hvo ene lader (Neumark)"
"I Jesu navn (Kingo)"
"Jeg vil mig Herren love (Zinck)"
"Jesu, dine dype vunder" ("Freu dich sehr")
"Jesu er mitt liv i live" ("Alle Menschen - Wessnitzer")
"Kirken den er et"
"Kjaere Guds barn (Folk)"
"Kom, Hellige Aand, Herre Gud (Walther)"
"Med sorgen og klagen"
"Med straalekrans om tinde (Vulpius)"
"Min Sjel, min Sjel (Kugelman)"
"Nu beder vi" ("Soldau")
"Nu hjertelig jeg langes" ("Herzlich tut mich verlangen")
"Nu hjertelig jeg langes" ("Valet")
"Nu hviler mark" ("Innsbruck")
"Nu rinner solen op (Zinck)"
"O Fader vaar" ("Vater Unser")
"O Hellig Aand (Strassburg)"
"O Herre Krist, dig til oss vend"
"O lad din Aand (Rung)"
"Op al den ting (Freiburg)"
"Op alle som paa jorden (Herman)"
"Paa Gud alene (Zinck)"
"Sjaa han gjeng (Vulpius)"
"Som den gylne (Schop)"
"Til dig alene (Wittenberg)"
"Uverdig er jeg" ("Old 130")
"Vreden din avvend (Crueger)"

Barlow, Wayne   American   1912-

Preludes for Hymns in the Worship Supplement (ed. Thomas)--Concordia
    "Forest Green"
Voluntaries on the Hymn of the Week, Part 3----------------Concordia
    "Christ lag in Todesbanden"
    "Gelobt sei Gott (Vulpius)"
    "Herr, wie du willst (Strassburg)"
    "Ich dank dir schon (Praetorius)"
    "Komm, Gott Schoepfer, Heil'ger Geist (Klug)"
    "Komm Heiliger Geist, Herre Gott (Walther)"
    "Kommt her zu mir (Leipzig)"
    "Nun freut Euch (Nuernberg)"
    "St. Columba (Irish)"
    "Vater Unser"

Barr, John   Contemporary

How Brightly Shines the Morning Star--------------------- H. W. Gray
    "Wie schoen leuchtet"

Bartelink, Bernard   Dutch   1929-

Consoliere, Vol. 3, #4---WLSM
    Lo How a Rose ("Es ist ein Ros' ")

Baumgartner, Henry Leroy   American   1891-1969

"In Te Domine Speravi"-------------------------------------J. Fischer
Variations on Hymn Tunes of William Bradbury--------------- Abingdon
  "He Leadeth Me"
  "Olive's Brow"
  "Pleasant Pastures"
  "Woodworth"

Baur, Juerg   German   1918-

Choral triptychon "Christ ist erstanden (Folk)"--------------------B&H

Beck, Theodore   American   1929-

Preludes for Hymns in the Worship Supplement (ed. Thomas)--Concordia
  "Consolation (Wyeth)"
Sacred Organ Folio---Lorenz
  Vol. 1:
    Processional on Let Us Ever Walk With Jesus
      ("Lasset uns mit Jesu – Boltze")
  Vol. 3:
    "Alles ist an Gottes Segen"
    Prelude on "St. Cross"
    Prelude on "Southwell"

Belli, P. Giulio   Italian   1560-1613

Cantantibus Organis, Vol. 10--------------------------------- Pustet
  "O Bone Jesu"
  "O Sacrum Convivium"
  "Quem Vidistis, Pastores"
  "Salve Sancte Parens"

Bender, Jan   Dutch-American   1909-

4 Variations on "Down Ampney"-----------------------------Augsburg
"O God, O Lord of Heaven and Earth (Bender)"--------------Augsburg
Partita on "Vater Unser"----------------------------------- Augsburg
Preludes for Hymns in the Worship Supplement (ed. Thomas)-- Concordia
  "Christum, wir sollen loben"
Sacred Organ Journal, Nov. 1969----------------------------- Lorenz
  Prelude and Chorale on "Nun danket alle Gott"

Berg, Gottfrid   Swedish   1889-1970

Introitus Preludier (ed. Runbaeck and Aahlen)-----------------Nordiska
  Vol. 1:
    "Goer porten hoeg" ("Gjoer doeren hoej")
    "Han lever! O min Ande, kaenn"
    "Snabbt som blixten de foersvinna"
  Vol. 2:
    "Ack, saella aero de"
    "Helige Ande, sanningens Ande"
    "Naer vaerldens hopp fortvinat stod (Rhau-Vulpius)"
    "Som harpoklangen foersvinner"
    "Var kristtrogen froejde sig"

Berg, G. (cont.)

Koralfoerspel (ed. Andersson and Norrman)-------------------Nordiska
"Jesu aer min haegnad" ("Jesu, meine Freude")
"O Gud vaar Broder Abels" ("Durch Adams Fall")

Bermudo, Juan   Spanish   1510-1560

Orgue et Liturgie, Vol. 47---------------------------Schola Cantorum
5 Hymnen:
"Ave Maris Stella (Mode 1)"
"Conditor Alme Siderum"
"Pange Lingua"
"Veni Creator (Sarum - Mode 8)"
"Vexilla Regis (Sarum - Mode 1)"

Berruyer, G.

10 Pièces: Nouveau Répertoire d'Oeuvres Religieuses---Schola Cantorum
#6: Choral Varié - "Herzliebster Jesu"

Bevan, Gwilym J.   English

Metrical Psalm-Prelude on "Abbey"------------------------- Waterloo

Beverst, George E.

Variations and Chorales for the Church Year-------Sacred Music Press
"Herzliebster Jesu"
"Lasst uns erfreuen"
"Lobe den Herren, den"
"Nun danket alle Gott"
"St. Anne"
"So nimm, denn, meine Haende (Silcher)"
"Wie schoen leuchtet"

Bielawa, Herbert   American   1930-

Chorale and Fugue on "Lasst uns erfreuen"------------------- Abingdon
Consoliere, Vol. 1, #3--------------------------------------- WLSM
"Lyons"
4 Preludes on Hymns of the Church------------------------- Abingdon
"Dundee"
"Erhalt uns, Herr, bei deinem Wort (Klug)"
"O Sacred Head"
"Pange Lingua"

Biggs, John   American   Contemporary

Invention for Organ and Tape---------------Mss. (Santa Barbara, Cal.)
"Old 100th"
"Veni Creator Spiritus (Sarum - Mode 8)"

Bijster, Jacob   Dutch   1902-1958

Ricercare, Passacaglia and Partita on When I Survey---------Ars Nova
"Hamburg"

Bingham, Seth   American   1882-1972

6 Soft Pieces by 6 American Composers---------------------- WLSM
    Introit on "Elton (Mason)"

Binkerd, Gordon   American   1916-

2 Variations on "Jesu meine Freude"-----American Composers Alliance

Bjarnegaard, Gustaf   Swedish   1907-

2 Dalakoraler--Verbum
    "Kom, Helge Ande, till mig in"
    "Saa hoegt har Gud, oss till stor froejd"
Dalakoral "Min vilotimma ljuder (Thomissoen)"----------------Verbum
Nordiskt Orgelalbum (ed. Anjou)----------------------private printing
    Partita "Glaed dig, du Kristi brud"
Orgelpartita "Aera ske Gud, som fraan sin tron"-------------Gehrmans

Blake, George

Sacred Organ Folio, Vol. 3----------------------------------Lorenz
    Prelude on "Euroclydon (Torrance)"

Blanchard, William G.

Sacred Organ Folio, Vol. 3----------------------------------Lorenz
    Chorale Prelude "Come, Come, Ye Saints"

Bloch, Waldemar

8 Choraele----------------------------------- ---------Doblinger (1967)
    "Aus tiefer Not (Phrygian)"
    "Es kommt ein Schiff (Andernach)"
    "Herzlich tut mich erfreuen"
    "Herzliebster Jesu"
    "Meinen Jesum lass ich nicht (Ulich)"
    "O Lamm Gottes (Decius)"
    "O Traurigkeit"
    "Wie schoen leuchtet"
Variationen und Fuge ("Wachet auf")------------------------Doblinger

Bock, Fred   American   1939-

4 Hymns for Organ-------------------------------------Th. Presser
    "Lead Me To Calvary (Kirkpatrick)"
    "Pleasant Pastures (Bradbury)"
    "St. Agnes (Dykes)"
    "They'll Know We Are Christians (Scholtes)"
Organ Sounds for Worship-----------------------Sacred Music Press
    "Arlington"   "Regent Square"
    "Divinum Mysterium"   "St. Dunstan's"
    "Old 100"   "We Three Kings"
    "Passion Chorale"

Boehm, Georg   German   1661-1733

80 Chorale Preludes by German Masters of the 17th and

Boehm, G. (cont.)

18th Centuries (ed. Keller)------------------------------Peters
"Ach wie fluechtig"
"Freu dich sehr"
"Herr Jesu Christ, dich zu uns"
"Wer nur den lieben Gott"
Organ Masters of the 17th and 18th Centuries-----------------Kalmus
"Christ lag in Todesbanden"
"Christum wir sollen"
"Vater Unser"
"Vom Himmel hoch"
Orgue et Liturgie #24: Notre Père------------------Schola Cantorum
"Vater Unser"
Saemtliche Werke (ed. G. Wolgast)--------------------------B. & H.
Band I: Partita "Jesu, du bist allzu schoene"
(plus preludes listed in Index)

Boëly, Alexandre Pierre François   French   1785-1858

Les Maîtres Français de l'Orgue------ Ed. Mus. de la Schola Cantorum
(17-18 siècles)
"Adoro Te Devote"

Bond, Anders   Swedish   1888-

Koralstudier II--- Gehrmans
Partita "En Herrdag i hoejden"
Partita "Min vilotimma ljuder (Thomissoen)"
Meditation oever en dalakoral------------------------------Gehrmans
"Ett spel om en vaag som till Himla baar"
Orgelpartita "Jag nu den paerlan funnit har"---------------- Gehrmans

Bornefeld, Helmut   German   1906-

Choralvorspiele 1930/70 (ed. Haenssler)-----------------------Peters
"Allein Gott in der Hoeh"
"Allein zu dir"
"Auf meinen lieben Gott"
"Aus meines Herzens Grunde"
"Aus tiefer Not (Phrygian)" (2)
"Christ, unser Herr, zum Jorden kam"
"Du, meine Seele, singe (Ebeling)"
"Durch Adams Fall"
"Ein feste Burg"
"Froehlich wir nun all fangen an"
"Gen Himmel aufgefahren (Franck)"
"Herr Jesu Christ, du hoechstes Gut (Goerlitz)" (2)
"Herzliebster Jesu"
"Ist Gott fuer mich (Augsburg)"
"Jauchzt alle Lande" ("Psalm 118")
"Jesus Christus, unser Heiland, der von uns (Erfurt)" (2)
"Kommt und lasst uns"
"Mit Fried und Freud"
"Nun bitten wir"
"Nun sich der Tag"
"O glaeubig Herz (Praetorius)" (2)
"Vater Unser"

Bornefeld, H. (cont.)

    "Verleih uns Frieden"
    "Wachet auf"
    "Was Gott tut"
    "Wer nur den lieben"
    "Wir glauben all an einen Gott, Schoepfer"
    Anhang: "Ach Gott vom Himmel"----------- Mozart (arr. Bornefeld)
Orgelstuecke - 10 Intonationen---------------------------Baerenreiter
    "Ach Gott vom Himmel"
    "Allein zu dir"
    "Christe Qui Lux Es"
    "Da Pacem Domine"
    "Erbarm' dich mein"
    "Ich ruf' zu dir"
    "Nun freut Euch lieben Christen"
    "Puer Nobis Nascitur"
    "Wir glauben all an einen Gott, Schoepfer"
    "Wo Gott der Herr nicht"

Bottazzo, Luigi   Italian   1845-

7 Short and Easy Pieces on Gregorian Themes----------------- Zanibon

Boulnois, Michel   French   1907-

    Orgue et Liturgie, Vol. 18--------------------------- Schola Cantorum
    Variations on "Sacris Solemnis"
    Paraphrase on "O Quam Suavis Est" and "Alleluja"

Brabanter, Jozef   Dutch   1918-

    Cantantibus Organis------------------------------------ Van Rossum
    Koraalvoorspel "Nu sijt wellecome"

Bracquemond, Martha   French   1898-

    Organistes Contemporains----------------------------Schola Cantorum
    Variations on a Noël

Braein, Edvard   Norwegian   1887-
        Edvard F.   1924-

29 Koralforspill av Norske Organister (ed. Sandvold)-------------Norsk
    "Hos Gud er idel glede (Norsk Folk)"

Braeutigam, Helmut   German   1914-1942

    Op. 14/1: Orgelmusik - "Wenn alle untreu werden"---------- B. & H.

Brandon, George   American   1924-

    Canonic Partita on "Duke Street"------------------------------ Brodt
    Consolaire---WLSM
        Vol. 1, #4: Chorale Prelude on "Chester"
                 Quiet Piece "Down Ampney"
        Vol. 1, #5: Christus Victor ("King's Weston")
        Vol. 2, #4: Meditation on "National Hymn"

Brandon, G. (cont.)

    Vol. 3, #1: Offertory Song "Munich"
Eureka Suite--- Brodt
    Fuguing Tune "Delight"
    March on "Royal Proclamation"
    Variations on "Dunlap's Creek"
    Variations on "Salem"
Fantasy on "Old 100"---Brodt
4 Liturgical Preludes---J. Fischer
    Dutch Easter Carol "Vruechten"
    "Gelobt sei Gott"
    "Lasst uns erfreuen"
    "O Filii et Filiae"
Manualiere, Vol. 2, #6 ---WLSM
    Variations on "Mear"
Variations on "Dix"--Brodt
Variations on "Sandringham"--- Brodt
Variations on 2 Spirituals---Brodt
    "Let Us Break Bread Together"
    "Were You There?"

Braun, H. Myron   American   Contemporary

    Voluntaries for the Christian Year, Vol. 2--------------------Abingdon
    "Peek (Peek)"

Broek, P. Van den   Belgian

    15 Organ Pieces from Modern Belgium-------------------------WLSM
    Meditation on "Vexilla Regis (Sarum – Mode 1)"

Broughton, Edward

    Organ Voluntaries for the Easter Season, #3------------------- Lorenz
    "St. Drostane"
    Sacred Organ Folio, Vol. 4--------------------------------- Lorenz
    "Adeste Fideles"

Brown, Rayner   American   1912-

    Chorale Preludes, Book 1------------------------ Western International
    "Allein zu dir"   "Jesu, meine Zuversicht"
    "An Wasserfluessen"   "O Haupt voll Blut"
    Chorale Prelude (Viola and Organ)----------------Western International
    "Aus tiefer Not"

Browne, Charles Foster   1910-

    5 Fugato Interludes on Plainsong Themes----------------------Novello
    "Adoro Te Devote (Plainsong)"
    "Asperges Me (Kyrial)"
    "Credo de Angelis"
    "Kyrie Dicta de Angelis"
    "Salve Regina (Mode 1)"

Brunner, Adolf   Swiss   1901-

    Chorale Variations on "Vater Unser"--------------------- Baerenreiter
    Pfingstbuch ueber den Chorale "Nun bitten wir"----------- Baerenreiter
    Short Partita on "Nun freut Euch"----------------------- Baerenreiter

Bunjes, Paul G.   American   1914-

    Preludes for Hymns in the Worship Supplement (ed. Thomas)--Concordia
    "Das neugebor'ne Kindelein"

Burkhart, Charles   American

    Hymn Preludes for the Mennonite Hymnal---------------Goshen College
    "Amazing Grace"
    "Bonar" (3)
    "Consolation (Wyeth)"
    "Goshen"
    "Gratitude"
    "Nettleton (Wyeth)"
    "St. Martin's (Tans'ur)"
    "Social Band"
    "Vernon"

Burnham, Cardon

    Sacred Organ Folio---Lorenz
    Vol. 1: Variations on Behold a Host ("Den store hvite
       flokk-Norwegian")
    Vol. 3: Prelude on "Detroit (Kentucky Harmony)"

Burns, William K.   American   Contemporary

    Voluntaries for the Christian Year, Vol. 2-------------------Abingdon
    "Cushman (Turner)"

Busarow, Donald   American   1934-

    Chorale Prelude "Nun freut Euch (Nuernberg)"-------------- Concordia

Buttstedt, Johann Heinrich   German   1666-1727

    80 Chorale Preludes by German Masters of the 17th and
       18th Centuries (Keller)--------------------------------- Peters
    "Gelobet seist du"
    Seasonal Chorale Preludes (Manuals) (ed. Trevor)--------------Oxford
    Book I: "Nun komm der Heiden"

Buxtehude, Dietrich   Danish-German   1637-1707

    80 Chorale Preludes by German Masters of the 17th and
       18th Centuries (Keller)--------------------------------- Peters
    "Auf meinen lieben Gott"
    "Herzlich tut mich verlangen"
    Organ Masters of the 17th and 18th Centuries----------------- Kalmus
    "Ach Herr, mich armen" ("Herzlich tut mich verlangen")
    "Gelobet seist du, Jesu Christ"
    "In Dulci Jubilo"

Buxtehude, Dietrich (cont.)

"Jesus Christus, unser Heiland, der den Tod (Klug)"
"Mensch, willst du leben"
"Puer Natus in Bethlehem"
"Wir danken dir, Herr Jesu Christ (Fischer)"
Orgue et Liturgie #24: Notre Père------------------Schola Cantorum
"Vater Unser"
Seasonal Chorale Preludes (Manuals) (ed. Trevor)-------------- Oxford
"Wie schoen leuchtet"

Campbell-Watson, Frank   American   1898-

Consoliere, Vol. 1, #1--- WLSM
"Jesus, My Lord, My God, My All"

Canning, Thomas   American   1911-

Preludes for Hymns in the Worship Supplement (ed. Thomas)--Concordia
"Greensleeves"

Cappelen, Christian   Norwegian   1845-1916

Hymne: "Nu la oss takke Gud"---------------------------------Norsk
6 Smaa Fantasier--- Norsk
"Aa hjertens ve"
"Din dyre Ihukommelse (Gesius)" (2)
"Lover den Herre"
"Naar mitt oeie (Lindeman)"
"O hjertenskjaere Jesus Krist" ("Vater Unser")
"Overmaade, fullt av naade (Freylinghausen)"
3 Postludier--- Norsk
#1: "Et barn er foedt (Lindeman)"

Carleton, Nicholas   English   16th Century

Cantantibus Organis, Vol. 12---------------------------------- Pustet
"Audi Benigne Conditor"

Carlman, Gustaf   Swedish   1906-1958

Introitus Preludier (ed. Runbaeck and Aahlen)--------------- Nordiska
Vol. I:
"Anamma from de dyra naadeorden"
"Ett klarligt ljus av dina bud"
"I naad och sanning bland"
Vol. II:
"Jesu, laat mig staedse boerja"
"O du haerlighetens sken"
Koralfoerspel (ed. Andersson and Norrman)------------------ Nordiska
"Den ljusa dag" ("Vergangen ist der-Kingo")
Postludier (ed. Runbaeck and Aahlen)----------------------- Nordiska
"Befall i Herrens haender"
"Bereden vaeg foer Herran"
"Hur froejdar sig i templets famn"
"Jag lyfter mina haender" ("Valet")
"Jeg vil mig Herren (Thomissoen)"

Carlman, Gustaf (cont.)

"O Kriste, du som ljuset aer"
"O min Jesu, dit du gaat"
"Uverdig er jeg (Old 130)"
"Vi tacke dig, O Jesu god"

Casner, Myron D.   American   1908-

Preludes for Hymns in the Worship Supplement (ed. Thomas)--Concordia
"Divinum Mysterium"
"Jefferson"

Cassler, G. Winston   American   1906-

Manuals Only (ed. Johnson)---------------------------------Augsburg
"Kyrie: Eucharistia"
Varied Accompaniments to 3 Easter Hymns------------------ Augsburg
(with 2 trumpets)
"Easter Glory"
"Lasst uns erfreuen"
"Llanfair"

Castegren, Nils   Swedish   1908-

Postludier (ed. Runbaeck and Aahlen)------------------------Nordiska
"Ack hjaertens ve"
"Jesu, dine dype" ("Freu dich sehr")
"Jesu Frelser" ("Liebster Jesu")
"Naer vaerldens hoop"
"Saasom hjorten traeget"
"Vad kan dock min sjael foernoeja"

Caurroy, Eustache du   French   1549-1609

Les Maîtres Français de l'Orgue------Ed. Mus. de la Schola Cantorum
(17 et 18 siècles)
Fantasie "Salve Regina (Mode 1)"

Cellier, Alexandre Eugene   French-South African   1883-

Orgue et Liturgie, Vol. 66-------------------------- Schola Cantorum
Theme and Variations on "Psalm 149" (with trumpet)

Charpentier, Marc-Antoine   French   ?-1704

4 Noëls-------------------------- Procure de Clergé--Music Sacrée
"A la venue de Noël"
"Noël - Or dites-nous"
"Noël - Où s'en vont ces"
"Noël - Une jeune pucelle"
"Noël - Laissez paître vos bêtes"-------------------------Concordia
(Flutes, strings and continuo)

Chaudeur, Roger

Consolaire, Vol. 1, #2------------------------------------ WLSM
Ye Sons and Daughters ("O Filii et Filiae")

Chauvin, Dori   French   1899-

   Consolaire--WLSM
      Vol. 1, #3: "Veni Creator Spiritus (Sarum – Mode 8)"
      Vol. 3, #3: Variations on "America"
   Manualiere, Vol. 1, #6--WLSM
      Noël - "Ilestné"

Clarke, F. R. C.   Canadian   Contemporary

   6 Hymn Tune Voluntaries------------------------------------ Waterloo
      "Iste Confessor (Rouen)"
      "Kingsland (Boyce)"
      "Lasst uns erfreuen"
      "Nicht so traurig (Bach)"
      "O Quanta Qualia"
      "Song 4 (Gibbons)"

Clifford, J.

   Manualiere, Vol. 1, #1--WLSM
      Recessional on "We Three Kings"

Clokey, Joseph Waddell   American   1890-1960

   35 Interludes on Hymn Tunes------------------------------J. Fischer
      "Binchester (Croft)"
      "Caerlleon (Welsh)"
      "Croft's 148th"
      "Evan (Havergal)"
      "Hanover (Croft)"
      "Herzliebster Jesu"
      "Jesu, meine Freude"
      "Jesu, meine Zuversicht"
      "Llangoedmor (Welsh)"
      "Llangollen (Welsh)"
      "Lobet den Herren, alle die ihn (Crueger)"
      "Old 107th (Geneva)"
      "Picardy"
      "Psalm 3 (Geneva)"
      "Psalm 42 (Geneva)"
      "Psalm 136 (Pierre)"
      "Psalm 140 (Geneva)"
      "Rhyddid (Welsh)"
      "Rockingham (Miller)"
      "St. Agnes (Dykes)"
      "St. Anne (Croft)"
      "St. Flavian"
      "St. John (Welsh)"
      "St. Matthew (Croft)"
      "Schmuecke dich"
      "Song 1 (Gibbons)"
      "Song 13 (Gibbons)"
      "Song 22 (Gibbons)"
      "Song 24 (Gibbons)"
      "Song 67 (Gibbons)"
      "Tallis First Mode"
      "Tallis Third Mode"

Clokey, Joseph Waddell (cont.)

    "Tallis Fifth Mode"
    "Tallis Canon"
    "Veni Creator (Tallis?)"

Coates, Douglas Marsden   English   1898-

    7 Short Improvisations----------------------------Bosworth (London)
    "Nun danket all und bringet Ehr"
    "Schoenster Herr Jesu"

Collot, Jean   Belgian   1907-

    Variations on a Noël---WLSM

Copes, V. Earle   American   1921-

    Voluntaries for the Christian Year, Vol. 2-------------------Abingdon
    "Welwyn"

Corina, John

    Suite for Christmas---Abingdon
    "Carol"
    "Divinum Mysterium"
    "Westminster Carol"
    "Yorkshire (Wainwright)"

Corrette, Michel   French   1709-1795

    L'Organiste Liturgique, Vol. 3-----------------------Schola Cantorum
    "A la venue de Noël"
    "Vous qui désirez"

Crane, Robert E.   American   1919-

    Choral Prelude on "In Dulci Jubilo"--------------R. E. Crane (Library
                                        of Congress)

Cundick, Robert   American   1926-

    A First Album for Church Organists----------------------- C. Fischer
        Prelude on "Coventry Carol"
    Diversions-- C. Fischer
        Variations on Swedish Folk Song "Ack Vaermeland"

Curry, W. Lawrence   American   1906-1966

    Chorale Prelude on "Bremen"------------------------------- Abingdon
    15 Hymn-Tune Preludes------------------------------------Abingdon
    "Away in a Manger"
    "Dix"
    "First Nowell"
    "Greensleeves"
    "Italian Hymn"
    "Lasst uns erfreuen"

Curry, W. Lawrence (cont.)

"Leoni"
"Old 100"
"St. Elizabeth"
"St. Theodulph"
"Spanish Hymn"
"Terra Beata"
"Veni Emmanuel"
"Victory"
"Vom Himmel hoch"

Damm, Sixten   Swedish   1899-

"Den Blomstertid nu kommer"-------------------------- mss. STIM'S
"En herrdag i hoejden"------------------------------- mss. STIM'S

Dandrieu, Jean François   French   1682-1738

Archives des Maîtes de l'Orgue (Guilmant) --------Durand (also Johnson
    "Ave Maris Stella (Mode 1)"   "O Filii et Filiae"   Reprint Ed.)
    "Magnificat" (6 tones)
Cantantibus Organis, Vol. 8------------------------------------- Pustet
    "O Filii et Filiae"
L'Organiste Liturgique------------Ed. Musicales de la Schola Cantorum
    Vol. 12:
        "A la venue de Noël"
        Noël - "Adam fut un pauvre homme"
        "Joseph est bien marié"
        "Noël - Chrétian qui suivez l'Eglise"
        "Noël - Je me suis levé"
        "Nous sommes en voie"
        "Or dites-nous"
        "Noël - Une jeune pucelle"
        "Noël - Voici le jour Solemnel"
    Vol. 16:
        "Noël - Adam, où es tu"
        "Noël - Bergers, allons voir dans ce lieu"
        "Noël - Chanton de Voix Hautaine"
        "Noël - Joseph, tu es bien joyeux"
        "Noël - Laissez paître vos bêtes"
        "Noël - Marchons, marchons, gaiement"
        "Noël de Saintonge"
        "Noël Poitevin"
        "Noël pour l'amour de Marie" ("Au ciel d'hiver")
        "Noël Suisse"
        "Noël - Une bergère jolie"
        "Quoy ma voisine" ("Noël - Ah ma voisine")
        "Noël - Sortons de nos chaumieres"
        "Noël - Un jour Dieu se résolut"
    Vol. 19 & 20:
        "A Minuit" (2)
        "Noël - Allons voir ce divin Gage"
        "Noël - Chantons, je vous prie" (2)
        "Noël - Il fait bon aimer"
        "Noël - Il n'est rien de plus tendre"

Dandrieu, Jean François (cont.)

    "Noël - Jacob que tu es habile"
    "Noël - Le Roy des Cieux"
    "Noël - Mais on san es allé nau"
    "Noël - Michau qui causoit ce grand bruit"
    "Noël cette journée"
    "Noël - O Nuit, heureuse Nuit"
    "Noël - Où s'en vont ces gais bergers"
    "Puer Nobis Nascitur"
    "Noël - Quand je méveillai"
    "Noël - Quand le Sauveur"
    "Noël - Savez-vous mon cher voisin"
    "Noël - Si c'est pour ôter la vie"
    "Noël - Tous les Bourgeois de Chartres"
    "Vous qui désirez"
  Vol. 22:
    "Noël - Chanson de St. Jacques"
    "O Filii et Filiae"

Dandrieu, Pierre   French   ca 1660-1733

  Consolaire, Vol. 1, #2------------------------------------- WLSM
    Variations on At The Cross ("Stabat Mater Dolorosa-Mainz")
  Les Maîtres Français de l'Orgue----- Ed. Mus. de la Schola Cantorum
    (17 et 18 siècles)
    Vol. 2:
      Noël - "Puer Nobis Nascitur"
      "Noël - Une jeune pucelle"
      "Noël - Or dites-nous, Marie"
  Venite Adoremus Book ---------------------------------McL. & R.
    "Puer Nobis Nascitur"

David, Johann Nepomuk   Austrian   1895-

  Choralwerk ---B. & H.
    Vol. 16: "O du armer Judas"
    Vol. 17: "Vater Unser"
    Vol. 18: "Nun komm der Heiden"
    Vol. 19: "Nun komm der Heiden"

de Grigny, Nicolas - See Grigny, Nicolas de

de Jong, Marinus - See Jong, Marinus de

de St. Martin, Leonce - See St. Martin, Leonce de

de Vallombrosa, Amédée - See Vallombrosa, Amédée de

Demessieux, Jeanne   French   1921-1968

  Répons pour le Temps de Pâques---------------------------- Durand
    "Victimae Paschali"

Desprez, Josquin   Flemish   1450-1521

    Cantantibus Organis, Vol. 8----------------------------------- Pustet
        "Victimae Paschali Laudes (Gregorian-Mode 1)"

Diemer, Emma Lou   American   1927-

    Fantasy on "O Sacred Head"------------------------ Boosey & Hawkes
    He Leadeth Me ("Aughton")------------------------------------- Oxford
    7 Hymn Preludes---Flammer
        "Greensleeves"
        "Hyfrydol"
        "Jesu, meine Freude"
        "Martyrdom"
        "Munich"
        "Picardy"
        "Pleading Saviour (Plymouth)"

Diruta, Girolamo   Italian   16th Century

    Cantantibus Organis, Vol. 12--------------------------------- Pustet
        "Hostis Herodes Impie"

Dobson, Charles

    Partita for Organ---------------- Ascherberg, Hopwood & Crew (1969)
        "In Dulci Jubilo"

Dornel, Louis-Antoine   French   1695-1765

    Les Maîtres Français de l'Orgue------ Ed. Mus. de la Schola Cantorum
        (17 et 18 siècles)
        Vol. 2: "Noël - Je me suis levé"

Doyen, Henri   French   1905-

    Manualiere, Vol. 1, #2---------------------------------------WLSM
        3 Short Easter Pieces
        "Ite Missa Est"
        "Victimae Paschali"

Dragt, Jaap   Dutch   1930-

    Prelude and Fugue on "Psalm 122 (Geneva)"------------------Ars Nova

Drayton, Paul

    Chorale Prelude and Fugue "Nun ruhen alle Waelder"--------J. Fischer
    Prelude on a 15th Century Carol to St. Stephen------------ J. Fischer
        "Eia Martyr Stephane"

Dressler, John   Austrian-American   1923-

    Service Album of Organ Pieces----------------------------J. Fischer
        "O Sanctissima"

Drischner, Max   German   1891-1971

Einfache Orgelvorspiele (H. Weber)----------------------- C. Kaiser
   "Komm, o komm, du Geist (J. C. Bach)"
   "Valet"
   "Wer kann der Treu vergessen"
   "Wer nur den lieben (Neumark)"
   "Wohlauf, die ihr hungrig seid"
Nordische Kanzonen ------------------------------------- K. Littman
Norske Kanzoner --------------[same as above]---------- Baerenreiter
   "Herre Gud, ditt dyre navn (Norwegian Folk Tune)"
   "Ingen vinner frem (Norsk Folk)"
   "Kjaerlighet er lysets (Norsk Folk)"
   "Med Jesus vil eg fara (Norsk Folk)"
   "Min lodd falt mig (Norsk Folk)"
   "Om nogen til ondt (Norsk-Ehrenborg)"

Druckenmueller, Georg Wolfgang German   1628-1675

   Choralbearbeitungen und Freie Orgelstuecke der Deutschen
         Sweelinck Schule (ed. Moser) Vol. 2 ---------------- Baerenreiter
   Fantasie on "Nun lob mein Seel (Kugelman)"

du Caurroy, Eustache - See Caurroy, Eustache du

Dub, Georges

   Noël for Organ--------------------------------------J. Fischer (1956)
      "Sicilian Mariners"

Dubois, Francis Clement Theodore   French   1837-1924

   Douze Pièces Nouvelles---Leduc
      Alleluia - "O Filii et Filiae"
      La Fête Dieu - "Ecce Panis (Mode 8)"
                     "Lauda Sion (Mode 7)"
      "Noël"
   Venite Adoremus Book-------------------------------------McL. & R.
      "Noël"

Duchow, Marvin   Canadian   1914-

   7 Chorale Preludes in Traditional Styles--------------------- Berandol
      "Aus tiefer Not (Phrygian)"
      "Freu dich sehr"
      "Herr, straf' mich nicht (Crueger)"
      "O Haupt voll Blut"
      "Sei gegruesset, Jesu guetig (Vopelius)"
      "Uns ist ein Kindlein heut' gebor'n (Praetorius)"
      "Wer nur den lieben Gott (Neumark)"

Dueben, Andreas   German   1594-1662

   Choralbearbeitungen und Freie Orgelstuecke der Deutschen
         Sweelinck Schule (ed. Moser), Vol. 2----------------Baerenreiter
      Variations on "Erstanden ist der heilig Christ (Triller)"
   Musikalische Denkmaeler, Band III ------------------B. Schott's Soehne
      46 Choraele fuer Orgel

Dueben, Andreas (cont.)

>"Allein Gott in der Hoeh"
>"Erstanden ist der heil'ge Christ (Triller)"
>"Wo Gott der Herr nicht bei uns"

Dufay, Guillaume   French   1395-1474

>Cantantibus Organis, Vol. 12----------------------------------- Pustet
>"Pange Lingua (Sarum-Mode 3)"

Duro, John   American   1911-

>Improvisation on O Little Town of Bethlehem --------------H. W. Gray
>"St. Louis"

Eder, Helmut   Austrian   1916-

>Op. 47: 5 Choralpartiten--------------------------------- Doblinger
>#1: "O Heiland reiss"
>#2: "Ach wie fluechtig"
>#3: "Es sungen drei Engel"
>#4: "Gen Himmel aufgefahren (Franck)"
>#5: "Nun danket all' und"
>Op. 48: Choral Suite-------------------------------------Doblinger
>7 Choralvorspiele ueber den Weg des Herrn
>"Da Jesu an dem Kreuze stund" & "O Haupt voll Blut"
>"Christ ist erstanden"
>"In Dulci Jubilo"
>"Maria durch den Dornwald"
>"Nun bitten wir den Heiligen Geist"
>"O du hochheilige Kreuze (Koeln)"
>"Und unser lieben Frauen"

Edlund, Lars   Swedish   1922-

>Koralfoerspel (ed. Andersson and Norrman)-------------------Nordiska
>"Ack bliv hos oss"
>"En syndig man, som laag"
>"Jag lever och upphoejer" ("Aus meines Herzens")
>"Tvaa vaeldiga strida"
>Tre Koraler---Gehrmans
>"Guds rena Lamm" ("O Lamm Gottes-Decius")
>"I moerker sjoenko"
>"Min sjael och sinne" ("Wer nur den lieben")

Edmundson, Garth   American   1893-1971

>3 Organ Preludes--J. Fischer
>Chorale ("Herzliebster Jesu")

Egebjer, Lars   Swedish   1930-

>Choraliter---Nordiska
>"Den dag du gav oss, Gud (Rung)"
>"En fridens aengel"

Egebjer, Lars (cont.)

    "Gammal aer kyrken" ("Die Kirche ist ein")
    "Herren aer min herde god" ("Wennerberg I")
    "Hvad roest, hvad ljuvlig roest (Ahlstroem)"
    "Hvem aer den stora skaran daer"
    "Jag lyfter mina haender"
    "Lover Gud i himmelshoejd"
    "O Gud, om allt mig saeger"
    "O Jesu Krist, till dig foervisst"
Improvisation "Et barn er foedt i Bethlehem"----------------- Nordiska
2 Medeltida Koraler------------------------------- Eriks Musikhandel
    "Dig Helge Ande, bedja vi" ("Nun bitten wir")
    "Vi lova dig, O store Gud"

Ehrlinger, Fr.

    Einfache Orgelvorspiele (ed. H. Weber)---------------C. Kaiser (1959)
    "Ach Gott vom Himmel (Erfurt)"
    "Ach wie fluechtig"
    "Alle Menschen (Mueller)"
    "Allein zu dir"
    "Alles ist an"
    "Auf, auf, mein Herz (Crueger)"
    "Auf diesen Tag"
    "Auf meinen Lieben Gott (Regnart)"
    "Aus meines Herzens"
    "Aus tiefer Not (Phrygian)"
    "Christ ist erstanden (Folk)"
    "Christe, du Lamm Gottes (Decius)"
    "Christe, du Schoepfer (Koenigsberg)"
    "Christus der uns selig"
    "Da Christus geboren war (Bohemian)"
    "Es ist das Heil"
    "Herzlich lieb hab' ich dich"
    "Jesu geh voran" ("Seelenbraeutigam")
    "O durchbrecher (Halle)"
    "Vater Unser"
    "Warum willst du draussen"

Ek, Gunnar   Swedish   1900-

Toccata oever "Vi lova dig, o store Gud"--------------------Gehrmans

Eliot, Dennis

Sacred Organ Folio---Lorenz
    Vol. 1: Fantasie on "Veni Creator (Sarum-Mode 8)"
          Prelude on "When Jesus Wept (Billings)"
    Vol. 4: "Wachet auf"
Sacred Organ Journal, Nov. 1969----------------------------- Lorenz
    Two Service Pieces for Advent
        "Stuttgart (Gotha)"
        "Veni Emmanuel"

Ellsasser, Richard   American   1926-1972

Christmas Carols for the Organ------------------------------Flammer
   "Bring a Torch"
   "Carol"
   "Comes the Snow"
   "Deck the Halls"
   "First Nowell"
   "Good King Wenceslas"
   "Holly and the Ivy"
   "St. Louis"
   "Veni Emmanuel (Plainsong)"
   "Wassail"
Meditation on the Eucharist ---------------------------------Flammer
   "Picardy"
The Sanctuary Organist ------------------------------- Sacred Songs
   "Austrian Hymn"
   "Brother James' Air"
   "Crusaders Hymn"
   "Ein feste Burg"
   "Hymn to Joy (Beethoven)"
   "Ton-y-Botel"

Elmore, Robert Hall   American   1913-

Meditation on an Old Covenanter's Tune------------------ H. W. Gray
   "Varina"
Mixture IV--Flammer
   Chorale Prelude on "Lancashire"
   Chorale Prelude on "Morecambe"
2 Chorale Preludes---------------------------------------Elkan-Vogel
   "Ave Maria (Arcadelt)"
   "St. Theodulph"

Emborg, Jens Larson   Danish   1876-1957

Op. 32: 26 Koralforspill for Orgel ----------------------- W. Hansen
   "Dejlig er den himmel blaa (Danish)"
   "Den lyse dag forgangen er (Kingo)"
   "Den signede dag som nu vi ser (Weyse)"
   "Fryd dig du Kristi Brud (Regnart)"
   "Gjoer doeren hoei" ("Old 100")
   "Herre jeg har handlet ille (Crueger)"
   "Jesu dine dype vunder" ("Freu dich sehr")
   "Jesu, Frelser" ("Liebster Jesu")
   "Jesu din soete forening (Koenig)"
   "Jesu er mitt liv i live" ("Alle Menschen-Wessnitzer")
   "Med sorgen og klagen"
   "Nu hviler mark og enge" ("Innsbruck")
   "Op al den ting (Freiburg)"
   "Se vi gaa upp (Kingo)"
Fire Orgelkomposisjoner----------------------------------- W. Hansen
   #3: "Aa hjertens ve"

Enger, Elling   Norwegian   1905-

29 Koralvorspill av Norske Organister (ed. Sandvold)------------ Norsk
   "Dyre bord som Jesus dekker (Lindeman)"

Enger, Elling (cont.)

>"Folkefrelsar (Sletten)"
>"Hos Gud er idel (Norse Folk)"
>"Hvor er det godt (Norsk Folk)"
>"Jesu, din soete forening (Norse Folk)"
>"Korset vil jeg aldri (Folk Tune)"

Englert, Eugene

>Consolaire, Vol. 1, #6-- WLSM
>   Communion Piece on "Rendez à Dieu"

Erbach, Christian   German   1570-1635

>Cantantibus Organis, Vol. 8----------------------------------- Pustet
>   "Victimae Paschali"

Faessler, Guido

>Die Orgel im Kirchenjahr, Vol. 3----------------------- Cron Luzern
>   "Ach Jesu mein"
>   "Bei stiller Nacht"
>   "Da Jesu an dem Kreuze stund"
>   "Gegruesst seid, Jesu Wunden, mir"
>   "Ich sehe dich, O Jesu, schweigen"
>   "Jesu, zu dir rufen wir"
>   "Laetare"
>   "O du mein Volk"
>   "O Haupt voll Blut" (2)
>   "O Traurigkeit" (2)
>   "Sei gegruesset, sei gekuesset"
>   "Tu auf, tu auf, du schoenes Blut"

Falcinelli, Rolande   French   1920-

>Orgue et Liturgie, #11----------------------------- Schola Cantorum
>   Op. 29: Rosa Mystica (on Gregorian Themes)
>   "Alma Redemptoris Mater (Plainsong)"
>   "Ave Maris Stella (Mode 1)"
>   "Ave Regina Caelorum (Mode 6)"
>   "Regina Coeli (Mode 6)"
>   "Salve Regina"
>   "Stabat Mater (Mode 1)"

Fasolo, Giovanni Battista   Italian   17th Century

>Annuale-- W. Mueller
>   (Additions to those already listed)
>   "Aurea Luce (3rd Tone)"
>   "Decus Morum (Tone 8)"
>   "Exultet Luminum"
>   "Fortem Virili Pectore (Plainsong)"
>   "Hostis Herodes (Plainsong)"
>   "Kyrie Orbis Factor"
>   "Proles de Coelo Prodiit (Tone 5)"
>   "Sanctorum Meritis (Plainsong)"

Fauchard, Auguste Louis Joseph   1881-1957

    Orgue et Liturgie, #12------------------------------Schola Cantorum
      Le Mystère de Noël: "Jesu Redemptor Omnium"

Feibel, Fred   American   1906-

    Postlude on Easter Themes--------------------Ethel Smith Music Co.
      "Fortunatus (Sullivan)"
      "Greenland (Haydn)"
      "Lyra Davidica"
      "St. Kevin"
      "Unser Herrscher (Neander)"

Fiebig, Kurt   German   1908-

    Organ Partita "Wer nur den lieben Gott"--------------------Concordia

Finkbeiner, Reinhold   German   1929-

    Chorale Fantasie "Wachet auf"------------------------------ B. & H.

Fischer, Irwin   American   1903-

    Chorale Preludes----------------------- American Composers Alliance
      "Als Jesus Christus in der Nacht"
      "Das walt Gott"
      "Jesu, meine Freude" #2
      "Nun ruhen alle Waelder"

Fischer, Johann Kaspar Ferdinand   German   ca 1660-1746

    Organ Masters of the 17th and 18th Centuries------------------ Kalmus
      "Ave Maria klare"
      "Christ ist erstanden (Christus Resurrexit-Plainsong)"
      "Da Jesu an dem Kreuze"
      "Der Tag der ist so"
      "Komm, Heiliger Geist, mit deiner Gnad" ("O Jesulein suess")

Fisher, Norman Zagal   American

    Toccata on a French Psalm Tune ("Psalm 81")----------------- Galaxy

Fissinger, Edwin   American   Contemporary

    6 Soft Pieces by 6 American Composers----------------------- WLSM
      "To Jesus Christ Our Sov'reign King"

Fleury, André   French   1903-

    Manualiere, Vol. 2, #6 ---WLSM
      Variations on "Adeste Fideles"

Forsberg, Roland   Swedish   1939-

    "Att bedja aer ej endast"------------------------------- mss. STIM'S
    "Ecce Novum Gaudium"--------------------------------   "

Forsberg, Roland (cont.)

"In Dulci Jubilo"--- mss. STIM'S
"Med tacksam roest och tacksam sjael"------------------   "
"Ingen vinner fram"--Norberg

Franck, César   French   1822-1890

Venite Adoremus Book---------------------------------- McL. & R.
    Offertory for Midnight Mass:
        "Nous allons, ma mie"   "Noël - Nous voici dans la ville"

Frank, René   German-American   1910-1965

11 Short Organ Hymns--Hope
    "Avon"
    "Azmon"
    "Coronation"
    "Crusaders Hymn"
    "Dix"
    "Germany"
    "Gordon (Gordon)"
    "Maryton"
    "Neumark"
    "Ortonville"
    "Regent Square"

Franzen, Bengt   Swedish   1914-1969

Koralfoerspel (ed. Andersson and Norrman)----------------- Nordiska
    "Herre, jag vil bida"
    "Jag lyfter mina haender" ("Valet")

Frescobaldi, Girolamo   Italian   1583-1644

Orgue et Liturgie, #11------------------------------Schola Cantorum
    "Ave Maris Stella (Mode 1)"

Fromm, Herbert   German-American   1905-

Partita on Let All Mortal Flesh---------------mss. Brookline, Mass.
    "Picardy"

Fronmueller, Frieda

Einfache Orgelvorspiele (ed. H. Weber)---------------C. Kaiser (1959)
    "Es ist ein Ros'"
    "Nun sich der Tag (Krieger)"
    "Sei Lob und Ehr (Crueger)"

Gantner, Albert   1916-

Die Orgel im Kirchenjahr, Vol. 2---------------------- Cron Luzern
    Wiehnachtskreis:
        "Da nun das Jahr (Vexilla Regis-German)"
        "Dominus Dixit"

Gantner, Albert (cont.)

> "Ecce Advenit"
> "Es ist ein Reis"
> Es kam ein Engel - "Vom Himmel hoch"
> Gloria In Excelsis - "Allein Gott in der"
> "Heilige Namen"
> "In Dulci Jubilo"
> "Jubilate Deo"
> "Lasst uns das Kindlein (Folk Tune)"
> "Puer Natus Est Nobis"
> "Te Deum Laudamus (Tone 3)" and "Hursley"

Gebhard, Hans   1897-

Einfache Orgelvorspiele (ed. H. Weber)-------------- C. Kaiser (1959)
    "Der Tag ist nun vergangen (Ahle)"
    "Du Volk, das du getaufet bist (Ebeling)"
    "Heil'ger Geist, du Troester mein (Crueger)"
    "Herzlich tut mich verlangen"
    "O glaeubig Herz, gebenedei"
    "O Herre Gott, dein goettlich Wort"
    "O Lamm Gottes, unschuldig (Decius)"
    "O suesser Herre Jesu Christe"
    "O Traurigkeit"
    "O wir armen Suender"
    "Sonne der Gerechtigkeit (Bohemian)"
    "Was Gott tut, das ist"

Gebhardi, Ludwig Ernst   German   1787-1862

12 Chorale Trios (ed. Boeringer)--------------------------- Augsburg
    "Allein Gott in der"   "Lobt Gott, ihr Christen (Herman)"(2)
    "Dir, dir, Jehova"   "Mach's mit mir Gott"
    "Es ist das Heil"   "Straf' mich nicht"
    "Herr Jesu Christ, dich zu uns" "Was Gott tut"
    "Herzliebster Jesu"   "Wer nur den lieben (Neumark)"
    "Jerusalem, du"

Gehring, Philip   American   1925-

2 Folk-Hymn Preludes---Augsburg
    "Amazing Grace"
    "They'll Know We Are Christians"

Geilsdorf, Paul

Einfache Orgelvorspiele (ed. H. Weber)--------------C. Kaiser (1959)
    "Es mag sein, dass alles faellt"
    "Ewig steht fest der Kirche Haus (Lindeman)"
    "Herr Jesu Christ, dich zu uns"
    "Jesu hilf siegen (Darmstadt)"
    "Komm Heiliger Geist, Herre Gott"
    "Lob Gott getrost mit singen (Bohemian)"
    "Morgenglanz"
    "Nun lasst uns den Leib"
    "Nun lasst uns Gott dem Herren (Selnecker)"

Genzmer, Harald   German   1909-

   Die Tageszeiten-- Peters
      Die Nacht - "Morgenglanz"
      "Die Sonn' hat sich"
      "Er weckt mich alle Morgen"

Geoffroy, Jean-Nicolas   French   17th Century

   Les Maîtres Français de l'Orgue------ Ed. Mus. de la Schola Cantorum
      (17 & 18 Siècles)
      Fugue "Lucis Creator Optime (Angers)"

Gigault, Nicolas   French   1624-1707

   Livre de Musique pour l'Orgue------------------------- Schott Frères
      "Veni Creator Spiritus (Mode 8)"

Gigout, Eugène   French   1844-1925

   Poèmes Mystique--- A. Durand
      Pèlerinage: "Ave Maris Stella (Lourdes)"
   Ten Pieces--- Leduc
      Rhapsodie on Noëls:
        "Adeste Fideles"
        "Joseph est bien marié"
        "Les Anges dans nos"

Giorgi, Pietro

   Consolaire, Vol. 1, #5------------------------------------ WLSM
      Lord, Who at Thy First Eucharist ("Unde et Memores")

Girod, Marie-Louise   French   1915-

   Orgue et Liturgie---------------------------------- Schola Cantorum
      #18: Triptyque on "Sacris Solemnis"
      #64: Suite on "The Lord Is My Shepherd (Bourgeois)"
      #66: "Estans assis aux rives (Goudimel)"

Goemanne, Noel   Belgian-American   1926-

   Church Windows Suite---WLSM
      A Christmas Carol ("Puer Natus Est")
   Sortie on Jesus Christ Is Risen Today------------------- Th. Presser
      "Lyra Davidica"

Goller, Fritz   German   1914-

   6 Organ Processionals (for coming into church) ----------------- WLSM
      Ciacona and Processional on "Pange Lingua (Sarum-Mode 3)"

Gore, Richard T.   American   1908-

   Orgelbuechlein II --------------------- private printing, Wooster, Ohio
      "Ach Gott, erhoer mein Seufzen (Erfurt)"
      "Ach Gott, tu dich erbarmen (Franck)"
      "Ach Gott und Herr (Schein)"

Gore, Richard T. (cont.)

"Ach Gott vom Himmel, sieh darein (Erfurt)"
"Ach Gott, wie manches Herzeleid (Leipzig)"
"Ach Herr, mich armen Suender" ("Herzlich tut mich verlangen")
"Ach lieben Christen, seid getrost"
"Ach, was ist doch unser Leben"
"Ach, was soll ich, Suender, machen (Altdorf)"
"Alle Menschen (Dretzel)"
"Allein Gott in der Hoeh' (Plainsong)"
"Allein nach dir, Herr Jesu Christ"
"Allein zu dir, Herr Jesu Christ (Wittenberg)"
"Allenthalben wo ich gehe (Nuernberg)"
"An Wasserfluessen Babylon (Dachstein)"
"Auf meinen lieben Gott (Regnart)"
"Aus meines Herzens Grunde (Hamburg)"
"Aus tiefer Not (Phrygian)"
"Christ, unser Herr, zum Jordan (Walther)"
"Christe, der du bist Tag und Licht (Old Church)"
"Christe, du bist der helle Tag (Bohemian)"
"Christus der ist mein Leben" ("Ach bleib mit deiner (Vulpius)")
"Danket dem Herrn, denn er ist sehr freundlich"
"Das walt mein Gott (Vopelius)"
"Der du bist drei (Plainsong)"
"Der Herr ist mein getreuer Hirt (Wittenberg)"
"Du Friedefuerst (Gesius)"
"Ein feste Burg (Luther)"
"Erbarm' dich mein (Walther)"
"Erhalt uns, Herr (Klug)"
"Es spricht der Unweisen Mund (Walther)"
"Es steh'n vor Gottes Throne (Burck)"
"Es wolle Gott uns gnaedig sein (Strassburg)"
"Frisch auf, mein Seel'"
"Gelobet sei der Herr, der Gott Israels (Wittenberg)"
"Gen Himmel aufgefahren (Franck)"
"Gib Fried, O frommer, treuer Gott (Schneegass)"
"Gott der Vater wohn uns bei (Wittenberg)"
"Gott des Himmels (Albert)"
"Gott hat das Evangelium (Alberus)"
"Gott ist mein Heil, mein Huelf und Trost (Gesius)"
"Gott sei gelobet und gebenedeiet (Walther)"
"Gott, Vater, der du deine Sonn (Herman)"
"Hast du denn, Jesu" ("Lobe den Herren, den")
"Herr Gott, dich loben alle wir" ("Old 100th")
"Herr Gott, dich loben wir (Babst)"
"Herr Gott, erhalt uns fuer und fuer (Burck)"
"Herr Jesu Christ, du hoechstes Gut (Goerlitz)"
"Herr Jesu Christ, ich weiss gar wohl"
"Herr Jesu Christ, meins Lebens Licht (Calvisius)"
"Herr Jesu Christ, wahr Mensch und Gott" ("Andernach")
"Herzlich lieb hab' ich dich (Schmid)"
"Herzliebster Jesu (Crueger)"
"Ich dank dir, lieber Herr (Bohemian)"
"Ich dank dir schon (Praetorius)"
"Ich weiss ein Bluemlein huebsch und fein (Dresden)" (2)
"In dich hab' ich gehoffet (Nuernberg)"
"In dich hab' ich gehoffet (Strassburg)"

Gore, Richard T. (cont.)

"Itzt komm ich als ein armer Gast" ("Nun freut Euch (Klug)")
"Jesus Christus, unser Heiland der von uns (Erfurt)"
"Jesu, der du meine Seele (Gregor)"
"Jesu, meines Herzens Freud (Ahle)"
"Keinen hat Gott verlassen (Crueger)"
"Komm, Heiliger Geist, erfuell die Herzen (Old Church)"
"Komm, Heiliger Geist, Herre Gott (Walther)"
"Kommt her zu mir (Leipzig)"
"Lass mich dein sein"
"Lob sei Gott in des Himmels Thron (Erfurt)"
"Lobet den Herren, denn er ist sehr (Crueger)"
"Mach's mit mir, Gott (Schein)"
"Mag' ich Unglueck (Klug)"
"Mein Wallfahrt ich vollendet hab (Cramer)"
"Meine Seele erhebt den Herren (Klug)"
"Mensch willst du leben (Walther)"
"Mitten wir im Leben sind (Walther)"
"Nun bitten wir (Walther)"
"Nun freut Euch, Gottes Kinder all' (Strassburg)"
"Nun freut Euch, lieben (Nuernberg)"
"Nun gibt mein Jesu gute Nacht (Eccard)"
"Nun lasst uns den Leib begraben (Stahl)"
"Nun lasst uns Gott dem Herren (Selnecker)"
"Nun lob', mein Seel (Kugelman)"
"Nun ruhen alle Waelder" ("Innsbruck")
"O Gott, du frommer Gott (Hannover)"
"O grosser Gott von Macht (Franck)"
"O Heiliger Geist, du goettlich Feuer (Vulpius)"
"O Heiliger Geist, O Heiliger Gott" ("O Jesulein suess")
"O Herre Gott, dein goettlich Wort (Erfurt)"
"O Jesu, du edle Gabe (Weberbeck)"
"O Jesu, wie ist dein' Gestalt (Franck)"
"O Traurigkeit (Mainz)"
"O wir armen Suender" ("Ach, wir armen Suender (German)")
"Schmuecke dich (Crueger)"
"Sei gegruesset, Jesu gutig (Vopelius)" (2)
"Singen wir aus" ("Da Christus geboren (Bohemian)")
"So wuensch' ich Euch ein gute Nacht"
"Spiritus Sancti Gratia (Schein)"
"Valet (Teschner)"
"Von Gott will ich nicht (Erfurt)"
"Waer Gott nicht mit uns (Walther)"
"Warum betruebst du dich (Eler's)"
"Was Gott tut (Erfurt)"
"Was Gott tut (Gastorius)"
"Was mein Gott will (French)"
"Weltlich Ehr' und zeitlich Gut (Weisse)"
"Wenn dich Unglueck tut (Vulpius)"
"Wenn mein Stuendlein (Wolff)"
"Wer Gott vertraut (Calvisius)"
"Werde munter (Schop)"
"Wie nach einer Wasserquelle" ("Freu dich sehr")
"Wie schoen leuchtet (Nicolai)"
"Wie's Gott gefaellt, so gefaellt mir's auch (Cassel)"
"Wir danken dir, Herr Jesu Christ, dass du das Laemmelein (Gesius)"

Gore, Richard T. (cont.)

    "Wir glauben all an einen Gott, Schoepfer (Wittenberg)"
    "Wir haben schwerlich (1648)"
    "Wo Gott, der Herr, nicht (Wittenberg)"
    "Wo Gott zum Haus nicht gibt (Klug)"
    "Wo soll ich fliehen hin (Regnart)"
    "Wohl dem, der in Gottes Furcht steht (Walther)"

Graham, Robert V.   American   1912-

    Sacred Organ Journal, July 1970------------------------------Lorenz
        Chorale Meditation on "Where He Leads Me (Norris)"

Grieb, Herbert C.   American   1898-

    Fantasia on "Nun danket alle"------------------------------Abingdon
    Moments for Worship--------------------------------------C. Fischer
        Vol. I:
            "Oblation"
            "St. Clement (Scholefield)"
        Vol. II:
            "Sacramentum Unitatis (Lloyd)"
            "St. Margaret"

Grigny, Nicolas de   French   1671-1703

    Pièces d'Orgue---Schott Frères
        "A Solis Ortus Cardine"
        "Veni Creator Spiritus (Mode 8)"

Grimes, Travis

    Consolaire, Vol. 2, #6-------------------------------------- WLSM
        Chorale Prelude on "Maria durch den Dornwald ging"
        4 Variations on "Puer Nobis Nascitur"

Groom, Lester H.   American   Contemporary

    3 Festival Preludes--Abingdon
        "Gaudeamus Pariter"
        "Kremser"
        "Veni Emmanuel"
    Voluntaries for the Christian Year, Vol. 2-------------------Abingdon
        "Judas Maccabeus"

Grunenwald, Jean-Jacques   French   1911-

    Fantasie on "Lauda Sion"------------------------------------Salabert

Guglielmi, Antonio

    Consolaire, Vol. 1, #1------------------------------------ WLSM
        Communion on "We Three Kings"

Guilain (Freinsberg), ?   French   17-18th Century

Archives des Maîtres de l'Orgue, Vol. 7----------------------Durand
   Pièces d'Orgue pour le "Magnificat" (8 Tones)

Guilmant, F. Alexandre   French   1837-1911

Noëls---Durand
   Vol. 1:
      Offertoire on "Noël - Grand Dieu" and "Noël - Allons pasteurs"
      Elévation on "Noël - Pastre dei mountagne (Saboly)"
      Offertoire on "Noël - Chantons, je vous prie" and "Noël - Le
         messie vient de Naître"
      Elévation on "Noël - Or dites-nous, Marie"
      Offertoire on "Joseph est bien marié"
      Communion on "Noël Ecossais"
      Elévation on "Noël - Entends ma voix fidêle"
   Vol. 2:
      Introduction and Variations on "Noël - Accourez bergers fidèles"
      Elévation on "Noël - Ecoute Michel (Carcassonnais)"
      Communion on "Noël Languedocien"
      Offertoire on "Noël - Nuit sombre, ton ombre"
   Vol. 3:
      2 Variations on "Puer Nobis Nascitur (Praetorius)"
      Offertoire on 3 Noëls:
         "Noël - Chantons les louanges"
         "Noël - Bergers prenons nos chalumeaux"
         "Noël Flamand"
      Elévation on "Noël Brabançon"
      Communion on "Noël - D'où viens-tu, bergère? (Languedocien)"
   Vol. 4:
      Offertoire on "Noël Espagnol"
      Elévation on 2 Noëls:
         "Noël - Ve noei blaizôte"
         "Noël - Noei ven, j'aivon criai si for"
      Sortie "Noël - Chant du Roi René (Provençal)"
      Elévation on "Noël - O Jour, ton divin flambeau"

Guinaldo, Norberto   Argentinian   1937-

   3 Litanies for Organ------------------------------------- J. Fischer
      "Dies Irae"
      "Kyrie (Lutheran 1528)"
      (3rd on an original theme)
   5 Spanish Carols for Organ------------------------------- Concordia
      "El cant dels ocells"
      "El Decembre congelat"
      "El tre pastorets"
      "Que li darem"
      "Venid Niños"
   Paraphrase on "Sine Nomine"-------------------------------------mss.

Gustafson, Dwight

   3 Hymn Preludes----------------------------------- Shawnee (1969)
      "Avon"
      "Evan"
      "Tallis Canon"

Gwinner, Volker

Choralvorspiele in tiefer Lage---------------------------Baerenreiter
"Ach Gott vom Himmel"
"Der Tag bricht an" (2)

Haarklou, Johannes   Norwegian   1847-1925

Op. 19: 5 Julepreludier---------------------------------------Norsk
"Dejlig er jorden"
"Glade Jul"
"O lue fra Guds (Weisse)"
Op. 20: 25 Lette Preludier--------------------------------- Norsk
"Akk Fader, la ditt ord (Lindeman)"
"Akk Herre Gud (Schein)"
"Alene Gud"
"Apostlene sad i Jerusalem (Lindeman)"
"Av dypest noed (Phrygian)"
"Av hoeiheten oprunnen er"
"Bryd frem, mit hjertes (Zinck)" (2)
"Bryd frem, mit hjertes (Lindeman)"
"Den Herre Krist i doedens Baand" ("Christus Resurrexit") (2)
"Den lyse dag forgangen (Kingo)"
"Den signede Dag (Weyse)"
"Den store hvite flokk (Lindeman)"
"Der mange skal komme (Stockholm)"
"Du hoeie fryd for rene sjele (Zinck)"
"Du som gar ut fra (Lindeman)"
"Du vaere lovet, Jesus Krist (Walther)"
"Et barn er foedt" ("Puer Natus in Bethlehem")
"Et barn er foedt (Lindeman)"
"Jeg vet mig (Schein)"

Haegg, Gustaf   Swedish   1867-1925

Orgelmusik vid Hoegmaessans Avslutning---------------------Nordiska
"Var haelsad, skoena Morgonstund" ("Wie schoen leuchtet")

Haeussler, Gerhard

Einfache Orgelvorspiele (ed. H. Weber)---------------C. Kaiser (1959)
"Brich den Hungrigen dein Brot"

Haffner, Walter

Einfache Orgelvorspiele (ed. H. Weber)---------------C. Kaiser (1959)
"Gott, heilger Schoepfer aller Stern" ("Creator Alme Siderum")
"Herr Christ, der du die deinen liebst"
"Herr Jesu Christ, du hoechstes (Goerlitz)"
"Herr, nun lass in Friede (Bohemian)"
"Waer Gott nicht mit uns (Walther)"
"Wie soll ich dich empfangen (Crueger)"
"Zeuch ein zu deinen (Crueger)"

Haigh, Morris   American   1932-

    Fantasie on a Lutheran Chorale (with horn)-------------------Shawnee
    "Vater Unser"

Hallnaes, Hilding   Swedish   1903-

    Annorlunda Koralfoerspel----------------------------- Verbum Forlag
       Fantasi och Preludium "Se vi gaa upp till Jerusalem"
    Koralfoerspel "Kom Helge Ande, Herre god"-------------mss. STIM'S

Hambraeus, Bengt   Swedish   1928-

    Op. 4: Koralfoerspel--------------------------------- mss. STIM'S
    "Christus der uns selig macht"
    "Es sungen drei Engel"
    "Ingen vinner fram"
    "Jesus Christus unser Heiland"
    "Warum betruebst du dich"

Hamburger, Poul   Danish   1901-

    Introitus Preludier (ed. Runbaeck and Aahlen)-----------------Nordiska
       Vol. 1: "Att bedja Gud" ("Vater Unser")

Hamill, Paul   American   Contemporary

    Voluntaries for the Christian Year, Vol. 2------------------ Abingdon
    "Hendon"

Hamm, Walter   German   1926-

    Einfache Orgelvorspiele (ed. H. Weber)---------------C. Kaiser (1959)
    "Du Schoepfer aller Wesen"
    "Jesu Kreuz, Leiden und Pein"
    "Jesu, meine Freude"
    "Jesu meines Lebens Leben (Wessnitzer)"
    "Lobt Gott, ihr Christen alle gleich (Herman)"
    "Lobt Gott, ihr frommen Christen"

Hasse, Peter   German   1585-1640

    Musikalische Denkmaeler, Band III------------------B. Schott's Soehne
    46 Choraele fuer Orgel
       "Allein Gott in der Hoeh"

Hastings, Edward H.   American   1923-

    Noël in Olden Style -------------------------------------J. Fischer

Hays, Robert Wilson

    Improvisation on a Plainsong Melody---------------------- H. W. Gray
    "Kyrie (Ite Missa Est)"

Hedwall, Lennart   Swedish   1932-

    Annorlunda Koralfoerspel----------------------------------- Verbum

Hedwall, Lennart (cont.)

"Vart flyr jag foer Gud och" ("Stockholm")
Koralpartita "Att bedja aer ej endast" ("Psalm 12-Geneva")----Nordiska
Koralpartita VI: "Den blomstertid nu kommer"--------------- Nordiska
Koralpartita VII: "Christe Qui Lux Es" ("Christe der du
    bist")--- Nordiska
Partita "Min sjael och sinne"--------------------------- mss. STIM'S
Partita "Vi prise dig, O Fader kaer"---------------------------WESS
Variationer "I himmelen (Laurinus)"--------------------- mss. STIM'S
2 Koralfoerspel--   "
    "Den signede dag"
    "Nu vilar hela jorden" ("Innsbruck")
3 Sommarpastoraler----------------------------------- mss. STIM'S
    "Den blomstertid nu kommer"
    "En vaenlig groenskas rika draekt"
    "I denna ljuva sommartid"
8 Koralfoerspel-------------------------------------- mss. STIM'S
    "Ditt namn, O Gud, jag lova vill"
    "Hit, O Jesu, samloms vi"
    "Nu glaed dig, min ande"
    "O Kriste, du som ljuset aer"
    "O liv, som blev taent"
    "Pro Pace et Principe"
    "Si Jesu aer ett troestrikt namn" ("Wenn wir in hoechsten")
    "Upp min tunga"
18 Koralfoerspel------------------------------------- mss. STIM'S
    "Alla Herrens vaeger"
    "Den ljusa dag framgaanger aer" ("Den lyse dag")
    "Dig vare lov och pris" ("Ter Sanctus")
    "Din spira, Jesu, straeckes ut"
    "Ditt namn, O Gud"
    "En dunkel oertagaard jag vet"
    "Fraan Gud vill jag ej vika" ("Von Gott will ich-Erfurt")
    "Glaed dig, du helga kristenhit"
    "Hela vaerlden froejdes Herran"
    "Hit, O Jesu, samloms vi"
    "Jesu, du som sjaelen spisar"
    "Jesus fraan Nasaret"
    "O Fader vaar, barmhaertig, god"
    "O Gud det aer min glaedje"
    "O Gud, ditt rike ingen ser"
    "Vaerldens fraelsare kom haer" ("Nun komm der Heiden") (2)
    "Vem aer den som troett"

Hegedus, Arpad

Consolaire, Vol. 1, #2-- WLSM
    Postlude on Jesus Christ Is Risen Today ("Lyra Davidica")

Heiller, Anton   Austrian   1923-

In Festo Corporis Christi---------------------------------- Doblinger
    "Bone Pastor"
    "Lauda Sion (Mode 7)"

Held, Wilbur   American   1916-

  2 Traditional Carols (with C Instrument)-------------------- Augsburg
    "Celestia"   "Christmas Eve (Knudsen)"
  6 Carol Settings--- Concordia
    "Divinum Mysterium"   "God Rest You Merry"
    "First Nowell"   "In Dulci Jubilo"
    "Forest Green"   "Vom Himmel hoch"
  Preludes and Postludes, Vol. 1---------------------------- Augsburg
    "Duke Street"   "O Store Gud (Swedish)"
    "Ellers"   "Restoration (Southern Harmony)"
    "Holy Manna (Moore)"   "They'll Know We Are Christians
    "Hyfrydol"   (Scholtes)"
    "New Britain"
  Preludes for Hymns in the Worship Supplement (ed. Thomas)-Concordia
    "Picardy"

Hellden, Daniel   Swedish   1917-

  Annorlunda Koralfoerspel ----------------------------------- Verbum
    "O huvud, blodigt saarat"

Hemmer, Eugene   American   1929-

  6 Soft Pieces by 6 American Composers---------------------- WLSM
    O Holy Lord ("Bohemian Brethren")
  Consolaire, Vol. 1, #2------------------------------------- WLSM
    Offertory on "Regina Caeli"

Hens, Charles   Belgian   1898-

  Cantantibus Organis--------------------------------------- Van Rossum
    Passacaglia ("Gaudeamus-Gregorian")

Herzogenberg, Heinrich von   Austrian   1843-1900

  Seasonal Choral Preludes (Pedals) (ed. Trevor)----------------- Oxford
    Book I: "Nun komm, der Heiden"

Hilf, Robert

  Consoliere, Vol. 1, #6----------------------------------- WLSM
    Away in a Manger ("Mueller")

Hillert, Richard   American   1923-

  Preludes for Hymns in the Worship Supplement (ed. Thomas)--Concordia
    "Shepherding"

Hilty, Everett Jay   American

  Fanfare, Toccata and Chorale in Echo------------------------- WLSM
    "Aurelia"

Hoegner, Friedrich   German   1897-

  Einfache Orgelvorspiele (ed. H. Weber)--------------------- C. Kaiser

Hoegner, Friedrich (cont.)

"Dein Koenig kommt in (Zahn)"
"Der du bist Drei"
"Der Tag bricht an (Vulpius)"
"Die helle Sonn' leucht jetzt herfuer (Vulpius)"
"Er weckt mich alle Morgen"
"O Durchbrecher (Halle)"
"Steht auf ihr lieben Kinderlein"
"Wie schoen leuchtet"

Hoeller, Karl   German   1907-

Op. 55: Improvisation (cello and organ)-----------------------Peters
"Schoenster Herr Jesu"

Hofer, Maria   Austrian   1894-

Op. 75: Fest Organist----------------------------------- Universal
(9 pieces for Christmas, Easter and Whitsuntide)

Hofhaymer, Paulus   Austrian   1459-1537

Liber Organi VIII--------------------------------B. Schott's Soehne
"Ave Maris Stella (Mode 1)"
Orgue et Liturgie----------------------------------- Schola Cantorum
#11: Salve Regina ("Ite Missa Est - Gregorian")
#25: Fantasia on "On freudt verzer"

Hokanson, Margrethe   American   1898-

Jesus In Thy Dying Woes----------------------------------- Augsburg
"Swedish Litany"

Hovdesven, Elmer Arne   American   1893-

Raise the Strain----------------------------------- Boston Music Co.
"Credition"
"Farrant"
"Freiburg"
"Innsbruck"
"Lyons"
"O Traurigkeit"
"St. Kevin"
"Swedish Melody" ("Tryggare")
"Truro"
"Warum sollt ich"
Sacred Organ Folio, Vol. 4----------------------------------Lorenz
2 Carol Preludes:
"Bring a Torch"
"When Christmas Morn Is Breaking (Swedish)"

Hovland, Egil   Norwegian   1924-

Chorale Partita "Herre Gud, ditt dyre navn (Norwegian Folk
Tune)"--- Norsk
100 Salmeforspill --- Lyche

"Aa hjertens ve"
"Paa Gud alene (Zinck)"
"Paaskemorgen"
"Se hvor nu Jesus (Kingo-Arrebo)"
"Soerg, O kjaere Fader" ("Christus der uns selig")
"Soerg, O kjaere Fader (Lindeman)"
"Sorgen og gleden (Lindeman)"
"Tvang til tro (Steenberg)"
"Underfulle Konge (Steenberg)"
"Vaakn op, du som sover (Lindeman)"
"Vaakn op og slaa" ("Winchester New")
"Vaar Gud han er" ("Ein feste Burg")

Huber, Klaus   German   1924-

"In Te Domine Speravi"-------------------------------Baerenreiter

Hughes, E. J.   Welsh

The Organist (Yr Organydd)------------------ Gwynn Publ. Co. (1938)
    Prelude on "Caerllyngoed"

Hughes, Robert J.   American   1916-

Sacred Organ Journal, Nov. 1970----------------------------- Lorenz
    Song of Thanksgiving ("Kremser")
Sacred Organ Folio-- Lorenz
    Vol. 3: "I Need Thee Every Hour"
    Vol. 4: Saviour Like a Shepherd ("Pleasant Pastures")

Hulse, Camil Van   American   1897-

Consolaire, Vol. 1, #2--- WLSM
    Lenten Meditation ("Audi Benigne Conditor-Mode 2")
Soli Deo Gloria--- Flammer
    Chorale Prelude on Tune of Praetorius
      "Keine Schoenheit hat die Welt (Joseph)"
    Variation and Finale "God, Father, Praise and Glory (Mainz)"

Hultin, Lennart   Swedish   1927-

"Den signade dag"--Verbum

Hunt, William   English

Chorale Prelude on "St. Columba (Irish)"----------------J. B. Cramer
Prelude on "Franconia"--------------------------------------- Novello

Hurford, Peter   English   1930-

Ceremonial Music for Organ----------------------------------- Oxford
    Fanfare on "Old 100th"

Hustad, Don   American   Contemporary

3 Organ Hymns for Weddings----------------------------------- Hope
    "Lauda Anima"

Hustad, Don (cont.)

    "Nun danket alle Gott"
    "O Perfect Love"
  Hymn Sketches--Hope
    "Amazing Grace"   "Holy Manna"
    "Arise"   "Hymn to Joy (Beethoven)"
    "Crimond"   "Spanish Hymn"
    "Cwm Rhondda"   "To God Be the Glory (Doane)"
    "Ein feste Burg"   "Toplady"
  Hymns for the Organ--Hope
    "Aberystwyth"
    "Adelaide"
    "Antioch"
    "Beecher"
    "Gordon"
    "Lasst uns erfreuen"
    "Mercy"
    "Old Rugged Cross" and "Passion Chorale"
    "Quietude (Green)"
    "St. Margaret"
    "Sanctuary (Runyan)"
    "The Solid Rock (Bradbury)"
    "Toplady"
    "Victory (Palestrina)"
  Sacred Harp for the Organ--------------------------------Broadman
    "Antioch (F. C. Wood)"
    "Foundation"
    "Green Fields"
    "Irwinton"
    "Jordan's Banks"
    "Pisgah"
    "Sweet Rivers of Redeeming Love"
    "Wondrous Love"

Hutchison, Warner

  Hymn Tune Suite----------------------------------- Shawnee (1969)
    "Hyfrydol"
    "Picardy"
    "Slane"

Hutson, Wihla

  Hymn-Tune Voluntaries for the Worship Service---------------Shawnee
    "Aberystwyth" and "Hamburg"
    "Ar-Hyd-Y-Nos"
    "Dundee"
    "Gardiner"
    "Hyfrydol"
    "Leoni"
    "Puer Nobis Nascitur"
    "St. Denio"

Huybrechts, August J.

  Consolaire, Vol. 2, #4----------------------------------- WLSM
    Communion on "Spires"

Huybrechts, Louis (Lode)   Belgian   1911-1973

6 Organ Processionals (for coming into church) ----------------- WLSM
Processional on "Asperges Me (Kyrial)"

Iderstine, A. P. Van

Sacred Organ Folio---Lorenz
Little Chorale Prelude on "Slane"

Islandsmoen, Sigurd   Norwegian   1881-

29 Koralvorspill av Norske Organister (ed. Sandvold)------------ Norsk
"Akk visste du (Lindeman)"
"Folkefrelsar (Sletten)"
"Hos Gud er idel (Norse Folk)"
"Jeg vil mig Herren love (Norse Folk)"

Jacob, Dom Clément   1906-

Orgue et Liturgie, Vol. 48-------------------------- Schola Cantorum
"Puer Natus Est Nobis"

Jader, Joens   Swedish   ca. 1889

Postludier (ed. Runbaeck and Aahlen) -----------------------Nordiska
"Jeg vil mig Herren love (Swedish Psalm)"

Janáček, Bedrich   Czech-Swedish   1920-

2 Orgelkoraler--Norberg
"Jag lyfter mina haender" ("Valet")
"Saa gaar en dag aen fraan vaar tid"
3 Passionskoraler-- Nordiska
"Min sjael, du maaste"
"O huvud, blodigt"
"Se, vi gaa upp" ("O Jesu for din pina")
Liten partita "Vart flyr jag foer Gud (Stockholm)"------------Nordiska

Jenkins, Joseph Willcox   American   1928-

6 Pieces for Organ--- WLSM
#1: Old English Hymn - "Lenox"

Jobs, Anders   Swedish   1876-1959

Introitus Preludier (ed. Runbaeck and Aahlen) ----------------Nordiska
Vol. I: "Hela vaerlden froejdes Herran"

Joelson, A. G.   Swedish   1891-

Koralfoerspel "Bereden vaeg foer Herran"---------------------Verbum

Johannesen, Grant

   Improvisation on a Mormon Hymn (arr. A. Schreiner)-----------Oxford
   "Come, Come, Ye Saints"

Johansson, Sven-Eric   Swedish   1919-

   2 Koralfoerspel -- mss. STIM'S
     "Hav i ditt minne Jesus Krist"
     "Jesus aer min vaen den baeste"
   2 Orgelkoraler--- mss. STIM'S
     "Eja mitt hjaerta"
     "I Herrens namn"
   "Allena Gud i himmelrik"--WESS
   "Du som var den minstes vaen" ("Liebster Jesu")---------mss. STIM'S
   Partita "Naer vaerldens hopp foertvinat"-----------------mss. STIM'S

Johns, Donald   American   1926-

   Introduction and Passacaglia------------------------------- Doblinger
     "Ich wollt, dass ich daheime waer"

Johnson, David N.   American   1922-

   Just As I Am ("Woodworth")------------------------------- Abingdon
   Music For Worship (Easy Trios)----------------------------Augsburg
     "Christe Sanctorum (French)"
     "Froehlich soll mein (Crueger)"
     "Geduld die soll'n (Gesius)"
     "Heinlein"
     "In Babilone"
     "Kedron"
     "King's Weston"
     "Noël (English)"
     "O Filii et Filiae"
     "Passion Chorale"
     "Quem Pastores"
     "Ringe recht (Kuhnau)"
     "St. Thomas (Wade)"
     "Victory (Palestrina)"
     "Warum sollt ich (Ebeling)"
   Music for Worship (Manuals)------------------------------ Augsburg
     "Adrian Michelle"
     "Conditor Alme Siderum"
     "Congleton"
     "Freiburg"
     "Gaudeamus Pariter"
     "Herzlich tut mich erfreuen"
     "Herzliebster Jesu"
     "In Dulci Jubilo"
     "Mach's mit mir, Gott (Schein)"
     "Macht hoch die Tuer (Freylinghausen)"
     "Vom Himmel hoch"
     "Werde munter"
   Manuals Only--- Augsburg
     "Enchiridion (Erfurt)"
     "Jordan (Sacred Harp)"

Johnston, Edward F.   American

    Resurrection Morn--------------------------------- J. Fischer (1912)
    "Lyra Davidica"

Johnston, Helen   American   Contemporary

    Hymn Preludes for the Mennonite Hymnal --------------Goshen College
    "Down Ampney"

Jones, Robert W.   American

    Consolaire, Vol. 1, #4----------------------------------- WLSM
    Chorale Prelude on "Adoro Te Devote"

Jong, Marinus de   Belgian   1891-

    15 Organ Pieces from Modern Belgium ----------------------- WLSM
    Prelude on "O Salutaris Hostia (Duquet)"
    Postlude on "Lobe den Herren, den"
    Postlude on "Ad Te Levavi (Mode 8)"

Jonsson, Josef   Swedish   1887-

    Postludium Funebre---Nordiska
    "Jag gaar mot doeden"

Jordahl, Robert

    Festival Prelude on O for a Thousand--------------------- H. W. Gray
    "Azmon"

Joubert, John   Union of South Africa   1927-

    Easy Modern Organ Music, Book 2---------------------------- Oxford
    Prelude on "Picardy"

Joulain, Jeanne   French   1920-

    Finale on "Ave Maris Stella"------------------------ Schola Cantorum
    Orgue et Liturgie, Vol. 48-------------------------- Schola Cantorum
    "Hosanna Filio David"

Jullien, Gilles   French   1650-1703

    Les Maîtres Français de l'Orgue------Ed. Mus. de la Schola Cantorum
       (17 & 18 Siècles)
    Fugue on "Ave Maris Stella (Mode 1)"

Kaminski, Heinrich   German   1886-1946

    "Meine Seel' ist stille"----------------------------------Baerenreiter
    ("Jesu, meine Freude-Crueger")

Kammeier, Hans   German   1902-

    Einfache Orgelvorspiele (ed. H. Weber)-------------------- C. Kaiser

Kammeier, Hans (cont.)

"Dir, dir, Jehova (Halle)"
"Froehlich wir nun all fangen an"
"Lob Gott getrost mit Singen (Bohemian)"
"Sollt ich meinem Gott (Schop)"
"Walt's Gott, mein Werk ich lasse"
"Wer weiss, wie nahe (Rudolfstadt)"

Karlsen, Kjell Moerk   Contemporary

Partita over Koralen "Nu kjaere menige Kristenhet"-------------Norsk
("Nun freut Euch - Nuernberg")

Karlsen, Rolf   Norwegian

6 Koralforspill --Musikk Huset
"Jeg ser dig, O Guds Lam (Norsk Folk)"
"Kirken den er et"
"Korset vil jeg aldri (Folk Tune)"
"O bliv hos mig (Steenberg)"
"Se solens skjoenne (Norsk Folk)"
"Underfulle Konge (Steenberg)"
29 Koralforspill av Norske Organister (ed. Sandvold)-------------Norsk
"Kjaerlighet er lysets (Lindeman)"
Julefantasi --Musikk Huset
"Et barn er foedt" ("Puer Natus in Bethlehem")
"In Dulci Jubilo"

Kauffmann, Georg Friedrich   German   1679-1735

Harmonische Seelenlust --------------------------------- Baerenreiter
"Ach Gott vom Himmel"
"Allein zu dir"
"Aus tiefer Noth (Strassburg)"
"Christus der uns selig macht"
"Ein feste Burg"
"Herr Christ der einig"
"Herzlich tut mich verlangen"
"Herzliebster Jesu"
"Ich ruf' zu dir"
"Lobt Gott, ihr Christen (Herman)"
"Nun lob, mein Seel' "
"Vater Unser"
"Von Gott will ich nicht (Erfurt)"
"Wenn mein Stundlein"
"Wenn wir in hoechsten"
"Wir glauben all an einen Gott, Schoepfer"
Orgue et Liturgie #24: Notre Père------------------- Schola Cantorum
"Vater Unser"
Seasonal Chorale Preludes (Manuals) (ed. Trevor)--------------Oxford
Book I: "Valet"

Keldermans, Raymond A.   American   1911-

Manualiere, Vol. 1, #3-- WLSM
Toccata on "Veni Creator Spiritus"

Kjeldaas, Arnljot   Norwegian   1916-

29 Koralvorspill av Norske Organister (ed. Sandvold)------------ Norsk
   "Gladelig vil vi halleluja (Lindeman)"
   "Gud er naadig (Lindeman)"
   "O bliv hos mig (Steenberg)"

Kjellsby, Erling   Norwegian   Contemporary

"Jeg synger Julekvad"--- Lyche
4 Forspill til Norske Folketoner------------------------------- Norsk
   "Eg veit i himmerik (Folk Tune)"
   "I himmelen (Norwegian)"
   "Ingen vinner frem (Norse Folk Tune)"
   "Jesu, din soete forening (Norse Folk)"

Klenz, William   American   Contemporary

An Organist's Year-------------- mss. (N.Y. University at Binghamton)
   "Ach Gott vom Himmel" (2)
   "Ach Gott, wie lang"
   "Alle Menschen muessen sterben (German-Bach)"
   "Alle Menschen muessen sterben (Mueller)"
   "An Wasserfluessen"
   "Christ ist erstanden" (3)
   "Christ ist erstanden von dem Tod"
   "Christ lag in Todesbanden"
   "Dankt den Herrn" ("Old 107")
   "Das alte Jahr"
   "De Profundis" ("Psalm 129-Calvin")
   "Durch Adams Fall"
   "Erfreut Euch in Gott"
   "Es wollt uns Gott (Psalm 67)"
   "Gelobet seist du"
   "Gott ist mein Licht (Psalm 27)"
   "Herr erhoere meine Klagen (Psalm 77)"
   "Herr hoere doch (Psalm 5-Geneva)"
   "Herr Jesu Christ, dich zu uns"
   "Herr straf' mich nicht"
   "Ich erhebe mein Gemuethe (Psalm 25)"
   "In dich hab' ich (Nuernberg)"
   "In Dulci Jubilo"
   "Komm' Heiliger Geist, Herre Gott"
   "Lobt den Herrn (Psalm 136)"
   "Louez le Seigneur"
   "Mein Gott, warum verlaesst du mich (Psalm 22)"
   "Mein Seel' erhebt den Herren"
   "Mit Fried und Freud"
   "Nun komm, der Heiden" (2)
   "O Haupt voll Blut"
   "Psalm 3 (Calvin)"
   "Psalm 24"
   "Psalm 27"
   "Psalm 31"
   "Psalm 32 (Calvin)"
   "Psalm 37 (O Mensch bewein)"
   "Psalm 47"

Klenz, William (cont.)

"Psalm 50 (Calvin)" (2)
"Psalm 55"
"Psalm 79"
"Psalm 88 (Dutch)"
"Psalm 105"
"Psalm 125"
"Psalm 137"
"Psalm 148 (Dutch)"
"Schmuecke dich"
"Steh' auf in deiner Macht (Dominus Sanctus-Pierre)"
"Truro"
"Vom Himmel hoch"
"Wer nur den lieben Gott (Neumark)"
"Wie der Hirsch" ("Freu dich sehr")
"Wie herrlich gibst du, Herr (Psalm 8)"
"Wie lieblich ist das Haus (Jervaulx Abbey)"
"Wie schoen leuchtet"
"Wo Gott zum Haus"

Kluge, Manfred   German   1928-

Choralvorspiele-- B & H
"Aus tiefer Not (Phrygian)"   "Herzliebster Jesu"
"Da Christus geboren war (Bohemian)" "Ich ruf' zu dir"
"Der Tag hat sich geneiget"   "Sonne der Gerechtigkeit
"Du grosser Schmerzensmann (Vopelius)"   (Bohemian)"
"Gelobt sei Gott (Vulpius)"
"Heil'ger Geist, du Troester (Crueger)"

Knutzen, Ingvar   Swedish   1932-

Gammal dalakoral "O Jesu naer jag haedan skall"---------mss. STIM'S
Toccata and Fugue "Si Jesus aer ett troestrikt namn"----- mss. STIM'S
("Wenn wir in hoechsten")

Koert, Hans Van   Dutch   1913-

Consolaire, Vol. 1, #2----------------------------------- WLSM
Prelude on The Paschal Victim
"Victimae Paschali (Gregorian-Mode 1)"
Consoliere, Vol. 1, #6---------------------------------- WLSM
Postlude on "Lourdes Pilgrim Hymn"

Kousemaker, Adriaan   Dutch   1909-

Koraalboek - Psalmen------------------------------------- Ars Nova
Psalmen 21-30

Krapf, Gerhard   German-American   1924-

All Praise to Thee------------------------------------- Augsburg
"Gelobet seist du, Jesu Christ"
Built on a Rock-- Augsburg
"Kirken den er et"

Krapf, Gerhard (cont.)

Dear Christians, One and All ------------------------------ Augsburg
   "Nun freut Euch (Nuernberg)"
Lord Jesus Christ, With Us Abide ------------------------- Concordia
   "Ach bleib bei uns"
Partita on "Ein Laemmlein geht (Dachstein)"----------------- Concordia
Partita for Organ ("Wachet auf") ------------------------- Hope (Agape)
Preludes for Hymns in the Worship Supplement (ed. Thomas)--Concordia
   "Freuen wir uns alle"
Reformation Suite--Concordia
   "Ach Gott vom Himmel (Erfurt)"
   "Ein feste Burg"
   "Nun bitten wir (Soldau)"
   "Wir glauben all an einen Gott, Schoepfer (Wittenberg)"
3rd Organ Sonata on Morning Chorales-------------------- J. Fischer
   "All Morgen ist ganz frisch (Walther)"
   "Die helle Sonn' leucht't (Vulpius)"
   "O Christe, Morgensterne (Gesius-Leipzig)"

Krause, Paul   German   1880-

Op. 9, #1: Orgelkonzert #15 (ed. Gauss) ------------------Coppenrath
   "Alle Menschen (Mueller)"

Krebs, Johann Ludwig   German   1713-1780

Seasonal Chorale Preludes (Manuals) (ed. Trevor) ---------------Oxford
   Book I: "Erbarm dich mein"

Krieger, Johann   German   1652-1735

Orgue et Liturgie #24: Notre Père------------------- Schola Cantorum
   "Vater Unser"
Seasonal Chorale Preludes (Manuals) (ed. Trevor)---------------Oxford
   Book II: "Vater Unser"

Kropfreiter, Augustinus Franz   Austrian   Contemporary

Partita: "Es kommt ein Schiff geladen"----------------------Doblinger
Triplum super "Veni Creator Spiritus (Sarum-Mode 8)-------- Doblinger

Kuhnau, Johann   German   1660-1722

6 Biblical Sonatas----------------------------------- Broude Bros.
   #1: Der Streit zwischen David und Goliath
     2nd Movement: Israelites Prayer for Help
      "Aus tiefer Not (Phrygian)"

Kullnes, Aake   Swedish   1910-

Koralfoerspel (ed. Andersson and Norrman) -------------------Nordiska
   Vol. 2:
     "Av hjaertat haver jag dig kaer"
     "Fader du vars hjaerta goemmer"
Partita: "Vi prise Dig, O Fader kaer"--------------------------WESS

Lagergren, August   Swedish   1848-1908

Laeff Uffoerbara Koralpreludier------------------------- A. Lundquist
   Vol. 1:
    # 1: "Wachet auf"
      3: "Jesus allt mit goda aer (Arrhenius)"
      4: "Wenn wir in hoechsten"
      6: "Hjaelp mig, min Gud (Waldis)"
      8: "Herzlich tut mich verlangen"
      9: "Aus tiefer Not (Phrygian)"
     11: "Din klara Sol" ("Stoerl I")
     12: "Tvivlan ur min sjael (Wessnitzer)"
     14: "Jesu, meine Freude"
     16: (Haeffner Hymn 187)
     17: "Die Tugend wird durch's (Halle)"
     19: "Gud ej sitt tryckta barn"
     22: "Wer nur den lieben (Neumark)"
     26: "Allein zu dir"
   Vol. 2:
    #28: "Ein feste Burg"
     30: "In Dulci Jubilo"
     32: "O Lamm Gottes (Decius)"
     34: "In dich hab' ich (Nuernberg)"
     35: "Jeg raaber, Herre Jesu Krist (Wittenberg)"
     36: "Wo Gott, der Herr (Wittenberg)"
     37: "Es wolle Gott uns (Strassburg)"
     38: "O Gott, du frommer (Hannover)"
     39: "Jesu, deine tiefen (Koenig)"
     40: "Von Gott will ich nicht (Erfurt)"
     41: "Fraelsta vaerld!"
     42: "Vad min Gud vill"
     44: "Nun lob mein Seel (Kugelman)"
     45: "O Jesu Christ, du hoechstes Gut (Crueger)"
     46: "Jesu aer min vaen den baeste (Dueben)"
     48: "Ter Sanctus"
     49: "I dag, om Herrens roest"
     51: "Hjaelp mig, Jesu"
     52: "O Gud, ditt rike ingen (Waldis)"
     53: "Lob sei den Allmaechtigen (Crueger)"
     55: "Jesu, du mitt liv"
     56: "Vater Unser"
   Vol. 3:
    #58, 59, 60, 61: "Stoerl I"
     64, 65: "Pax"
     69, 70, 71: "O Lamm Gottes (Decius)"
     74, 75: "Werde munter (Schop)"
     79, 80, 81: "Liebster Jesu (Briegel)"
     83, 84, 85: "Wachet auf"
   Vol. 4:
    #87, 88, 89, 90: "Vom Himmel hoch"
     92: "Old 130th"
     94, 95: "Schmuecke dich"
     97, 98, 99: "Praise (Swedish)"
    101, 102, 103, 104: "Foerlossningen"
    106, 107, 108: "Jesus, du dig sjaelf uppvaeckte"
    110, 111: "Auf meinen lieben Gott (Regnart)"
    112, 113: "Freu dich sehr"

Lagergren, August (cont.)

    #115, 116, 117: "Nun freut Euch (Klug)"
    118, 119: "Wie schoen leuchtet"

Langlais, Jean François   French   1907-

    Op. 2: Poemes Evangéliques ----------------------------- H. Hérelle
      1: L'Annonciation ("Magnificat-Tone 6")
      3: Les Rameaux ("Hosanna Filio David")
    Folkloric Suite--- FitzSimons
      Canzona on "Durch Adams Fall"
      Fugue on "O Filii et Filiae"
      Rhapsody on 2 Noëls
    Livre Oecuménique--------------------------------------- Bornemann

"Allein Gott in der Hoeh'"	"Kyrie Orbis Factor"
"Aus tiefer Not (Phrygian)"	"Meine Seele erhebet den Herrn (Klug)"
"Ave Maris Stella (Mode 1)"	"Pater Noster (Liturgical)"
"Ein feste Burg"	"Sacris Solemnis (Mode 4)"
"Gloria Orbis Factor"	"Vater Unser"
"Kyrie, Gott Vater in Ewigkeit"	"Verbum Supernum (Plainsong-Mode 8)"

Lasceux, Guillaume   French   1740-1831

    Les Maîtres Français de l'Orgue ------Ed. Mus. de la Schola Cantorum
      (17 & 18 Siècles)
      Vol. 2: "Noël Lorraine"

LeBêgue, Nicolas Antoine   French   1631-1702

    Archives des Maîtres de l'Orgue, Vol. 9----------------------Durand
      "Magnificat" (All 8 Tones)
    Cantantibus Organis, Vol. 12---------------------------------- Pustet
      "Stabat Mater (Mode 1)"
    Les Maîtres Français de l'Orgue------ Ed. Mus. de la Schola Cantorum
      (17 & 18 Siècles)
      Vol. 1:
        Offertory on "O Filii et Filiae"
        "A la venue de Noël"
        "Noël pour l'amour de Marie"
      Vol. 2:
        "Noël - Où s'en vont ces gays bergers"
    Orgues et Liturgie, Vol. 16: Noëls Variés------------Schola Cantorum
      "A la venue de Noël" (2)
      "Noël - Laissez paître vos bestes" (3)
      "Noël - Le petit nouveau né"
      "Noël - Les Bourgeoises de Chartres"
      "Noël cette journée"
      "Noël pour l'amour de Marie"
      "Noël - Or nous dites Marie"
      "Noël - Où s'en vont ces gays bergers"
      "Puer Nobis Nascitur"
      "Noël - Une vierge pucelle"

Lechat, J.

    Consolaire, Vol. 2, #2--------------------------------------- WLSM
      Communion on "Ubi Caritas Et Amor"

Leguay, Jean Pierre   French   1939-

L'Organiste Liturgique, Vol. 53---------------------- Schola Cantorum
    Versets on "Veni Creator"

Lehr, Mangham David

Partita on "Veni Emmanuel"------------------------------- Ars Nova

Leighton, Kenneth   English   1929-

Op. 49: Fantasy and Fugue on "Et Resurrexit"---------------- Novello

Lenel, Ludwig   German-American   1914-

Preludes for Hymns in the Worship Supplement (ed. Thomas)--Concordia
    "Conditor Alme Siderum"

Lesur, Daniel Jean Yves   French   1908-

4 Hymnes----------------------------Ed. Musicale Transatlantiques
    "A Solis Ortus"
    "Coelestis Urbs Jerusalem"
    "Creator Alme Siderum"
    "Crudelis Herodes"

Lindberg, Knut   Swedish   1909-

Postludier (ed. Runbaeck and Aahlen)------------------------Nordiska
    "Beredd mig haall, Herre Jesu Krist"

Lindberg, Oskar Fredrik   Swedish   1887-1955

Gammal Faebodpsalm--- Nordiska
Liten Partita "Naer stormens lurar skalla"------------------- Nordiska
Orgelspelets Teknik (Anrep-Nordin)------- Elkan, Schildknecht, Carelius
    Koralfantasi "Jag haver en gaang varit ung"
Variationer oever en Gammal Dalakoral---------------------Nordiska

Lindegren, Johan   Swedish   1842-1908

Postludier (ed. Runbaeck and Aahlen)----------------------- Nordiska
    "Du bar ditt kors, O Jesu mild" ("So gehst du nun")

Lindorff-Larsen, Eilert   Danish   1902-

Partita on "Lasst uns zum Kreuze (Gesius)"--------------Baerenreiter

Lindroth, Henry   Swedish   1910-

Koralfoerspel (ed. Andersson and Norrman), Vol. 2----------- Nordiska
    "Den signade dag"
    "Oss kristna boer"
    "Som faagelen vid ljusan dag"
"Vid evighetens brunner"-----------------------------------Nordiska

60   Organ Preludes Supplement

Lindstroem, Martin   Swedish   1929-

  Tva Stilla Koraler--- Gehrmans
    "En dunkel oertagaard jag vet"
    "O min Jesu, dit Du gaatt" ("Schwing dich auf - Crueger")

Linke, Norbert   Contemporary

  Organ Pops: Choralvorspiele fuer Orgel -------------------W. Mueller
    "Vater Unser"
    "Wachet auf"
    "Wunderbarer Koenig"

Liszt, Franz   Hungarian   1811-1886

  Historical Recital Series-----------------------------------H. W. Gray
    "Ave Maria (Arcadelt)"
  Kirchliche Fest-Ouvertuere----------------------------------Hofmeister
    "Ein feste Burg"
  "Salve Regina (Mode 1)"--------------------------------------- Kahnt

Loewe, Andreas L.   17 ?-1826

  Consoliere, Vol. 1, #1--------------------------------------- WLSM
    Chorale Prelude: "Jesus, You Are My Life"

Long, Page C.   American   Contemporary

  Lenten Elegy on "Passion Chorale"------------------------J. Fischer

Lorentz, Johann   German   1610-1689

  Choralbearbeitungen und Freie Orgelstuecke der Deutschen
    Sweelinck Schule (ed. Moser), Vol. 2---------------Baerenreiter
  Variations on "Vater Unser"
  Prelude on "Herr Christ, der einig (Erfurt)"

Lovelace, Austin Cole   American   1919-

  Christ the Lord Is Risen Today--------------------------------- Hope
      (with trumpets and trombones)
    "Easter Hymn"

Luebeck, Vincent   German   1654-1740

  Orgelwerke---Klecken Verlag
    "Ich ruf' zu dir"
    "Nun lasst uns Gott dem Herren"

Lundborg, Geosta   Swedish   1903-

  3 Orgelstycken-- Norberg
    Fantasi "Den ljusa dag framgaangen aer (Kingo)"
    Introduction and Fughetta "I denna ljuva sommartid"
    Variations "Himmelriket liknas vid tio jungfrur"
  Orgelmusik vid jordfaestning (ed. Runbaeck)----------------- Nordiska
    Gammal dalakoral fraan Boda

Lundell, Carl   Swedish   1859-1916

Introitus Preludier (ed. Runbaeck and Aahlen)---------------- Nordiska
   Vol. I: "Ack hjaertens ve"
   Vol. II: "Ande, full av naad" ("Brunnquell aller Guete")
Postludier (ed. Runbaeck and Aahlen)----------------------- Nordiska
   "Av hjaertat haver jag dig kaer"

Lunden, Lennart   Swedish   1914-1966

   "Till himmelen, dit laengtar jag"---------------------------- Verbum
   (Sacred Song from Skoeldinge)

Lundh, Lars August   Swedish   1838-1916

   Op. 94: 50 Smaa Koralpreludier (out of print)----------------Nordiska

Lynn, George Alfred   American   1915-

   To God on High (20 Preludes on Hymns)------------------ Th. Presser
   "Adeste Fideles"
   "Allein Gott in der Hoeh"
   "Carol"
   "Chartres"
   "Easter Hymn"
   "Gloria (French Noël)"
   "Hyfrydol"
   "Lasst uns erfreuen"
   "Laudes Domini"
   "O Filii et Filiae"
   "Olivet"
   "Penitence (Lane)"
   "St. Kevin"
   "St. Louis"
   "Salzburg"
   "Stille Nacht"
   "Stuttgart (Gotha)"
   "Veni Emmanuel"
   "Were You There?"
   "Winchester New"

Mader, Clarence   American   1904-1971

   Passiontide Fantasy (on a melody by J. W. Franck)---------J. Fischer
   "Komm, Seele (Franck)"

Maekelberghe, August   American   1909-

   3 Hymn Preludes---H. W. Gray
   "Hursley"
   "Rendez à Dieu"
   "Veni Emmanuel"

Manz, Paul   American   1919-

   Op. 9: 10 Chorale Improvisations, Set III-------------------Concordia
   "Gelobet seist du, Jesu Christ"

Manz, Paul (cont.)

    "Herr Jesu Christ, dich zu uns"
    "In Dulci Jubilo"
    "Jesu, meine Freude"
    "Lobe den Herren, O meine"
    "Nun komm der Heiden"
    "O dass ich tausend (Koenig)" (2)
    "O Gott, du frommer Gott (Stoerl)"
    "Schmuecke dich"
  Op. 10: 10 Chorale Improvisations, Set IV --------------- Concordia
    "Aus meines Herzens"
    "Christe, du Lamm Gottes (Decius)"
    "Gott der Vater wohn uns bei"
    "Komm Gott, Schoepfer (Klug)"
    "Nun freut Euch, lieben (Nuernberg)"
    "Old 100"
    "Valet"
    "Veni Emmanuel"
    "Wachet auf"
    "Werde munter"
  Op. 11: 10 Short Intonations on Well-Known Hymns-----------Augsburg
    "Ein feste Burg"
    "Freu dich sehr"
    "Herzliebster Jesu"
    "Kirken den er et"
    "Komm Heiliger Geist, Herre Gott"
    "Liebster Jesu (Ahle)"
    "Schmuecke dich"
    "Sine Nomine"
    Tantum Ergo ("Alleluia Dulce Carmen")
    "Te Deum (Vienna)"

Marckhl, Erich   Austrian   1902-

  7 Choraltrios-- Doblinger

Mareschall, Samuel   Belgian   1554-1641

  Consoliere, Vol. 3, #4-------------------------------- WLSM
    "In Dulci Jubilo"

Martin, Gilbert M.   American   1941-

  2 Preludes on American Hymn Tunes---------------------H. W. Gray
    "Amazing Grace"   "Nettleton"
  Sacred Organ Folio, Vol. 4----------------------------------Lorenz
    Variations on "Foundation"
    "Marosa"
  Sacred Organ Journal--------------------------------------- Lorenz
    July 1970:
      Toccata on "Duke Street"   Fantasia on "O Filii et Filiae"
    Nov. 1970:
      Meditation on "Silent Night"

Marx, Karl Julius   German   1897-

  Einfache Orgelvorspiele (ed. H. Weber)--------------------C. Kaiser

Marx, Karl Julius (cont.)

    "Der Herr ist mein getreuer Hirt (Wittenberg)"
    "Die gueld'ne Sonne (Ebeling)"
    "Froehlich soll mein Herze (Crueger)"

Matthison-Hansen, Gottfried   Danish   1832-1909

    Album Nordischer Komponisten, Vol. 1--------------------- W. Hansen
    #21: "Det er saa yndigt (Weyse)"
    #23: "Kjaere Guds barn (Folk)"

Maurer, Otto   Swiss   1898-1959

    Praeludien und Choralbearbeitungen-------------------------------Hug
    "Auf meinen lieben Gott (Regnart)"
    "Ein feste Burg"
    "Erschienen ist der"
    "Jesu, meiner Seele Licht (Vulpius)" ("Jesu, Leiden, Pein und Tod")
    "Nun komm, der Heiden"
    "Treuer Heiland, wir sind hier (Swiss Hymnal)"
    "Wenn mein Stuendlein (Wolff)"

McKay, George Frederick   American   1899-1970

    3 Pastoral Preludes ------------------------------------ J. Fischer
    "Den store hvide flok (Norwegian)"
    American Folk Hymn (Tune name not identified)
    (Green Fields and Meadows--not on a hymn tune)

McKinney, Howard D.   American   1890-

    Christmas At the Organ----------------------------------J. Fischer
    "Adeste Fideles"
    "Antioch (Handel)"
    "Auf, ihr Hirten (German)"
    "Away in a Manger (Murray)"
    "Bring a Torch (French)"
    "Deck the Halls"
    "Es ist ein Ros' "
    "First Nowell"
    "Gesu Bambino (Yon)"
    "God Rest You Merry"
    "Greensleeves"
    "Herald Angels"
    "I Saw Three Ships"
    "Ihr Kinderlein kommet"
    "In Dulci Jubilo"
    "Kommet, ihr Hirten (Bohemian)"
    "Les Anges dans nos"
    "Morgen kommt der Weihnachtsmann"
    "Noël - Tous les Bourgeois"
    "O Holy Night (Adam)"
    "O Tannenbaum"
    "St. Louis"
    "Shepherds, Shake Off"
    "Stille Nacht"

McKinney, Howard D. (cont.)

    "Three Kings"
    "Twelve Days of Christmas"
    "Wassail"
    "We Wish You a Merry Christmas"
    "Wie schoen leuchtet"
Preludes for 55 Well-Known Hymn Tunes------------------ J. Fischer
    "Adeste Fideles"
    "Albany (Jeffery)"
    "Alford (Dykes)"
    "All Saints New (Cutler)"
    "America"
    "Amsterdam"
    "Aurelia"
    "Austrian Hymn"
    "Coronation"
    "Crusaders Hymn"
    "Dennis"
    "Dominus Regit Me"
    "Duke Street"
    "Easter Hymn"
    "Ellers"
    "Evan"
    "Eventide"
    "Gerontius"
    "Grace Church"
    "Hamburg"
    "Italian Hymn"
    "Kremser"
    "Lancashire"
    "Langran"
    "Lasst uns erfreuen"
    "Lobe den Herren, den"
    "Louvan"
    "Lyons"
    "Marion"
    "Materna"
    "Mendebras"
    "Merrial"
    "Munich"
    "Nicaéa"
    "Nun danket alle"
    "Old 100"
    "Old 124"
    "Olivet"
    "Pentecost"
    "Rathbun"
    "Regent Square"
    "Rockingham"
    "Russian Hymn"
    "St. Agnes"
    "St. Anne"
    "St. Asaph"
    "St. Catherine"
    "St. Christopher"
    "St. Crispin"

McKinney, Howard D. (cont.)

    "St. Gertrude"
    "Sicilian Mariners"
    "Toulon"
    "Veni Emmanuel"
    "Victory (Palestrina)"
    "Webb"

Mead, Edward Gould   American   1892-

   Sacred Organ Folio, Vol. 4----------------------------------Lorenz
      Prelude on "Eucharistic Hymn"

Means, Claude   American   1912-

   Carol Prelude: "A Babe Lies in the Cradle (Corner)"----- H. W. Gray
   Joseph Dearest ("Joseph lieber, Joseph mein")---------------Concordia

Meek, Kenneth   Canadian   1908-

   Organ Music of Canada (ed. Peaker)------------------- Berandol Music
      Voluntary for St. Crispin's Day ("Agincourt Song")

Melin, Hugo   Swedish   1907-

   Introitus Preludier (ed. Runbaeck and Aahlen)-----------------Nordiska
      "O Fader vaar, barmhaertig god"
   Koralpartita "Jag vet paa vem (Copenhagen)"-------------- mss. STIM'S
   6 Orgelkoraler-- Norbergs
      "Aera ske Herren"
      "Hela vaerlden froejdes Herran (Swedish)"
      "Naer vaerldens hopp foertvinat stod"
      "Nu tackar Gud allt folk" ("Nun danket alle")
      "Vaar Gud aer oss en vaeldig borg"
      "Var haelsad skoena morgonstund"

Merkel, Gustav Adolf   German   1827-1885

   Seasonal Chorale Preludes (Pedals) (ed. Trevor)---------------- Oxford
      Book I: "Ach Gott wie manches" ("Breslau")

Merritt, Charles   American   Contemporary

   Voluntaries for the Christian Year, Vol. 2--------------------Abingdon
      "Slane"

Merulo, Claudio   Italian   1533-1604

   Orgue et Liturgie #11: Notre Dame------------------ Schola Cantorum
      "Kyrie Cum Jubilo"

Metzger, Hans Arnold   German   1913-

   Preludes for Hymns in the Worship Supplement (ed. Thomas)- Concordia
      "Adeste Fideles"

Micheelsen, Hans Friedrich   German   1902-

   Einfache Orgelvorspiele (ed. H. Weber) --------------------- C. Kaiser
     "Brich uns, Herr (Micheelsen)"
     "O Christenheit, sei hoch erfreut (Micheelsen)"
     "Troestet, troestet (Micheelsen)"
   Grenchener Orgelbuch, Part 1 ---------------------------- W. Mueller
     "Des Tages Glanz erloschen ist"
     "Heil'ger Geist, du Troester mein"
     "Herr Gott, dich loben alle wir (Old 100)"
     "Herr Jesu, deine Angst und Pein (Goerlitz)"
     "In Dir ist Freude"
     "Komm Heiliger Geist, Herre Gott"
     "O dass ich tausend (Koenig)"
     "O Welt, ich muss dich lassen"
     "Schmuecke dich"
     "Sei Lob und Ehr (Crueger)"
   Orgelkonzert IV: "Nun freut Euch" ----------------------- W. Mueller

Miles, George Theophilus   English   1913-

   Preludes for Hymns in the Worship Supplement (ed. Thomas)-- Concordia
     "Deo Gracias (Agincourt Hymn)"

Miles, Russell Hancock   American   1895-

   3 Communion Meditations------------------------------------G. Schirmer
     "Jesu, meine Freude"
     "Martyrdom"
     "Something for Jesus (Lowry)"

Moeller, Svend-Ove   Swedish   1903-1949

   Op. 4: 20 Orgelstykker-------------------------------------- Lohse
     "Jesu, dine dype vunder" ("Freu dich sehr")
     "Nu beder vi"
     "O Hellig Aand (Strassburg)"
     "Op alle som paa Jorden (Crueger)"

Monnikendam, Marius   Dutch   1896-

   2 Themes with Variations---------------------------------- Donemus
     "Veni Creator Spiritus (Sarum-Mode 8)"
     (Second theme is Frère Jacques)

Moseng, Sigvart   Norwegian

   29 Koralvorspill av Norske Organister (ed. Sandvold) ------------ Norsk
     "Eg veit i himmerick (Folk Tune)"
     "Herre Gud, ditt dyre navn (Norwegian Folk Tune)"
     "I Himmelen (Norwegian)"
     "Ingen vinner frem (Norse Folk Tune)"

Mourant, Walter   American   1910-

   Chorale Prelude----------------------- American Composers Alliance
     "O Welt, sieh hier dein Leben"

Moyer, J. Harold   American   1927-

Hymn Preludes for the Mennonite Hymnal --------------Goshen College
    "Aberystwyth"
    "Bound for the Promised Land"
    "Consolation (Wyeth)"
    "Foundation"
    "Resignation"
    "Rhyddid"
    "St. Denio"
    "Wondrous Love"
    "Zion's Pilgrim"

Mozart, Wolfgang Amadeus   Austrian   1756-1791

H. Bornefeld: Choralvorspiele 1930/70 (ed. Haenssler)---------Peters
    "Ach Gott vom Himmel" (from The Magic Flute)

Mueller, Carl F.   American   1892-

Organist's Solo Book-----------------------------------G. Schirmer
    Chorale Prelude on "Ein feste Burg"
O Worship the Lord------------------------------------ Broadman
    Carol and Hymn for Christmas: "Mueller" and "Mendelssohn"
    Festive Prelude on "St. Anne"
    Festive Prelude on "St. Theodulph"
    Meditation on "Crusaders Hymn"
    Meditation on "St. Christopher (Maker)"
    Prelude on 2 Advent Hymns: "Picardy" and "Veni Emmanuel"
    Prelude on "Lancashire (Smart)"

Naess, Sten

4 Orgelkoraler--Norsk

Near, Gerald   American   1942-

Preludes on 4 Hymn Tunes-------------------------------- Augsburg
    "Eisenach"
    "Hyfrydol"
    "Old 113th"
    "Seelenbraeutigam"

Nees, Staf (Gustaf F.)   Belgian   1901-

15 Organ Pieces from Modern Belgium ----------------------- WLSM
    Communion on "O Filii et Filiae"

Neubauer, Heinz

Einfache Orgelvorspiele (ed. H. Weber)---------------C. Kaiser (1959)
    "Christus, der ist mein Leben"
    "Ein feste Burg"
    "Ein Laemmlein geht"
    "Eins ist Not (Crueger)"
    "Erschienen ist der"

Neubauer, Heinz (cont.)

   "Erstanden ist der Heilig Christ"
   "Es geht daher des Tages Schein (Bohemian)"
   "Es glaenzet der Christen (Freylinghausen)"
   "Es ist das Heil"
   "Es ist gewisslich (Klug)"
   "Es jamm're, wer nicht glaubt (Hirschberg)"
   "Es kommt ein Schiff"
   "Gottes Sohn ist kommen (Weisse)"
   "Ich ruf' zu dir"
   "Ringe recht (Kuhnau)"
   "Schaffe in mir, Gott (Witt)"
   "Wer weiss, wie nahe mir (Crasselius)"
   "Wunderbarer Koenig (Neander)"

Nielsen, Ludvig   Norwegian   1906-

  Orgelkoraler--Norsk
   "Jeg ser dig, O Guds Lam (Norsk Folk)"
   "Jeg vil mig Herren love (Zinck)"
   "Jesu, din soete forening (Koenig)"
   "Kirken den er et"
   "Korset vil jeg aldri (Folk Tune)"
  Variasjoner--Norsk
   "Ingen vinner frem (Norse)"

Nilsson, Gunnar   Swedish

  "O Fader vise"--- Eriks

Nilsson, Torsten   Swedish   1920-

  Annorlunda Koralfoerspel---------------------------------- Verbum
   "Hell morgonstjaerna, mild och ren"
  Communionmusik--Nordiska
   "Agnus Dei (Liturgy)"
   Partita "Gud vare lovad"
  Partita: "Ave dypest noed (Phrygian)"---------------------- Nordiska

Norrman, Rudolf   Swedish   1903-1965

  Koralfoerspel (ed. Andersson and Norrman)----------------- Nordiska
   "Ack hjaertans ve"
   "Aera ske Herren" ("Lobe den Herren, den")
   "Den kaerlek du till" ("Bangor-Tans'ur")
   "Dig skall min sjael" ("Winchester New")
   "En herrdag i hoejden"
   "En jungfru foedde ett"
   "Gud har av sin barmhaertighet" ("Es ist das Heil - Wittenberg")
   "Herre dig i naad foerbarma"
   "Hit, O Jesu, samloms vi (Briegel)"
   "Hoega Majestaet vi alla" ("Wie schoen leuchtet")
   "I denna ljuva sommartid (Soederblom)"
   "I oester stiger solen opp (Lindberg)"
   "Jag lyfter mina haender" ("Valet")
   "Jesu, aer min vaen den baeste"

Norrman, Rudolf (cont.)

"Jesu, du mit liv min haelsa"
"Kom Helge Ande, till mig in" ("Kommt her zu mir - Leipzig")
"Lova Herren Gud, min sjael" ("Hoechster Priester - Basel")
"Min Fraelsare"
"Min hoegsta skatt" ("O Jesu Christ, du hoechstes Gut-Crueger")
"Min sjael du maaste nu glomma"
"Naer stormens lurar (Lindberg)"
"Nu vilar hela jorden" ("Innsbruck")
"O Gud, vaar hjaelp" ("St. Anne")
"O Jesu Krist, som mandom tog" ("Aus tiefer Not - Strassburg")
"O min Jesus, dit du gaatt"
"Oss Kristna boer"
"Saa aelskade Gud vaerlden" ("Old 100")
"Statt upp, O Sion" ("In Dulci Jubilo")
"Tiden flyr: naer vill du boerja"
"Tvivlan ur min sjael (Wessnitzer)"
"Uppfaren aer vaar Herre Krist"
"Vaar Herres Jesu Kristi" ("Jesu din Ihukommelse")
"Vaelsignat vare Jesu namn"
"Vaend av din vrede"
"Vaka, sjael, och bed" ("Seelenbraeutigam")
"Var kristtrogen froejde sig" ("Joseph lieber, Joseph")
"Var man maa nu vael" ("Nun freut Euch - Nuernberg")
Postludier (ed. Runbaeck and Aahlen)------------------------Nordiska
"Allt vad vi paa jorden aega"

Nystedt, Knut   Norwegian   1915-

Op. 44:   Partita "Hos Gud er idel glede (Norsk Folk Tune)"-----Peters
Variasjoner--Norsk
"Med Jesus vil eg fara (Norsk Folk)"

Nyvall, Jacob   Swedish   1894-1961

Introitus Preludier (ed. Runbaeck and Aahlen)-----------------Nordiska
    Vol. I: "Goer porten hoeg (Swedish)"
             "Jesu, du dig sjaelv uppvaeckte"
             "Se vi gaa upp (Swedish)"
    Vol. II: "Den haerlighet och aera"
             "Helig, helig, helig (Dykes)"
             "Helige Ande, laat din roest"
             "Kriste, som ditt ursprung leder"
             "Upplys vaar sjael"
             "Vi lova dig, O store Gud"
Koralpartita "Jesu aer min haegnad (Crueger)"----------------Nordiska
Koralpartita "Vad kan dock min sjael"-----------------------Nordiska
Postludier (ed. Runbaeck and Aahlen)------------------------Nordiska
    "Helig, helig, helig (Dykes)"
    "Jeg vet mig en soevn (Schein)"
    Partita "Gud skal all ting (Crueger)"
    Partita "Herre i din naad foerbarma"
    Partita "Vad kan dock min sjael foernoeja"
    Partita "Vaend av din vrede"
Variation and Fughetta: "Kaerlek av hoejden"---------------- Nordiska
Variationer och Fuga: "Vaar blick mot helga berget gaar"------Nordiska

Ohlsson, Sven-Olof   Swedish   1932-

Orgelkoral "Se kaerlet brast" ------------------------------- Verbum

Olson, Daniel   Swedish   1898-

3 Gammalkyrkliga Melodier------------------------------- Gehrmans
    "Helig, helig, helig (Dykes)"
    "Lov vare dig, O Jesu Krist" ("Gelobet seist du")
    "O du som skapar stjaernors haer"
3 Julpastoraler--- Verbum
    "En stjaerna gick"
    "Vaerldens Fraelsare"
    "Var Kristtrogen"
3 Koralfantasier--Norbergs
    Ps. 89 - "Du bar ditt kors"   Ps. 279 - "Till dig av hjaertens
    Ps. 102 - "Vad ljus oever griften"   grunde"
3 Koralsatser--- WESS
    "Allena Gud i himmelrik"
    "O Helge And, goer sjaelen from"
    "O Jesu Krist, Guds ende son"
4 Orgelkoraler --- Gehrmans
    "Dig skall ditt Sion sjunga se"
    "Glaed dig, du helga Kristenhet"
    "Guds rena lamm oskuldig se (Decius)"
    "O du min aedla skatt (Hannover)"
En gammal andlig folkmelodi -------------------------------Gehrmans
    "Foerdenskull, Jesu"
Fantasi "Var haelsad, skoena morgonstund"----------------- Gehrmans
Gammal faebodpsalm "Lovad vare Herren"----------------------Eriks
Introduktion, Fuga och Koral "Vad ljus oever griften
    (Jesperson)"-- Gehrmans
Introitus Preludier (ed. Runbaeck and Aahlen) ---------------- Nordiska
    Vol. I: "Alla Herrens vaegar"
              "Du segern oss foerkunnar"
              "Mitt fasta hopp till Herren"
    Vol. II: "Att tacka dig, O Gud, mig laer"
              "Herren Gud i alla tider"
              "Jesu, laat mig staedse boerja"
              "Tvivlan ur min sjael (Wessnitzer)"
Koralpartita "Himmelriket aer naera" ---------------------- Gehrmans
Koralpartita "Var aer den vaen, som oeverallt"------------- Gehrmans
Kyrkoaarets Ingaangspreludier------------------------------Gehrmans
    "Aa hjertens ve"
    "Me hoeyrer stundom (Thomissoen)" ("Den signede dag")
    "Med sorgen og klagen" ("Iam Moesta")
    "Min sjel, min sjel (Kugelman)"
    "Nu hjertelig jeg langes" ("Valet")
    "Nu kjaere menige (Nuernberg)"
    "Nu la oss takke Gud"
    "Naar vi i stoerste (Lyons)"
    "O Gud, du gode Gud (Hannover)"
    "O Gud som tiden (Erfurt)"
    "O Guds Lam Uskyldig"
    "O Jesu, som har" ("Ich ruf' zu dir")
    "O naadens sol (Erfurt)"
    "Sions vekter" ("Wachet auf")

Olson, Daniel (cont.)

"Sjaa han gjeng (Vulpius)"
"Tig dig alene"
"Uverdig er jeg" ("Old 130")
"Vaakn op og slaa" ("Winchester New")
Liten Toccata "Vart flyr jag foer Gud (Stockholm)"-----------Gehrmans
Partita "I Himmelen"---Norbergs
Postludier (ed. Runbaeck and Aahlen)------------------------Nordiska
"I himmelen, i himmelen (Laurinus)"
"Vaar blick mot det heliga berget gaar"
"Vi lova dig, O store Gud"
Prelude, Ricercare och Passacaglia------------------------ Gehrmans
"Hit, O Jesu, samloms vi"
Prelude, Trio and Fuga-----------------------------------Gehrmans
"Den signade dag (Thomissoen)"
Vaara Nattvardspsalmer-----------------------------------Gehrmans
"Av helig laengtan hjaertat slaar"
"Dig vare lov och pris"
"Du livets broed, O Jesu Krist"
"Du oeppnar, O evige"
"Du sanna vintraed, Jesu kaer"
"Gud, vaar loesta tunga"
"Hur kan och skall jag dig"
"Jag kommer, Gud, och soeker dig"
"Jag vill i denna stund"
"Jesus Kristus aer vaar haelsa"
"O Jesu, aen de dina"
"Som spridda saedeskornen"
"Vaar Herres, Jesu Kristi doed" ("Saell den som haver")
"Vad roest, vad ljuvlig roest"

Olsson, Lennart   Swedish   1925-

3 Smaa Orgelstycken------------------------------------- Norbergs
"Giv att ditt ord oss lysa maa"
"Jesu aer min vaen den baeste" (3rd not on a hymn)

Olsson, Otto Emanuel   Swedish   1879-1964

Op. 29: Fantasi och Fuga--------------------------------- Koerlings
"Vi lova dig, O store Gud"
Op. 30: Gregorianska Melodier---------------------------Gehrmans
"Angelus Autem Domini"
"Creator Alme Siderum"
"O Quot Undis Lacrimarum"
"Salve Regina"
"Veni Creator Spiritus (Mode 8)"
"Vexilla Regis Prodeunt"
Op. 36: 12 Orgelstycken oever koralmotiv------------------Koerlings
"Av himlens hoejd oss kommet aer"
"Bereden vaeg foer Herran"
"Foerlossningen"
"Gud, trefaldig, statt oss bi"
"Herre, dig i naad foerbarma"
"Kom Helge Ande, Herre Gud (Walther)"
Laangfredag

Olsson, Otto Emanuel (cont.)

    "Min sjael skall lova Herran"
    "Se Jesus aer ett troestrikt" ("Wenn wir in hoechsten")
    "Till haerlighetens land igen (Schein)"
    "Vad ljus oever griften"
    "Var haelsad, skoena"
Introitus Preludier (ed. Runbaeck and Aahlen)-----------------Nordiska
    "Som den gylne" ("Werde munter")

Olsson, Thure V.   Swedish   1905-1960

Introitus Preludier (ed. Runbaeck and Aahlen)-----------------Nordiska
    "Dett finns ett ord"
    "Lyft, min sjael, ur jordegruset"
    "O Gud, det aer en hjaertans troest"
Koralvorspel (ed. Andersson and Norrman)------------------- Nordiska
    Vol. 2:
        "Aelskar barnet modersfamnen"
        "Att bedja aer ej" ("Psalm 12 - Geneva")
        "Av djupets Noed (Phrygian)"
        "Gud, vaar loesta tunga"
        "Kaerlek av hoejden"
        "O Gud, det aer min glaedje (Vulpius)"
        "Vaenligt oever jorden"
        "Vak upp, bed Gud om kraft och mod"
Postludier (ed. Runbaeck and Aahlen)------------------------Nordiska
    "Den korta stund jag vandrar"
    "I maenskors barn"
    "Vaka, sjael och bed"

Ore, Charles W.

11 Compositions for Organ--------------------------------Concordia
    "All' Ehr und Lob"
    "Allein Gott in der Hoeh'"
    "Erhalt uns, Herr"
    "Lasst uns erfreuen"
    "Nun komm, der Heiden"
    "O dass ich tausend (Dretzel)"
    "O Heilige Dreifaltigkeit (Herman)"
    "O Welt ich muss dich"
    "Puer Nobis Nascitur"
    "Schmuecke dich"
    "Winchester Old"

Ossewaarde, Jack   American   Contemporary

Improvisation for a Requiem----------------------------- H. W. Gray
    "O Quanta Qualia"

Ourgandjian, Raffi   1937-

L'Organiste Liturgique, Vol. 53----------------------Schola Cantorum
"Veni Creator Spiritus"----------[same as above]--------- Baerenreiter

Owens, Sam Batt

Consoliere, Vol. 3, #1--- WLSM
    Postlude on "Jefferson"
    Prelude on "Restoration"
Voluntaries for the Christian Year, Vol. 2--------------------Abingdon
    "All the World (McCutchan)"

Pachelbel, Johann   German   1653-1706

Orgue et Liturgie #24: Notre Père------------------- Schola Cantorum
    "Vater Unser"
Organum: Reihe 4, #14----------------------------Kistner and Siegel
    "Magnificat" Fugen (Tones 1, 2, 3, 4, 5, 6, 7, 8) also D.T.O., Vol. 17
Seasonal Chorale Preludes (Manuals) (ed. Trevor)---------------Oxford
    Book I: (add)
       "Es woll' uns Gott"
    Book II: (add)
       "Durch Adams Fall"
       "Nun lasst uns Gott"
Seasonal Chorale Preludes (Pedals) (ed. Trevor)--------------- Oxford
    Book I:
       "Ach Gott vom Himmel"
    Book II:
       "Der Herr ist mein getreuer Hirt" ("Psalm 23")
       "Herr Gott, dich loben alle wir" ("Old 100")

Panel, Ludovic   French   1887-1952

Orgue et Liturgie, Vol. 23 ------------------------- Schola Cantorum
Stuecke fuer Trauerfeiern --------[same as above]------Baerenreiter
    "Aus tiefer Not (Phrygian)"

Papale, Henry

Consolaire, Vol. 1, #1-- WLSM
    Postlude on "Dix"

Paponaud, Marcel   French   1893-

Orgue et Liturgie, Vol. 19------------------------- Schola Cantorum
    "Nun komm, der Heiden Heiland"

Parisot, Octave

6 Pièces d'Orgue --- Ed. Costallat
    #3: Offertoire "Les Anges dans nos campagnes"
    #6: Offertoire "Il est né"

Parker, Alice   American   1925-

Hymn Preludes for the Mennonite Hymnal ---------------Goshen College
    "Geneva 42"
    "Herr Jesu Christ, dich zu uns"
    "West End"
    "Wondrous Love"

Pasquet, Jean   American   1896-

9 Chorale Preludes--Augsburg
  "Dir, Dir, Jehova (Halle)"
  "Eisenach"
  "Es liegt ein Schloss" ("Op al den ting - Freiburg")
  "Freu dich sehr"
  "Jesu, meines Leben's Leben (Mueller)"
  "Lobt Gott, ihr Christen (Herman)"
  "Salzburg"
  "Stuttgart (Gotha)"
  "Werde munter"

Paulson, Gustaf   Swedish   1898-1966

Op. 40: 18 Laetta Koralfoerspel ----------------------- mss. STIM'S
  "Av himlens hoejd"
  "Befall i Herrens haender"
  "Det aer en Ros"
  "Dig skall min sjael" ("Winchester New - Crasselius")
  "Din klara sol" ("Stoerl I")
  "Din spira, Jesu" ("Nun freut Euch - Klug")
  "Du segern oss" ("Herr Christ, der einig")
  "Du tunga, soemn" ("In dich hab' ich - Nuernberg")
  "Gammal aer kyrkan"
  "Glaed dig, du Kristi brud" ("Auf meinen lieben")
  "Guds rena Lamm (Decius)"
  "Huru laenge skall" ("Schmuecke dich")
  "Min sund, O Gud" ("Ach Gott und Herr")
  "Nu tacker Gud allt folk"
  "Si, Jesu aer ett" ("Wenn wir in hoechsten")
  "Vaar Gud aer oss" ("Ein feste Burg")
  "Vaar herras, Jesu Kristi, doed" ("Jesu, din Ihukommelse")
  "Vad roest, vad ljuvlig roest" ("St. James - Stockholm")
Op. 87: 66 Koralfoerspel-------------------------------mss. STIM'S
  Ps. 308 - "Ach bleib mit deiner (Vulpius)" (2)
  Ps. 41 - "Auf meinen lieben (Regnart)" (2)
  Ps. 474 - "Blomstertid" (2)
  Ps. 355 - "Blott en dag (Ahnfelt)" (2)
  Ps. 438 - "Den ljusa dag"
  Ps. 420 - "Din klara sol" ("Stoerl I") (2)
  Ps. 198 - "Du oeppnar, O evige"
  Ps. 124 - "Ein feste Burg"
  Ps. 51 - "Es ist ein Ros' "
  Ps. 77 - "Freu dich sehr" (2)
  Ps. 62 - "Gelobet seist du"
  Ps. 42 - "Goer porten hoej (Swedish)"
  Ps. 396 - "Gott des Himmels (Albert)"
  Ps. 202 - "Gud vaar loesta tunga (Lindstroem)"
  Ps. 95 - "Herzlich tut mich verlangen"
  Ps. 14 - "Hoechster Priester (Basel)"
  Ps. 68 - "In Dulci Jubilo"
  Ps. 120 - "Jesu aer min vaen den baeste (Dueben)"
  Ps. 35 - "Jesu, du dig sjael uppvaekte"
  Ps. 76 - "Jesu, du mitt liv (Swedish)"
  Ps. 519a - "Jesu foer vaerlden (Ekstroem)"
  Ps. 48 - "Jesus fraan Nasaret (Nordquist)" (2)

Paulson, Gustaf (cont.)

   Ps. 511 - "Lobe den Herren, den"
   Ps. 238 - "Lobet den Herren, alle die (Crueger)" (3)
   Ps. 43 - "Messiah" (2)
   Ps. 33 - "Naer vaerldens hopp (Rhau - Vulpius)"
   Ps. 4 - "Nicaea"
   Ps. 12 - "Nun danket alle Gott"
   Ps. 58 - "Nun komm, der Heiden Heiland"
   Ps. 434 - "Nun sich der Tag (Krieger)"
   Ps. 292 - "O Gud ditt rike ingen (Waldis)" (3)
   Ps. 94 - "O Lamm Gottes (Decius)" (2)
   Ps. 332 - "O liv som blev taant"
   Ps. 31 - "Old 100th"
   Ps. 470 - "St. Anne"
   Ps. 70 - "Se vi gaa upp (Swedish)"
   Ps. 53 - "Sicilian Mariners"
   Ps. 89 - "So gehst du nun, mein Jesu" (2)
   Ps. 52 - "Stille Nacht"
   Ps. 127 - "Uppfaren aer var Herre"
   Ps. 306 - "Valet"
   Ps. 63 - "Vom Himmel hoch" (2)
   Ps. 66 - "Wenn wir in hoechsten" (3)
   Ps. 136 - "Werde munter" (2)
   Ps. 55 - "Wie schoen leuchtet" (2)
   Ps. 15 - "Winchester New (Crasselius)" (2)
Op. 92: 31 Preludier till Koraler----------------------mss. STIM'S
   Ps. 283 - "Ach Gott und Herr (Schein)"
   Ps. 278 - "Aus tiefer Not (Phrygian)"
   Ps. 474 - "Blomstertid"
   Ps. 438 - "Den ljusa dag"
   Ps. 424 - "Den signade dag (Thomissoen)" (2)
   Ps. 124 - "Ein feste Burg"
   Ps. 8 - "Hela vaerlden froejdes (Swedish)"
   Ps. 131 - "Helige Ande, sanningens (Scandelli)"
   Ps. 475 - "I denna ljuva (Soederblom)" (2)
   Ps. 144 - "I Himmelen (Laurinus)"
   Ps. 68 - "In Dulci Jubilo"
   Ps. 433 - "Innsbruck"
   Ps. 120 - "Jesu aer min vaen den baeste (Dueben)"
   Ps. 181 - "Liebster Jesu (Ahle)"
   Ps. 104 - "Lob sei dem Allmaechtigen (Crueger)"
   Ps. 129 - "Lobet den Herren, ihr (Vulpius)"
   Ps. 125 - "Mach's mit mir (Schein)"
   Ps. 445 - "O Kriste, du som ljuset aer"
   Ps. 298 - "Old 130th"
   Ps. 45 - "Schmuecke dich"
   Ps. 21 - "Schoenster Herr Jesu"
   Ps. 345 - "Seelenbraeutigam"
   Ps. 162 - "Ter Sanctus"
   Ps. 106 - "Upp min tunga (Ridderholm)"
   Ps. 102 - "Vad ljus oever griften (Jesperson)"
   Ps. 448 - "Vak upp min sjael, giv aera"
   Ps. 96 - "Vi tacke dig (Swedish)"
   Ps. 476 - "Was Gott tut"
   Ps. 66 - "Wenn wir in hoechsten"
Op. 95: 57 Preludier till koraler i den Svenska
     Koralboken--------------------------------------- mss. STIM'S

Paulson, Gustaf (cont.)

    Ps. 283 - "Ach Gott und Herr"
    Ps. 79 - "An Wasserfluessen"
    Ps. 37 - "Aus tiefer Not (Phrygian)"
    Ps. 474 - "Blomstertid" (2)
    Ps. 355 - "Blott en dag (Ahnfelt)"
    Ps. 137 - "Brunnquell aller Guter (Crueger)"
    Ps. 424 - "Den signade dag (Thomissoen)"
    Ps. 163 - "Die Kirche ist ein (Lindeman)"
    Ps. 5 - "Dieses ist der Tag (Dretzel)"
    Ps. 149 - "Durch Adams Fall"
    Ps. 38 - "Es ist das Heil"
    Ps. 305 - "Fader, du vars kjaerta"
    Ps. 428⎱
        439⎰- "Fraan Gud vill jag"
    Ps. 78 - "Fraelsta vaerld"
    Ps. 187 - "Franzen"
    Ps. 77 - "Freu dich sehr"
    Ps. 202 - "Gud, vaar loesta tunga"
    Ps. 8 - "Hela vaerlden (Swedish)"
    Ps. 50 - "Herr Christ, der einig (Erfurt)"
    Ps. 287 - "Herre, jag vill bida"
    Ps. 189 - "Hvad roest, hvad ljuvlig roest (Aahlstroem)"
    Ps. 144 - "I Himmelen (Laurinus)"
    Ps. 432 - "I oester stiger solen opp (Lindberg)"
    Ps. 150 - "Iam Moesta"
    Ps. 100 - "In dich hab' ich (Nuernberg)"
    Ps. 190 - "Jesu, din Ihukommelse"
    Ps. 35 - "Jesu, du dig sjaelv (Swedish)"
    Ps. 75 - "Jesu, laer mig (Albert)"
    Ps. 138 - "Kommt her zu mir (Leipzig)"
    Ps. 212 - "Liebster Jesu (Briegel)"
    Ps. 4 - "Nicaea"
    Ps. 12 - "Nun danket alle Gott"
    Ps. 118 - "Nun freut Euch (Klug)"
    Ps. 37 - "Nun freut Euch (Nuernberg)"
    Ps. 1 - "Nun lob', mein Seel (Kugelman)"
    Ps. 363 - "O Gott, du frommer (Hannover)"
    Ps. 119 - "O Jesu Christ, du hoechstes Gut" (2)
    Ps. 298 - "Old 130th"
    Ps. 24 - "Praise (Swedish)"
    Ps. 147 - "Pro Omnibus Sanctis (Barnby)"
    Ps. 22 - "Ratisbon"
    Ps. 286 - "Ringe recht (Kuhnau)"
    Ps. 45 - "Schmuecke dich"
    Ps. 114 - "Schwing dich auf (Crueger)"
    Ps. 331 - "So nimm den meine Haende (Silcher)"
    Ps. 52 - "Stille Nacht"
    Ps. 260 - "Stockholm"
    Ps. 162 - "Ter Sanctus"
    Ps. 217 - "Tvivlan (Wessnitzer)"
    Ps. 325 - "Vad min Gud vill"
    Ps. 3 - "Wachet auf"
    Ps. 55 - "Wie schoen leuchtet" (2)
    Ps. 15 - "Winchester New (Crasselius)"

Paxton, David

Sacred Organ Journal -- Lorenz
    Nov. 1970:   Scherzino on a French Carol "Noël Nouvelet"
    Nov. 1972:   Fanfare Prelude on "Gwalchmai"

Pedemonti, Guiseppe

Manualiere, Vol. 1, #6 ------------------------------------- WLSM
    Offertory on "Silent Night"

Pedersen, Gottfred   Norwegian

6 Forspill --- Musikk Huset
    "Herre Gud, ditt dyre (Norwegian Folk)"
    "Ingen vinner frem (Norsk Folk)"
    "Kjaerlighet er lysets (Norse Folk)"
Prelude and Fugue "Kirken den er et" ------------------------- Norsk

Peek, Richard M.   American   1927-

6 Organ Processionals (for coming into church)----------------WLSM
    Processional March on "Vexilla Regis (Sarum - Mode 1)"
Chaconne on "O Filii et Filiae" (with brass)-------------------- Brodt
Partita on Fairest Lord Jesus--------------------------------- Brodt
    "Schoenster Herr Jesu"
Partita on "St. Paul (Aberdeen)"-----------------------------Abingdon
Voluntaries for the Christian Year, Vol. 2--------------------Abingdon
    "Arnsberg"

Peeters, Emil   1893-

Die Orgel, Reihe I, #21-------------------------- Kistner and Siegel
    Kleine Partita "Froehlich soll mein Herze (Crueger)"

Peeters, Flor   Belgian   1903-

Cantantibus Organis---------------------------------- Van Rossum
    Twe Trios op O Hoofd vol Bloed en Wonden
    ("O Haupt voll Blut")
Orgue et Liturgie, #11----------------------------- Schola Cantorum
    Op. 73 A: "Alma Redemptoris Mater (Plainsong)"

Pelz, Walter

Fantasy on O Sons and Daughters ("O Filii et Filiae")-------- Augsburg
    (with brass and timpani)

Pepping, Ernst   German   1901-

Praeludia Postludia------------------------------- B. Schott's Soehne
    Vol. 1:
        "Allein zu dir"
        "Christe, du Lamm Gottes (Agnus Dei - Liturgy)"
        "Gott sei gelobet (Walther)"
        "Im Frieden dein (Dachstein)"
        "Jesus Christus, unser Heiland, der von uns (Erfurt)"

Pepping, Ernst (cont.)

    "Vater Unser"
    "Verleih uns Frieden (Nuernberg)"
    "Wir danken dir, Herr Jesu Christ, dass du (Wittenberg)"
    "Wunderbarer Koenig (Neander)"
  Vol. 2:
    "Aus tiefer Not (Phrygian)"
    "Befiehl du deine Wege (Gesius)"
    "Bis hierher hat mich (Elbing-Sohren)"
    "Dir, dir, Jehova (Winchester-New - Halle)"
    "Ich ruf' zu dir"
    "In dich hab' ich (Nuernberg)"
    "Nun jauchzt dem Herren (Hannover)"
    "Nun lob' mein Seel (Kugelman)"
    "O glaeubig Herz (Praetorius)"

Perdigon, Pierre   French   1940-

  L'Organiste Liturgique, Vol. 53--------------------- Schola Cantorum
    Versets on "Veni Creator"

Pethel, James

  Consoliere, Vol. 3, #4--------------------------------------- WLSM
    2 Seasonal Preludes: "Kremser"   "Silent Night"
  Sacred Organ Folio--Lorenz
    Vol. 3: Prelude on "Hursley"
    Vol. 4: Fanfare on "Ein feste Burg"
              "In Dulci Jubilo"
  Sacred Organ Journal ------------------------------------- Lorenz
    July, 1970: Prelude on "Diademata"
    March, 1972: Chorale Prelude on "St. Theodulph"

Pfiffner, Ernst   German   1922-

  Partita "Gott sei gelobt"---------------------------------- Doblinger
  Partita "Herr, send herab nun deinen Sohn"------------------- Schwann
    ("Creator Alme Siderum")

Pikéthy, Tibor K.   Hungarian   1884-

  Op. 27: Klein Praeludien und Fughetten ueber: ---------- Editio Musica
    "Ite Missa Est"   (Budapest)
    "Te Deum Laudamus"
    "Veni Sancte Spiritus (Dublin - Mode 1)"

Pineau, Charles   French   1877-

  Consolaire, Vol. 2, #2---WLSM
    Easter Postlude "Victimae Paschali Laudes"

Pisk, Paul Amadeus   Austrian-American   1893-

  Op. 75: Choral-Phantasy on When I Survey ------American Composers
    "Hamburg"   Alliance

Plé-Caussade, Simone   French   1897-

    Orgue et Liturgie, Vol. 24-------------------------- Schola Cantorum
       Gregorian Paternoster
         "Pater Noster (Liturgical)"

Plettner, Arthur   American   1904-

    Improvisation on Father in Whom We Live------------------- Abingdon
       "Dover"
    O Trinity, Most Blessed Light----------------------------- Abingdon
       "O Lux Beata Trinitas"

Polifrone, Jon   American   1937-

    Chorale Prelude-------------------------------- Western International
       "In God and Love We Trust"

Post, Piet   Dutch   1919-

    Manuals Only (ed. Johnson) ---------------------------------Augsburg
       Chorale and Variations
         "Warum sollt ich"

Powell, Robert J.   American   1932-

    15 Chorale Preludes---------------------------- Sacred Music Press
       "Aberystwyth"
       "Allein Gott"
       "Carey's"
       "Cradle Hymn (Harmonia Sacra)"
       "Duke Street"
       "Dulce Carmen"
       "Gardiner"
       "London New"
       "Mendon"
       "Mentzer"
       "Picardy"
       "St. Bernard (Cologne)"
       "St. Magnus (Clark)"
       "Selnecker"
       "Steadfast"
    Chorale Prelude on "Angelus"--------------------------------Abingdon
    Easy Organ Pieces (Collection) ----------------------------- Flammer
       Chorale Prelude on "Martyrdom"
    Voluntaries for the Christian Year, Vol. 2--------------------Abingdon
       "Tryggare kan ingen vara"

Powell, Wilfred

    2 Fantasias on Welsh Hymn Tunes---------------- Quintopus Music Co.
       "Bryn Calfaria"   (Toronto)
       "Rachie"

Praetorius, Hieronymus   German   1560-1629

    Organ Magnificats (ed. C. G. Raynor) ----------- American Institute of
       "Ach Gott vom Himmel (Erfurt)"   Musicology (1963)

Praetorius, Hieronymus (cont.)

    "Magnificat" (one on each tone)

Praetorius, Jacob   German   1586-1651

    Musikalische Denkmaeler, Band III ------------------B. Schott's Soehne
       46 Choraele fuer Orgel
          "Christum wir sollen (A Solis Ortus)"
          "Durch Adams Fall"
          "Grates Nunc Omnes"
          "Herr Gott, dich loben wir (Babst)"
          "Magnificat Germanicae" ("Meine Seele erhebet")

Preston, Thomas   English   16th Century

    Cantantibus Organis, Vol. 12--------------------------------- Pustet
       "Reges Tharsis"

Proctor, Robert E.   American

    Deck Thyself, My Soul---Brodt
       "Schmuecke dich"

Proulx, Richard   American   Contemporary

    Prelude on "Land of Rest"---------------------------------Augsburg

Purvis, Richard   American   1915-

    5 Folk Hymn Orisons----------------------------------- Sacred Songs
       "Beulah Land"
       "Dwelling in Beulah Land"
       "Have Thine Own Way"
       "Materna"
       "Pilot"
    Mixture IV --Flammer
       Passepied for a Joyous Festival ("Veni Creator")

Quignard, J. René   French   1887-

    Consoliere, Vol. 3, #4----------------------------------- WLSM
       Sortie-Carillon on "Adeste Fideles"

Quinn, James

    Consolaire, Vol. 1. ----------------------------------- WLSM
      #3: In Memoriam: J. F. Kennedy "Crusaders Hymn"
      #4: Postlude on "Battle Hymn of the Republic"
    Manualiere, Vol. 1. ----------------------------------- WLSM
      #5: Postlude on "To Jesus Christ Our Sov'reign King (Peoples
        Mass Book)"
      #6: Prelude, Fragmentation on Come Ye Thankful ("St. George's
        Windsor")

Raison, André   French   ca 1650-1719

   Second Livre d'Orgue: L'Organiste Liturgique --------Schola Cantorum
       Vol. 39:
           "A la venue de Noël"
           "Joseph est bien marié"
           "Noël Poitevin"
           "Noël - Or nous dites, Marie"
           "Noël - Une jeune pucelle"
           "Noël - Voici le Jour Solemnel"
       Vol. 43-44:
           "A Minuit"
           "Noël - Laissez paître"
           "Noël - Les Bourgeois de Chartres"
           "Noël - Cette journée"
           "Noël de Sts. Innocens"
           "Noël - O Createur"
           "Noël - O Dieu! que n'etois je en vie"
           "Noël - Où s'en vont ces gais bergers"
           "Puer Nobis Nascitur"
           "Quoy! ma voisine"
           "Vous qui désirez" (2)

Raphael, Gunther   German   1903-1960

   Op. 27, #2: Variations on "Durch Adams Fall"-----------------B & H
   Fantasy and Fugue on "Christus, der ist mein Leben"-----------B & H

Reboulat, Antoine

   L'Organiste Liturgique, Vol. 3 -----------------------Schola Cantorum
       "Noël (Bresson)"
   Orgue et Liturgie, Vol. 24: Notre Père ---------------Schola Cantorum
       "Pater Noster (Liturgical)"

Reda, Siegfried   German   1916-1968

   In Meditationem -- Baerenreiter
       Choralfantasie "Herzlich lieb hab' ich dich"
   "Ich weiss ein lieblich Engelspiel" ----------------------Baerenreiter
       Chorale Concerto

Rehm, P. Otto

   Kleines Konzert in D
       "Salve Regina"

Reichert, James A.   American   1932-

   Prelude and Fugue on "Duke Street"----------------------------mss.

Renauld, Pierre

   Consolaire, Vol. 1, #1---------------------------------- WLSM
       Offertory on "Reges Tharsis"

Ricek, Walter

    21 Choralvorspiele---------------------------------Waldheim-Eberle

Richardson, Harriette Anne

    Chorale Prelude on "Liebster Jesu (Ahle)"------mss. Library Congress
                                                  (1968)

Rippen, Piet   Dutch

    Muziek Voor Pasen-------------------------------------- Ars Nova
       "Song 58" (Halleluja de blijde)

Roelstraete, Herman   Dutch   1925-

    Cantantibus Organis-------------------------------------Van Rossum
       Op. 32, #2: "Ic sie die Morgensterne"

Rohlig, Harald   German-American   1926-

    Voluntaries for the Christian Year, Vol. 2--------------------Abingdon
       "In Dulci Jubilo"

Rohwer, Jens   Danish   1914-

    Das Juengste Gericht--Doblinger
       "Aus tiefer Not (Phrygian)"
       "Es ist gewisslich (Klug)"
       "Ich wollt, dass ich daheime (Strassburg)"
       "Mitten wir im Leben (Walther)"
       "O wir armen Suender (German)"
       "Vater Unser" and "Kyrie: Herr erbarme dich"
       "Wachet auf"

Rooper, Jasper Bonfay   English   1898-

    Prelude on 2 Christmas Carols--------------------------------Novello

Roper, Edgar Stanley   English   1878-1953

    "Greensleeves"-- Concordia

Roques, Jean Leon   French   1839-

    Consoliere, Vol. 3, #4--------------------------------------- WLSM
       Angles We Have Heard on High
       ("Les Anges dans nos")

Rosenberg, Gunnar   Swedish   1913-

    Koralfoerspel (ed. Andersson and Norrman)-------------------Nordiska
       "Av himlens hoejd"
       "Se, vi gaa upp"
       "Skaader, skaader nu"

Rosenberg, Hilding   Swedish   1892-

    Koralvariationer "Lover Gud i himmelshoejd"-------------------- Eriks

Rosenquist, Carl Eric   Swedish   1906-

    Introitus Preludier (ed. Runbaeck and Aahlen)-----------------Nordiska
        Vol. I:
            "Glad jag staedse vill bekaenna"
            "Gud har av sin barmhaertighet"
            "Jesu, du mitt liv, min haelsa"
        Vol. II:
            "Gud, laer mig dock besinna"
            "Min sjael skall lova Herren"
            "Si, Herrens ord aer rent"
            "Vaenligt oever jorden glaenser"
            "Var man maa nu vael (Nuernberg)"
    Koralfoerspel (ed. Andersson and Norrman)-------------------Nordiska
        Vol. 2:
            "Det ringer till vila (Wideen)"
            "Dig, ljusens Fader"
            "Hjaelp mig, Jesu, troget vandra"
            "Jesus allt mitt goda aer"
            "Kom Helge Ande, Herre Gud"
            "Naer ingen dager oegat skaadar"
            "Sion klagar med stor smaerta"
            "Tvivlan ur min sjael (Wessnitzer)"
    Postludier (ed. Runbaeck and Aahlen)------------------------Nordiska
        Vol. 1:
            "Bereden vaeg foer herran"
            "Den korta stund jag vandrar"
            "Du bar ditt kors"
            "Du som haerlig staellde"
            "I denne verdens sorger (Swedish Psalm - Haeffner)"
            "Jesu dine dype" ("Freu dich sehr")
            "Nu kjaere menige (Nuernberg)"
            "Vad ljus oever griften"
        Vol. 2:
            "Behall oss vid ditt rena ord"
            "Der mange skal komme (Stockholm)"
            "Foergaeves all den omsorg"
            "I levernets bekymmer saenkt"
            "Ingen herde kan saa leta" (2)
            "Kommen alla, som arbeten"
            "Oss Kristna boer"
            "Vart flyr jag foer Gud (Stockholm)"
        Vol. 3:
            "Den lyse Dag (Kingo)"
            "En dalande dag"
            "Tiden flyr: naer vill du boerja"
            "Var man maa nu vael glaedja sig (Nuernberg)"

Roth, Daniel François   French   1942-

    L'Organiste Liturgique, Vol. 53----------------------Schola Cantorum
        Versets on "Veni Creator"

Roth, Robert N.

    Improvisation on "The Infant King" ----------------------H. W. Gray

Roucairol, J.

    Manualiere, Vol. 1, #6---------------------------------------WLSM
        Variation on a Noël Provencal

Rouher, Marcel

    4 Sorties - Marches (on Noëls) --------------------------- L. J. Biton
      #1: "Noël - Voici le Jour Solemnel"
            "Noël - Promptement levez-vous mon voisin"
      #2: "Noël - Suivons les Rois dans l'étable"
            "Noël - Chantans tous avoué"
      #3: "Noël - Rangeans nous tretous"
            "Noël - Lei mage dius Jerusalem"
      #4: "Noël - Réveillez-vous belle endormie"
            "Noël - A minuit fut fait un réveil"

Rowley, Alec   English   1892-1958

    4 Meditations on Communion Hymns--------------------------Ashdown
        "Adoro Te Devote"
        "Albano"
        "Old 124th"
        "Pange Lingua"

Runbaeck, Albert   Swedish   1894-

    Efter Sammanrigningen---Nordiska
        "Av hoeiheten oprunnen er" ("Wie schoen leuchtet")
        "Dejlig er jorden" ("Schoenster Herr Jesu")
        "Du vaere lovet Jesus Krist (Walther)"
        "Fryd dig, du Kristi Brud (Regnart)"
        "Helig, helig, helig (Dykes)"
        "Her ser jeg da et Lam" ("An Wasserfluessen")
        "Hvo ene lader Herren raade (Neumark)"
        "In Dulci Jubilo"
        "Kom hit til mig (Folk Tune)"
        "Me hoeyrer stundom (Thomissoen)"
        "Min sjel, min sjel (Kugelman)"
        "Naar vi i stoerste (Lyons)"
        "Nu hjertelig jeg" ("Valet")
   * "Nu kjaere menige (Nuernberg)"
        "Nu la oss takke Gud"
        "O Guds Lam uskyldig"
        "O Jesu som har" ("Ich ruf' zu dir")
        "O naadens sol og sete (Erfurt)"
        "Sions vekter" ("Wachet auf")
        "Sjaa han gjeng (Vulpius)"
        "Tig dig alene"
        "Uverdig er jeg" ("Old 130th")
        "Vaakn op og slaa" ("Winchester New")
    Fantasi "Kom Hellige Aand, Herre Gud (Walther)"-------------Nordiska
    Introitus Preludier (ed. Runbaeck and Aahlen)-----------------Nordiska

Runbaeck, Albert (cont.)

Vol. 1:
  "Aen vaarder och foeder"
  "Du gaar, Guds Lamm"
  "Goer porten hoeg"
  "Helige, som bor i ljuset"
  "Herren aer min Herde god"
  "Jesus allt mitt goda aer"
  "Jesu, du som sjaelen spisar"
  "Livets ande, kom fraan ovan"
  "Min sjael, ditt hopp till Herran"
  "Naer mitt hjaerta maaste"
  "O Herre Gud, O aendelig"
  "Snabbt som blixten"
  "Taenk paa honom som var frestad"
  "Vaar raetta spis vid hemmets"
  "Vaart paaskalamm, O Jesu Krist"
  "Vad ljus oever griften" (2)
  "Var haelsad skoena" ("Wie schoen leuchtet")
Vol. 2:
  "Ack, att i synd vi slumra bort"
  "Allt maenskoslaektet"
  "Allt vad vi paa jorden"
  "Att tacka dig, O Gud, mig laer"
  "Den blomstertid nu kommer"
  "Din spira, Jesu, straeckes ut"
  "En gaang doe, och sedan domen" (2)
  "Herre, dig i naad foerbarma"
  "Hjelp mig, Jesu, troget vandra"
  "I dag om Herrens roest"
  "Jag nu den saekra grunden vunnit"
  "Min sjael, ditt hopp till Herran"
  "Mitt vittne vare Gud"
  "Naer dombasuners straenga ljud"
  "O Jesu Krist, dig till oss vaend"
  "Saa skoen gaar morgonstjaernan"
  "Salig, salig den som kaende"
  "Saliga de som ifraan vaerldens oeden"
  "Till dig, av hjaertens grunde"
  "Vaar kraft, O Gud, foeroeka"
Koralfoerspel (ed. Andersson and Norrman)-------------------Nordiska
  Vol. 2:
    "Gaa varsamt min kristen"
    "Helige Ande, sanningens Ande"
    "Hoega Majestaet, vi alla"
    "O du som ser, o du som vet"
    "Om Kristus doeljes nu foer dig"
    "Sorgen och glaedjen"
Orgelmusik vid Hoegmaessans Avslutning---------------------Nordiska
  Ciaconna "Naer vaerldens hopp"
  Fantasi oever 2 Pingstkoraler
    "Helige Ande, sanningens Ande"
    "Kom, Helge Ande, Herre Gud"
  Improvisation "Av himlens hoejd"
  Liten Partita "O Fader, stor i makt" ("Lucis Creator - Sarum,
    Mode 8")

Runbaeck, Albert (cont.)

Postlude "O Gud, foer de tragna Martyrer" ("Iam Moesta")
"Upp min tunga (Swedish)"
Orgelmusik vid Jordfaestning--------------------------------- Nordiska
"Aar och vaenner flykta"
"Gud laer mig dock besinna"
"Laer mig, du skog"
"Nu laemna vi stoftet"
"Saa skoen gaar morgonstjaernan"
"Saa snart aer det med"
"Vaara stunder ila"
Orgelmusik vid Vigsel --------------------------------------- Nordiska
"Aera ske Herren"
"Befall i Herrens haender"
"Vi oenska nu vaar brudgum"
Postludier (ed. Runbaeck and Aahlen) ------------------------Nordiska
Vol. 1:
"Ack jordens barn vaar tid"
"Goer porten hoeg"
Vol. 2:
"Dig klad i helighetens skrud"
"Din spira, Jesu (Klug)"
"Hit, O Jesu, samloms vi"
"Hjaelp mig, min Gud, ack fraels (Waldis)"
"O Jesu Krist, till dig foervisst"
Vol. 3:
"Behall oss Herre, vid det hopp"
"Gud vaelsigna dessa hjaertan"
"Jag gaar mot doeden"
"Jag lyfter mina haender" ("Valet")
"Jeg vil mig Herren (Zinck)"
"Jeg vil mig Herren (Swedish Psalm)"
"Min vilotimma ljuder (Thomissoen)"
Variationer oever en Estlaendsk Aftonkoral ------------------ Norbergs
"Nu haver denna dag"

Russell, Olive Nelson   American   Contemporary

Consoliere---WLSM
Vol. 1, #2:   Vol. 2, #1:
"Herzliebster Jesu"   Improvisation on "Morning Star"
"St. Theodulph"
Vol. 1, #3:
"Schmuecke dich"

St. Martin, Leonce de   French   1886-1954

Oeuvres d'Orgue--H. Hérelle
Postlude de fête "Te Deum Laudamus (Tone 3)"
Le Salut à la Vierge: Ave Maria, Ave Maris Stella
("Ave Maris Stella - Mode 1")

Salonen, Sulo   Finnish   1899-

Op. 7: Variationer och Fuga oever en Finsk Koraler------- Gehrmans
"Liksom vandraren i laengtau"

Sandahl, Helge   Swedish   1905-

  3 Orgelkoraler--- mss. STIM'S

Sandvold, Arild   Norwegian   1895-

  30 Inn- og Utgangspill --Norsk
    "Aa hjertens ve"
    "Dejlig er jorden"
    "Den signede dag (Thomissoen)"
    "Det er saa yndig (Weyse)"
    "Gjoer doeren hoei" ("Old 100")
    "Hvo ene lader (Neumark)"
    "Naglet til et Kors (Zinck)"
    "Nu beder vi"
    "Se solens skjoenne (Norse Folk)"
    "Vaar Gud han er saa"
  Orgelsonate (F Minor)----------------------------------- Norsk
    "Naglet til et Kors (Zinck)"
  Variationer oever "Eg veit i himmerick (Folk Tune)"------------ Norsk
  Variationer oever "Herre jeg hjertelig (Folk)"------------------ Norsk

Saxton, Stanley E.   American   1904-

  Prelude and Fugue on "Adeste Fideles" -------------------------Brodt
  Prelude on "Vater Unser"-------------------------------------Brodt

Schack, David A.

  9 Chorale Preludes--- Concordia
    "Herr Jesu Christ, dich zu uns"
    "Hyfrydol"
    "Jesu, meine Freude"
    "Lasst uns erfreuen"
    "Lobet den Herrn, ihr" (2)
    "Nun danket alle Gott"
    "O dass ich tausend (Dretzel)"
    "Vom Himmel hoch"

Schehl, J. Alfred   American   1882-1959

  Songs of Syon, Vol. 1 ----------------------------------J. Fischer
    "Adoro Te Devote"
    "Ave Maria (Arcadelt)"
    "Creator Alme Siderum"
    "Deo Gratias (Latin)"
    "Domine Non Sum Dignus"
    "Eventide"
    "Herzliebster Jesu"
    "Jesus, My Lord"
    "Jesu Tibi Vivo"
    "Lauda Sion, Salvatorem (German)"
    "Nun danket alle Gott"
    "Nun haben wir den grossen Bund"
    "O Come Emmanuel (German)"
    "O Filii et Filiae"
    "O Sacrament Most Holy (Schehl)"

Schehl, J. Alfred (cont.)

    "O Sanctissima"
    "Salve Mater"
    "Schmuecke dich"
    "Schoenstes Kindlein"
    "Stille Nacht"
    "Tantum Ergo (Novello)"
    "Wahrer Gott, wir glauben Dir"
    "Wir beten an die Macht"
    Toccata on All Glory, Laud and Honor ("Valet")------------ J. Fischer

Scheidemann, Heinrich   German   1595-1663

    Magnificat Bearbeitungen---------------------------------Baerenreiter
      "Magnificat" (Tones 1, 2, 3, 4, 5, 6, 7, 8(2))
    Musikalische Denkmaeler, Band III -----------------B. Schott's Soehne
      46 Choraele fuer Orgel:
        "Gott sei gelobet (Walther)"
        "In dich hab' ich gehofet (Zuerich)"
        "Jesu wollest uns weisen"
        "Komm Heiliger Geist, Herre Gott"
        "Lobet den Herren, denn er ist sehr freundlich (Scandelli)"
        "Mensch willst du leben seliglich"
        "Nun bitten wir"
        "Vater Unser" (3)

Scheidt, Gottfried   German   1593-1661

    Musikalische Denkmaeler, Band III ----------------- B. Schott's Soehne
      46 Choraele fuer Orgel:
        "Allein Gott in der Hoeh' "

Scheidt, Samuel   German   1587-1654

    Liber Organi, VI---------------------------------- B. Schott's Soehne
      "Magnificat (Tone 8)"
    Manuals Only (ed. Johnson)---------------------------------Augsburg
      "Verzage nicht, o frommer Christ"
    Musikalische Denkmaeler, Band III ----------------- B. Schott's Soehne
      46 Choraele fuer Orgel:
        "Allein Gott in der Hoeh"
    Organ Masters of the 17th and 18th Centuries----------------- Kalmus
      Credo in Unum Deum ("Wir glauben all' an einen Gott,
        Schoepfer - Wittenberg")
    Orgue et Liturgie #24: Notre Père------------------Schola Cantorum
      "Vater Unser"
    Preludes for Hymns in the Worship Supplement (ed. Thomas)--Concordia
      "Herr Christ, der einig Gott's Sohn"

Scheller, Helmut   German

    Einfache Orgelvorspiele (ed. H. Weber) ------------- C. Kaiser (1959)
      "Das alte Jahr vergangen ist"
      "Gott des Himmels (Alberti)"
      "Hilf, Herr Jesu, lass gelingen (Kocher)"
      "Wir Christenleut (Crueger)"

Schildt, Melchior   German   1592-1667

Die Orgel, Reihe II, #24: Choralbearbeitungen------------- F. Kistner
   "Allein Gott in der Hoeh' "
   "Herr Christ, der einig (Erfurt)"
   "Herzlich lieb hab' ich dich (Schmid)"
   "Magnificat (Tone 1)"
Musikalische Denkmaeler, Band III------------------B. Schott's Soehne
   46 Choraele fuer Orgel:
     "Allein Gott in der Hoeh' "
     "Herr Christ, der einig (Erfurt)"
     "Herzlich lieb hab' ich dich (Schmid)"

Schilling, Hans Ludwig   German   1927-

Versetten "O Welt, ich muss dich" ----------------------------B & H

Schlick, Arnolt   German   1460?-1521

Masterpieces of Organ Music, Folio 51--------- Liturgical Music Press
   "Ad Te Clamamus"
   "Eia Ergo Advocata"
   "O Dulcis Maria"
   "O Pia"
   "Salve Regina"
Orgelkompositionen--------------------------------B. Schott's Soehne
   (on Plainsong Chants)

Schmidt, Warren

Consoliere, Vol. 1, #6--------------------------------------- WLSM
   Thanksgiving Suite:
     "Nun danket all und"
     "Nun danket alle Gott"
     "O dass ich tausend (Koenig)"

Schmidt-Arzberg, Georg

Einfache Orgelvorspiele (ed. H. Weber)--------------C. Kaiser (1959)
   "Da Jesu an dem Kreuze"
   "Du Lebensbrot, Herr Jesu Christ (Sohren)"
   "Es sind doch selig"
   "Ewig steht fest der Kirche Haus"
   "Morgenglanz"
   "O Lebensbruennlein (Goerlitz)"
   "So fuehrst du doch recht selig (Gregor's 192nd)"
   "Wacht auf, ihr Christen alle"

Schmutz, Albert D.   American   1887-

Chorale Prelude on It Came Upon a Midnight Clear-------- H. W. Gray
   "Carol"

Schneider, Johann   German   1702-1788

Orgue et Liturgie #24: Notre Père------------------- Schola Cantorum
   "Vater Unser"

Schneidt, Hanna-Martin   German   1930-

   Einfache Orgelvorspiele (ed. H. Weber)--------------------C. Kaiser
    "Gott sorgt fuer dich"
    "Ich weiss' woran ich glaube (Schuetz)"
    "Mach's mit mir Gott"
    "Macht hoch die Tuer (Freylinghausen)"
    "Mein Seel, O Herr, muss loben dich (Gesius)"
    "Mitten wir im Leben"
    "Nun bitten wir"
    "Nun danket alle Gott"
    "Nun jauchzt dem Herren (Hannover)"
    "Nun komm, der Heiden"
    "Nun lob, mein Seel, den Herren"

Schoenberg, Stig Gustav   Swedish   1933-

   Annorlunda Koralfoerspel (ed. Jansson)-----------------------Verbum
    "Tvaa vaeldiga strida"
   Koralfantasi "Vaar Gud aer oss en vaeldig borg"----------mss. STIM'S
   Koralpartita "Att bedja Gud han sjaelv"------------------mss. STIM'S

Schroeder, Hermann   German   1904-

   12 Organ Carols for Christmas----------------------------------Concordia
    "Auf, ihr Hirten (Tyrolean)"
    "Es flog ein Taeublein weisse (German Folk)"
    "Es wird schon gleich dunkel"
    "Freu' dich Erd' und Sternenzelt"
    "Ihr Hirten erwacht"
    "In Dulci Jubilo"
    "Kindelein zart"
    "Lasst uns das Kind'lein wiegen"
    "O schlafe, lieblicher Jesu"
    "Schlummerlied der Hirten"
    "Singen wir mit Froehlichkeit"
    "Zu Bethlehem geboren"

Schultz, Ralph   American   1932-

   Preludes for Hymns in the Worship Supplement (ed. Thomas)--Concordia
    "Tempus Adest Floridum"

Schwartz, Gerhard von

   Einfache Orgelvorspiele (ed. H. Weber)-------------- C. Kaiser (1959)
    "Christe, du bist der helle Tag (Bohemian)"
    "Jesu, meine Zuversicht"
    "Lobet den Herren, alle die ihn ehren"
    "Schmuecke dich"
    "Wie schoen leuchtet"
    "Wo Gott, der Herr, nicht bei uns haelt"
    "Wo Gott zum Haus nicht gibt"
    "Zion klagt mit Angst und Schmerzen (Crueger)"

Schwartz, Paul   Austrian-American   1907-

   Op. 20: Organ Sonata (4 Chorale Fantasias)   American Composers
    "Allein Gott in der Hoeh'"   Alliance

Schwartz, Paul (cont.)

   "Gottes Sohn ist kommen"
   "Herr, ich habe missgehandelt"
   "Zeuch ein zu deinen Toren (Crueger)"
   Reflections on an Irish Hymn Tune------- American Composers Alliance
   "Slane"

Schwarz-Schilling, Reinhard   German   1904-

   Consolaire, Vol. 1, #1--- WLSM
   "Members of One Mystic Body (Holland 1609)"

Segond, Pierre   Swiss   1913-

   L'Organiste Liturgique, Vol. 15--------------------- Schola Cantorum
   Stuecke fuer Trauerfeiern----------[same as above]------- Baerenreiter
   "Aus tiefer Not (Phrygian)"

Seiler, Gustav

   Einfache Orgelvorspiele (ed. H. Weber) --------------C. Kaiser (1959)
   "Herr Gott, dich loben alle wir"
   "Kommet, ihr Hirten"
   "O Jesu Christe, wahres Licht (Nuernberg)"
   "Versuchet euch doch selbst"
   "Wenn wir in hoechsten Noeten"

Senfl, Ludwig   German   1492-1555

   Liber Organi VIII --------------------------------B. Schott's Soehne
   "Also heilig ist der Tag"

Sergisson

   Jesus, Thou Joy of Loving Hearts---------------- Sacred Music Press
   "Quebec"

Siedel, Mathias

   2 Hymnen--- Baerenreiter
   "O Lux Beata"
   "Te Lucis Ante Terminum"

Siefert, Paul   German   1586-1666

   Musikalische Denkmaeler, Band III ------------------B. Schott's Soehne
   46 Choraele fuer Orgel:
      "Puer Natus in Bethlehem"

Sifler, Paul J.   American   1911-

   4 Nativity Tableaux------------------------------------- H. W. Gray
   "First Nowell"
   "Gloria (French Noël)"
   "Stille Nacht"
   "Veni Emmanuel"

Sister M. Theophane   American   1915-

   Postlude Partita on "Old 100th" ------------ Gregorian Institute (Chicago)

Sjoegren, Albert, Jr.   Swedish   1934-

   Partita "Jesus aer min haegnad"----------------------- mss. STIM'S
   "Vakna upp! en staemma bjuder"----------------------- mss. STIM'S

Skaalen, Peter A.

   Processional and Recessional on "Herr Jesu Christ,
      dich zu uns wend" (with trumpets) --------------------- Augsburg

Skoeld, Yngve   Swedish   1899-

   "Det spirar i Guds oertagaard"----------- Elkan, Schildknecht, Carelius

Skottner, Finn   Norwegian

   29 Koralvorspill av Norske Organister (ed. Sandvold)------------ Norsk
      "Hjerte loeft din (Steenberg)"
      "Kjaerlighet fra Gud (Steenberg)"
      "Med Straalekrans (Lindeman)"
   Ti Koralvorspil --- Musikk-Huset
      add:
         "Hvor er det godt (Norsk)"
         "I Himmelen (Norwegian)"
         "Nu rinner solen op (Zinck)"

Smart, David

   4 Seasonal Preludes--- Hope
      "Cradle Song (Kirkpatrick)"
      "Lyra Davidica"
      "O Sacred Head"
      "Veni Emmanuel"

Smith, Glanville

   A Christmas Wreath---------------------------------------C. Fischer
      "Angel's Song (Gibbons)"
      "Annunciation Carol (Provençal)"
      "Antigua Carol"
      "Noël (Provençal)"
      "O Sanctissima"
      "Puritan Nativity Hymn"

Smith, Lani

   Organ Voluntaries for Easter Season #3 -----------------------Lorenz
      "Were You There?"
   Sacred Organ Folio -- Lorenz
      Prelude on "Materna"

Soederholm, Valdemar   Swedish   1909-

   Op. 21: Koralbearbetningar-------------------------------- Norbergs

Soederholm, Valdemar (cont.)

    "Jag vet paa vem jag tror"
    "Jesus aer min vaen den baeste"
    "Nu tacker Gud allt folk"
    "Saa gaar en dag aen fraan"
4 Smaa Orgelkompositioner ---------------------------------Norbergs
    Partita "I Himmelen (Laurinus)"
    Passacaglia "O Gud, vaar broder Abels blod"
    Prelude and Fugue "Glaed dig du helga kristenhet"
    Toccata "Av himlens hoejd"
Introitus Preludier (ed. Runbaeck and Aahlen)-----------------Nordiska
    Vol. 2:
        "Gud vare tack och aera"
        "O maa vi noga maerka"
Koralpartita "Dig vare lov och pris" ("Ter Sanctus")---------- Nordiska
Orgelkompositioner ---Norbergs
    Partita: "Saeg mig den vaegen"
    Trio: "Hit, O Jesu, samloms vi"
Orgelmusik vid Hoegmaessons Avslutning ---------------------Nordiska
    Toccata "Gud laater sina trogna haer (Klug)"
Orgelpartita: "Jesus aer min haegnad" --------------------- Norbergs
Postludier (ed. Runbaeck and Aahlen)------------------------Nordiska
    Vol. 3: "Fryd dig du Kristi Brud"

Soedersten, Gunno   Swedish   1920-

Koralpartita: "Befall i Herrens haender" ("Old 130")--------- Nordiska

Soerenson, Torsten   Swedish   1908-

2 Orgelkoraler-- mss. STIM'S
    "Beproeva mig, min Gud"
    "Jag lyfter mina haender"
Improvisationer "Vi lova dig, O store Gud"--------------- mss. STIM'S
Introitus Preludier (ed. Runbaeck and Aahlen)-----------------Nordiska
    Vol. 1:
        "Foer mig sitt liv"
        "Jag vet paa vem (Hannover)"
    Vol. 2:
        "Herre, var de trognas styrka"
        "Hit, O Jesu, samloms vi"
Koralfoerspel (ed. Andersson and Norrman)------------------- Nordiska
    Vol. 2:
        "Kom Helge Ande, Herre god" ("Veni Creator Spiritus -
            Sarum") (2)
        "O Gud, all sannings kaella"
    Vol. 3:
        "Jesu, du min froejd"
        "Min vilotimma ljuder (Thomissoen)"
Koralvariationer "Lova vill jag Herran"---------------------Norbergs
"O Jesu, aen de dina (Thomissoen)"--------------------- mss. STIM'S

Southbridge, James

Organ Portfolio, Dec. 1969------------------------------------Lorenz
   How Firm a Foundation ("Foundation")

Southbridge, James (cont.)

Sacred Organ Folio--Lorenz
    Vol. 1:   Prelude on a Shaker Hymn ("Simple Gifts")
    Vol. 3:   Prelude on "St. Christopher"
    Vol. 4:   "Divinum Mysterium"
Sacred Organ Journal, Nov. 1970---------------------------- Lorenz
    "Coventry Carol"

Sowande, Fela   Nigerian   1905-

"Joshua Fit de Battle ob Jericho"----------------------------Chappell
Introduction, Theme and Variations on "Oyigiyigi"--------------Ricordi
Prayer on "Oba a ba ke"-------------------------------------Ricordi

Sowerby, Leo   American   1895-1968

"Snow Lay on the Ground"------------------------------- H. W. Gray

Speller, Frank N.   American   Contemporary

Triptych of Praise and Thanksgiving -----------------------J. Fischer
    "Dix"   "St. Denio"   "St. George's Windsor"

Spong, Jon   American   Contemporary

Scenes from the Life of Christ -------------------------Electro Voice
    Festal Voluntary on "Coronation"
    Variations on "Three Kings of Orient"

Stearns, Peter Pindar   American   Contemporary

3 Chorale Preludes------------------------Amer. Composers Alliance
    "Ein feste Burg"
    "Es ist genug (Muehlhausen)"
    "Lobe den Herren, den"
12 Chorale Preludes on Well-Known Hymns-- Amer. Composers Alliance
                                (included in 20 Hymn Preludes)
    "Auch jetzt macht Gott (Koch)"   "Expectation (Berggreen)"
    "Benediction (Hopkins)"   "Gottlob, es geht nunmehr"
    "Consolation (Webbe)"   "Liebster Jesu (Ahle)"
    "Es ist ein Ros' "   "Missionary Hymn"
    "Eventide"   "Rutherford"
    "Ewing"   "Serenity (Wallace)"
20 Hymn Preludes------------------------------------+------ Coburn Press
    "Auch jetzt macht Gott (Koch)"   "Gerald (Spohr)"
    "Bethany (Mason)"   "Gloaming (Stainer)"
    "Carol Melody"   "Gottlob, es geht nunmehr"
    "Communion (Brackett)"   "Guidance (Brackett)"
    "Consolator"   "Herzlich tut mich verlangen"
    "Ellers (Hopkins)"   "Liebster Jesu (Ahle)"
    "Es ist ein Ros' "   "Missionary Hymn"
    "Eventide"   "Oldown"
    "Ewing"   "Rutherford"
    "Expectation (Berggreen)"   "Serenity (Wallace)"
Fantasie on "Christ, unser Herr, zum Jordan"-- Amer. Comp. Alliance
Hymn Improvisation on "Dix"------------------ Amer. Comp. Alliance

Steenberg, Per   Norwegian   1870-1945 ?

2 Fuger--- Norsk
    "Sions Vekter"
4 Orgelstykker--Norsk
    "Av hoeiheten"
    "Konge er du visst (Steenberg)"
    "Saligheten er oss naer (Lindeman)"
5 Inngangsstykker-- Norsk
    "Jesu, dine dype vunder (Lindeman)"
Festpreludier--- Norsk
    "Du som gaar ut fra (Lindeman)"
    "Fra Himlenhoeit jeg" ("Christum wir sollen")
    "Jesu i det hoeie (Lindeman)"
    "Krist stod opp av doede (Lindeman)"
    "Min sjel, min sjel" ("Nun lob mein Seel' ")
    "Nu la oss takke Gud"
Introitus Preludier (ed. Runbaeck and Aahlen)-----------------Nordiska
    "Av hoeiheten" ("Wie schoen leuchtet") (2)
Orgelkoraler-- Lyche
    "Apostlene satt i Jerusalem (Lindeman)"
    "Den tro som Jesum favner"
    "Folkefrelsar, til oss kom (1524)"
    "Herre, du et hjem oss gav (Solheim)"
    "Herre Gud, ditt dyre navn og aere (Steenberg)"
    "Med straalekrans om tinde (Vulpius)"
    "Naar mitt oeie (Lindeman)"
    "Opstanden er den Herre Krist"
    "Underfulle Konge (Steenberg)"

Steigleder, Johann Ulrich   German   1593-1635

Orgue et Liturgie, #24: Notre Père------------------ Schola Cantorum
    "Vater Unser"
Seasonal Chorale Preludes (Manuals) (ed. Trevor) --------------Oxford
    "Vater Unser"

Stevens, Halsey   American   1908-

3 Pieces--- Mark Foster
    Prelude on "Christ lag in Todesbanden"

Stockmeier, Wolfgang   German   1931-

Die Orgel, Reihe I, #18 --------------------------- Kistner & Siegel
    Partita on "Jauchzt alle Lande, Gott zu ehren"
Die Orgel, Reihe I, #19--------------------------- Kistner & Siegel
    Choralvorspiele:
        "Du, meine Seele, singe (Ebeling)"
        "Ihr lieben Christen, freut Euch nun (Herman)"
        "Ist Gott fuer mich (Augsburg)"
        "O Koenig, Jesu Christe (13th Century)"
        "Was Gott tut (Gastorius)"
Die Orgel, Reihe I, #24: Choralvorspiele und Begleitsaetze
            zu Advents und Passionslieder--------------- Kistner & Siegel
    "Auf, auf, ihr Reichsgenossen (Selle)"
    "Christe, du Schoepfer aller Welt (Koenigsberg)"
    "Du grosser Schmerzensmann (Vopelius)"

Stockmeier, Wolfgang (cont.)

    "Nun sei uns willkommen (Dutch)"
    "O Heiland, reiss (Rheinfels)"
    "O Welt, sieh hier dein Leben (Friese)"
    "Wie soll ich dich (Crueger)"
    "Wir danken dir, Herr Jesu Christ, dass du fuer uns (Wittenberg)"

Stollberg, Oskar

    Einfache Orgelvorspiele (ed. H. Weber)-------------- C. Kaiser (1959)
    "Kommt her zu mir (Leipzig)"
    "Was mein Gott will"
    "Wer nur den lieben (Neumark)"

Stout, Alan   American   1932-

    3 Organ Chorales--- Augsburg
    "Schmuecke dich"
    "Wer nur den lieben Gott (Neumark)"
    "Wo soll ich fliehen hin (Regnart)"
    Forspil over "O Gud vors lands"--------- American Composers Alliance

Stow, Douglas G.

    Prelude on Fairest Lord Jesus--------------------------------- Brodt
    "Schoenster Herr Jesu"

Sventelius, Harald   Swedish   1922-

    "Till himmelen dit laengtar jag"----------------------------Nordiska

Swann, Frederick L.   American   Contemporary

    "Agincourt Hymn"---------------------------------------G. Schirmer

Sweelinck, Jan Pieterszoon   Dutch   1562-1621

    Musikalische Denkmaeler, Band III------------------B. Schott's Soehne
      46 Choraele fuer Orgel:
        "Ach Gott vom Himmel"
        "Allein zu Dir"
        "Christe Qui Lux Es"
        "Da Pacem Domine"
        "Dies sind die heiligen"
        "Durch Adams Fall"
        "Erbarm' dich mein"
        "Es ist das Heil"
        "Es spricht der Unweisen Mund"
        "Herr Christ, der einig"
        "Herzlich lieb hab' ich dich (Schmid)"
        "Ich ruf' zu dir"
        "Nun freut Euch (Klug)"
        "Nun freut Euch (Nuernberg)"
        "Nun komm, der Heiden"
        "O Lux Beata Trinitas"
        "Psalm 116"
        "Psalm 140"

Sweelinck, Jan Pieterszoon (cont.)

> "Puer Nobis Nascitur"
> "Vater Unser"
> "Wie nach einer Wasserquelle"
> "Wir glauben all an einen Gott, Schoepfer (Wittenberg)"
> "Wo Gott, der Herr, nicht bei uns haelt"

Opera Omnia, Vol. 1, Fascicle II (ed. A. Anne-
> garn) --- Ver. Voor Nederlandse Muziekgeschiedenis (Amsterdam)
> "Allein Gott in der Hoeh' "
> "Allein zu Dir"
> "Christe Qui Lux Es"
> "Da Pacem Domine"
> "Erbarm' dich mein"
> "Ich ruf' zu dir"
> "Nun freut Euch (Nuernberg)"
> "Ons ist gheboren" ("Puer Nobis Nascitur")
> "Onse Vader" ("Vater Unser")
> "Psalm 36 (Geneva)"
> "Psalm 116"
> "Psalm 140"
> "Wir glauben all an einen Gott, Schoepfer (Wittenberg)"
> Spurious: "Herzlich lieb hab' ich (Schmid)"
>   "Onse Vader"

Telemann, Georg Philipp   German   1681-1767

Recent Researches in Music of Baroque Era, Vol. II -----
> (ed. A. Thaler) -------------------------------- A R Editions
>   (New Haven)
> "Ach Gott vom Himmel" (2)
> "Ach Herr, mich armen" (2) ("Herzlich tut mich verlangen")
> "Alle Menschen (Mueller)" (2)
> "Allein Gott in der Hoeh' " (2)
> "Christ lag in Todesbanden" (2)
> "Christus, der uns selig macht" (2)
> "Durch Adams Fall" (2)
> "Erschienen ist der" (2)
> "Gott, der Vater, wohn uns bei" (2)
> "Herr Christ, der einig Gottes" (2)
> "Herr Jesu Christ, dich zu uns wend" (4)
> "Ich ruf' zu dir" (2)
> "Jesu, meine Freude" (2)
> "Komm Heiliger Geist, Herre Gott" (2)
> "Nun danket alle Gott" (2)
> "O Lamm Gottes" (2)
> "O wir armen Suender" (2)
> "Schmuecke dich" (2)
> "Straf' mich nicht" (2)
> "Vater Unser" (2)
> "Was mein Gott will" (2)
> "Wer weiss wie nahe (Neumark)" (2)
> "Wie schoen leuchtet" (2)

Seasonal Chorale Preludes (Manuals) (ed. Trevor) -------------- Oxford
> Book I:
> "Allein Gott in der Hoeh' "
> "O Lamm Gottes"

Telemann, Georg Philipp (cont.)

    Book II:
      "Christ lag in Todesbanden"
      "Vater Unser"

Teutsch, Walter   German-American   Contemporary

    Chorale Prelude "Gen Himmel aufgefahren (Franck)"---------------ms.

Thalben-Ball, George   English   1896-

    113 Variations on Hymn Tunes for Organ----------------------Novello

"Aberystwyth"	"Lasst uns erfreuen"
"Abridge"	"Laus Deo"
"Angel's Song"	"Les Commandemens"
"Arden"	"Liebster Jesu (Ahle)"
"Bedford"	"Llanfair"
"Belgrave"	"London New"
"Bellwoods"	"Love Divine (Stainer)"
"Bishopthorpe"	"Marching"
"Breslau"	"Maria jung und zart"
"Bromsgrove"	"Martyrdom"
"Buckland"	"Martyrs"
"Caithness"	"Meine Hoffnung (Neander)"
"Cannock"	"Melcombe"
"Capel"	"Mendip"
"Capetown"	"Metzler's Redhead"
"Carlisle"	"Meyer"
"Caswall"	"Miles Lane"
"Church Triumphant"	"Monkland"
"Collingwood"	"Monksgate"
"Crucis Victoria"	"Morning Hymn (Bartholemon)"
"Crueger"	"Moscow"
"Darwall's 148th"	"Narenza"
"Dominus Regit Me"	"Nativity"
"Dundee"	"Neander"
"Dunfermline"	"O Traurigkeit"
"Eisenach"	"Old 100th"
"Eventide"	"Old 104th"
"Ewing"	"Oriel"
"Fitzwilliam"	"Picardy"
"Franconia"	"Praise My Soul"
"Fulda"	"Ratisbon"
"Gopsal"	"Regent Square"
"Gott sei Dank (Halle)"	"Rockingham"
"Gott will's machen (Steiner)"	"St. Anne"
"Gwalchmai"	"St. Bernard"
"Hanover"	"St. Clement"
"Harts"	"St. Denio"
"Herongate"	"St. Ethelreda"
"Hyfrydol"	"St. Ethelwald"
"Illsley"	"St. Hugh (Hopkins)"
"Intercessor"	"St. James (Courteville)"
"Irby"	"St. Leonard"
"King's Lynn"	"St. Magnus"
"Ladywell"	"St. Matthew (Croft)"

Thalben-Ball, George (cont.)

"St. Michael (Old 134)"   "Veni Sancte Spiritus (Webbe)"
"St. Stephen (Jones)"   "Vienna"
"St. Thomas (Wade)"   "Vruechten"
"Song 67 (Gibbons)" (2)   "Vulpius"
"Stockton (Wright)"   "Wareham"
"Stracathro"   "Warwick (Stanley)"
"Stuttgart (Gotha)"   "Westminster (Turle)"
"Surrey (Carey)"   "Wigtown"
"Tallis Ordinal"   "Wiltshire"
"Ton-Y-Botel"   "Windsor"
"Uffingham"   "Wolvercote"
"University College"   "Woodlands"

Thatcher, Howard Rutledge   American   1878-1973

Organ Fantasy on "Sine Nomine"-------------------------C. Fischer

Thiman, Eric Harding   English   1900-1959

4 Easy Pieces on English Hymn Tunes---Ascherberg, Hopwood, & Crew
"Albano (Novello)"
"Lauda Anima (Goss)"
"Melcombe (Webbe)"
"Sharon (Boyce)"
Meditation on a Traditional Hymn Tune--------------------G. Schirmer
"Cleansing Fountain"

Thomas, Brander

Consolaire, Vol. 1, #4--WLSM
Postlude on "Grosser Gott, wir loben dich"

Thomas, Paul Lindsley

Variations on Welsh Hymn "Aberystwyth"-----------------------Oxford

Thompson, Randall   American   1899-

20 Chorale Preludes, 4 Inventions and a Fugue---------E. C. Schirmer
"Aus tiefer Noth (Phrygian)"
"Christus, der ist mein Leben (Vulpius)" (2)
"Erhalt uns Herr (Klug)"
"Erschienen ist der (Herman)"
"Gott des Himmels (Alberti)"
"Herr, ich habe missgehandelt (Crueger)"
"Jesu, meine Zuversicht (Crueger)" (3)
"Liebster Jesu (Ahle)"
"Meine Seele erhebet (Klug)" (3)
"Nun sich der Tag (Krieger)" (2)
"O Ewigkeit, du (Schop)"
"Wenn wir in hoechsten"
"Wer nur den lieben Gott (Neumark)" (3)

Thompson, Van Denman   American   1890-1969

Laudamus Te ("Old 100th")----------------------Sacred Music Press

Thorkildsen, John   Norwegian

29 Koralvorspill av Norske Organister (ed. Sandvold)-------------Norsk
    "Hjerte loeft din (Steenberg)"
Jule Pastorale-- Norsk
    "Glade Jul"
    "In Dulci Jubilo"
Prelude and Fugue on "Jeg er rede til (Darmstadt)"-------------Norsk

Thyrestam, Gunnar   Swedish   1900-

Annorlunda Koralfoerspel------------------------------------Verbum
    "Jesus aer min vaen den baeste"
Koralfoerspel (ed. Andersson and Norrman)------------------ Nordiska
    Vol. 2:
        "Den blomstertid nu kommer"
        "Den korta stund jag vandrar haer"
        "Huru laenge skall mitt hjaerta"
        "Jag hoeja vill till Gud min saang (Klug)"

Timme, Traugott

Choralevorspiele in tiefer Lage--------------------------- Baerenreiter
    "Christe, der du bist Tag und"

Ulrich, E. J.

Consolaire, Vol. 1, #5 ---------------------------------------WLSM
    "Ein feste Burg"
Consoliere, Vol. 1, #2--------------------------------------- WLSM
    When I Survey ("Hamburg")

Vallombrosa, Amédeé de   French   1880-

Cantantibus Organis--------------------------Société Anonyme (Nancy)
    Prelude on "Jesu Corona Virginum (Mode 8)"

Van den Broek, P. - See Broek, P. Van den

Van Hulse, Camil - See Hulse, Camil Van

Van Iderstine, A. P. - See Iderstine, A. P. Van

Van Koert, Han - See Koert, Han Van

Vermulst, Jan

Consolaire, Vol. 2, #6 --------------------------------------WLSM
    Communion on "We Come To You With Longing (Vermulst)"

Verschraegen, Gabriel   Dutch   1919-

Cantantibus Organis----------------------------------- Van Rossum
    Prelude on "Puer Natus Est Nobis"
    Interlude on "Puer Natus Est Nobis"
    Partita on "Veni Creator (Sarum - Mode 8)"

<u>Vetter</u>, Andreas Nikolaus   German   1666-1710

   Seasonal Chorale Preludes (Pedals) (ed. Trevor)---------------- Oxford
     Book I: "Nun komm, der Heiden"

<u>Videroe</u>, Finn   Danish   1906-

   Koralpartiter "Kirken den er et"-----------------Engstroem & Soedring
   Koralpreludier och Orgelkoralen til Koraler i
        Svenska Koralboken-------------------- Engstroem & Soedring
    "Der mange skaal komme (Stockholm)"
    "I prektige himler (Wideen)"
    "In Dulci Jubilo"
    "Naar vi i stoerste" ("Wenn wir in hoechsten")
    "O hjelp mig, Gud (Waldis)"
    "Vaakn op og slaa" ("Winchester New")
   21 Hymn Intonations ------------------------------------Concordia

"Adeste Fideles"	"Mit Freuden zart"
"Aus tiefer Not (Phrygian)"	"Munich (Stoerl)"
"Coronation (Holden)"	"Potsdam (Bach)"
"Diademata"	"Regent Square"
"Ein feste Burg"	"Resignation (U.S. Southern)"
"Es ist das Heil"	"St. Magnus (Clarke)"
"Gaudeamus Pariter"	"St. Michael (Geneva)"
"Herzliebster Jesu"	"St. Thomas (Williams)"
"Iste Confessor (Rouen)"	"Song 13 (Gibbons)"
"Leoni"	"Ton-Y-Botel"
"Lyons"	

<u>Vogt</u>, Emanuel

   Einfache Orgelvorspiele (ed. H. Weber)---------------C. Kaiser (1959)
    "Christe, du Beistand (Loewenstern)"
    "Dein Wort, O Herr, bringt uns zusammen"
    "Freut Euch, ihr lieben Christen all (Gesius)"
    "Herz und Herz vereint zusammen (Basel)"
    "Heut triumphieret Gottes Sohn (Gesius)"
    "Hilf, Herr Jesu, lass gelingen (Schop)"
    "Hosianna, David's Sohne"
    "Ich will, so lang ich lebe"
    "In Gottes Namen fahren wir" ("Dies sind die")
    "Jauchzt alle Lande (Psalm 118)"
    "Valet"
    "Wenn mein Stuendlein (Wolff)"
    "Wir danken dir, Herr Jesu Christ, dass du fuer uns (Wittenberg)"

<u>von Herzogenberg</u>, Heinrich - See <u>Herzogenberg</u>, Heinrich von

<u>von Schwartz</u>, Gerhard - See <u>Schwartz</u>, Gerhard von

<u>Vretblad</u>, Patrik   Swedish   1876-1953

   Op. 40, #1: Koralfantasi----------------Elkan, Schildknecht, Carelius
   Op. 47: Jul Meditation oever gamla julsaanger ---------------Nordiska
    "Es ist ein Ros' "   "Sicilian Mariners"
    "Julsaanger"   "Stille Nacht"
    "Naer juldags-morgon"

Vyverman, Jules   Belgian   1900-

    15 Organ Pieces from Modern Belgium ----------------------- WLSM
        Prelude on "Asperges Me (Kyrial)"

Walcha, Helmut   German   1907-

    Cantantibus Organis----------------------------------- Van Rossum
        "Christ ist erstanden (Folk)"

Walter, Samuel   American

    Cardinal Suite--------------------------------------- McL. & R.
        "Tantum Ergo"
        Toccata on "Grosser Gott, wir loben dich"
        Variations on "O Filii et Filiae"
    Sacred Organ Journal, Nov. 1970----------------------------- Lorenz
        "What Is This Lovely Fragrance?"

Walther, Johann Gottfried   German   1684-1748

    Seasonal Chorale Preludes (Manuals) (ed. Trevor)-------------- Oxford
        Book I:
            "Allein Gott in der"
            "Christus der ist"
            "Herr Christ, der einig"
            "Jesu, Leiden, Pein und Tod"
            "Liebster Jesu"
            "Lobt Gott, ihr Christen"
            "O Lamm Gottes"
            "Vom Himmel hoch"
            "Wachet auf"
        Book II:
            "Christus der ist mein"
            "Ein feste Burg"
            "Erschienen ist der"
            "Erstanden ist der (Triller)"
            "Mache dich, mein Geist"
            "Mach's mit mir"
            "Meine Seele erhebet (Klug)"
            "Von Gott will ich nicht (Erfurt)"
            "Werde munter"

Warner, Richard L.   American   1908-

    5 Spirituals for Organ -------------------------------------- Shawnee
        "Deep River"
        "Let Us Break Bread"
        "Lord, I Want to Be a Christian"
        "Steal Away to Jesus"
        "Were You There?"

Webber, William S. Lloyd   English   1914-

    Trumpet Tune--- Novello
        "Lobe den Herren, den"

Weckmann, Matthias   German   1619-1674

   Consolaire, Vol. 2, #6 --WLSM
     "Nun freut Euch (Nuernberg)"

Weegenhuise, Johan   Dutch   1910-

   6 Communion Pieces by 6 Dutch Composers---------------------WLSM
     O Saving Victim ("O Salutaris Hostia-Duquet")

Weiss, Ewald   Polish-German   1906-

   10 Orgelchoraele-- B & H
     "Christe, du bist der helle Tag (Bohemian)"
     "Erhalt uns Herr (Klug)" (2)
     "Froehlich wir nun all fangen an (Strassburg)"
     "Ich weiss', mein Gott, dass all mein Tun (Schein)"
     "Ich wollt, dass ich daheime war (Strassburg)"
     "Jauchz' Erd', und Himmel (Strassburg)"
     "Jerusalem, du (Franck)"
     "Jesus Christus, unser Heiland, der den Tod (Klug)"
     "Nun freut Euch, lieben (Nuernberg)"
   Einfache Orgelvorspiele (ed. H. Weber)--------------------- C. Kaiser
     "Liebster Jesu (Ahle)"
     "Verleih uns Frieden (Nuernberg)"
     "Warum sollt ich mich denn graemen"
     "Wenn meine Suend' mich (Leipzig)"

Weitz, Guy   Belgian-English   1884-1970

   Prière-- Hinrichsen
     "Salve Regina"

Welander, Waldemar   Swedish   1899-

   3 Passionskoraler------------------------------------- mss. STIM'S
     "Den kaerlek du till (Tans'ur)"
     "Jesu, dig i djupa noeden"
     "Skaader, skaader nu haer alle"

Werner, Fritz E. H.   German   1898-

   Einfache Orgelvorspiele (ed. H. Weber)--------------------- C. Kaiser
     "Der Tag, der ist so"
     "Der Tag ist seiner Hoehe nah (Werner)"
     "Der Tag mit seinem Lichte"
     "Gott der Vater wohn uns bei"
     "Lobe den Herren, O meine Seele"
     "Mit Freuden zart"
     "Wir wollen alle froehlich (Spangenberg)"

Wetherill, Edward H.

   10 Chorale Fantasies for Organ ----------------------------C. Fischer
     "Cwm Rhondda"
     "Diadem"
     "Flemming"

Wetherill, Edward H. (cont.)

    "Liebster Jesu (Ahle)"
    "Mendon"
    "Petra"
    "Rockingham (Miller)"
    "Sandon"
    "Spanish Hymn"
    "Ton-Y-Botel"

Whitford, Homer P.   American   1892-

    2 Chorale Preludes----------------------------- Sacred Music Press
      "Rathbun"
      "St. Margaret (Peace)"
    Fantasie on National Songs---ms.
      America the Beautiful ("Materna")
      "Austrian Hymn"
      "God Save the Queen"
      "Marseillaise"
      "Netherlands"
      "Song of the Rhine"

Wideen, Ivar   Swedish   1871-1951

    150 Koralfoerspel----------------------- Elkan, Schildknecht, Carelius
    Orgelspelets Teknik (Anrep, Nordin and Asploef)--- Elkan, Schildknecht,
      "Ave Maris Stella (Mode 1)"   Carelius
    Introitus Preludier (ed. Runbaeck and Aahlen)---------------- Nordiska
      Vol. 1: "Skaader, skaader nu haer alle"

Wiebe, Esther   American   Contemporary

    Hymn Preludes for the Mennonite Hymnal --------------Goshen College
      "Picardy"
      "Zion's Pilgrim"

Wiemer, Wolfgang   German   1934-

    Choralvorspiele II (1969)--B & H
      "Aus tiefer Not (Phrygian)"
      "Christe, du bist der helle Tag"
      "Froehlich soll mein Herze (Crueger)"
      "Jesu, meine Freude"
      "Macht hoch die Tuer (Freylinghausen)"
      "Wenn wir in hoechsten Noeten (Bourgeois)"

Wikander, David   Swedish   1884-1955

    Introitus Preludier (ed. Runbaeck and Aahlen)----------------- Nordiska
      Vol. 1:
        "Min sjael, du maaste"
      Vol. 2:
        "Nu tacker Gud allt folk"
        "Till den himmel, som bliv allas"
        "Upp min sjael, att korset baera"
    Postludier (ed. Runbaeck and Aahlen)----------------------- Nordiska

Wikander, David (cont.)

> Vol. 1:
>> "De herdar vakta de deras hjord"
>> "En dalande dag, en flyktig stund"
> Vol. 3:
>> "Guds rena lamm, oskyldig (Decius)"
>> "O naadens sol (Erfurt)"

Willcocks, David   English

> Ceremonial Music for Organ --------------------------------- Oxford
>> Fanfare on "Gopsal"

Wilson, Roger   American   1912-

> Chorales for Organ --- Lorenz
>> "Allein Gott in der"
>> "Angelus (Joseph)"
>> "Bemerton"
>> "Christ ist erstanden (Folk)"
>> "Erhalt uns, Herr"
>> "Ermunt're dich"
>> "Herzliebster Jesu"
>> "Jesu, meine Freude"
>> "Jesu, meines Lebens Leben (Mueller)"
>> "Liebster Jesu (Ahle)"
>> "O dass ich tausend (Koenig)"
>> "St. Theodulph"
>> "Seelenbraeutigam"
>> "Vom Himmel hoch"
>> "Wer nur den lieben (Neumark)"
>> "Wunderbarer Koenig (Neander)"

Winter-Hjelm, Otto   Norwegian   1837-1931

> 72 Lette Koralvorspil------------------------------------- W. Hansen
>> "Aa hjertens ve"
>> "Akk Herre Gud (Schein)"
>> "Alene Gud"
>> "Av dypest noed (Phrygian)"
>> "Av hoeiheten oprunnen er"
>> "Den tro som Jesum"
>> "Et trofast hjerte (Praetorius)"
>> "Fra Himlen hoejt kom"
>> "Fryd dig du Kristi Brud (Regnart)"
>> "Frykt mit barn"
>> "Gud skal all ting (Crueger)"
>> "Guds soenn er kommet" ("Es ist das Heil")
>> "Herre gud Fader, du vaar (10th Century)"
>> "Herre, jeg har handlet ille (Crueger)"
>> "Hvad kan oss komme (Klug)"
>> "Hvo ene lader (Neumark)"
>> "I Jesu navn (Kingo)"
>> "I Kristne som toer (Geneva)"
>> "Jesu, din soete forening (Koenig)"
>> "Jesu, dine dype vunder" ("Freu dich sehr")

Winter-Hjelm, Otto (cont.)

    "Jesu, er mitt haap" ("Jesu, meine Zuversicht")
    "Jesu, er mitt liv i live (Crueger)"
    "Jesu, Frelser, vi er her"
    "Kom, Hellig Aand, med" ("Veni Creator Spiritus")
    "Kom, Hellige Aand, Herre Gud (Walther)"
    "Kom, hit til mig (Folk Tune)"
    "Kom Hjerte, ta ditt regnebrett" ("Mein' Seel' erhebt")
    "Lover den Herre"
    "Med Sorgen og Klagen"
    "Midt i livet (Walther)"
    "Min Glede i min Gud (Kingo)"
    "Min Sjel og Aand (Thomissoen)"
    "Naar mig min synd (Thomissoen)"
    "Naar mitt oeie (Lindeman)"
    "Naar vi i stoerste (Lyons)"
    "Naglet til et kors (Zinck)"
    "Nu beder vi"
    "Nu hjertelig jeg lenges (Hassler)"
    "Nu hviler mark"
    "Nu kjaere menige (Nuernberg)"
    "Nu la oss takke Gud"
    "Nu rinner solen op (Zinck)"
    "O Fader vaar i himmerik"
    "O Gud, du gode Gud (Hannover)"
    "O Gud som tiden (Erfurt)"
    "O Hellig Aand (Strassburg)"
    "O Herre Krist, dig til oss vend"
    "O Jesu som har"
    "O lue fra Guds (Weisse)"
    "Op al den ting (Freiburg)"
    "Overmaade fullt av naade (Freylinghausen)"
    "Paa Gud alene (Zinck)"
    "Sions Vekter" ("Wachet auf")
    "Soerg, O kjaere Fader" ("Christus, der uns selig")
    "Tig dig alene (Wittenberg)"
    "Uverdig er jeg (Old 130)"
    "Vaakn op og slaa" ("Winchester New")
    "Vaar Gud han er saa"
    "Vaer troestig, Sion" ("Ach Gott vom Himmel")
    "Vi tror og troester (Walther)"

Withrow, Scott S.   American   Contemporary

    Voluntaries for the Christian Year, Vol. 2--------------------Abingdon
        "Geneva 124"

Wood, Dale   American   Contemporary

    Organ Book of American Folk Hymns-------------- Sacred Music Press
        (from the Sacred Harp)
        "Antioch (F. C. Wood)"
        "Bleeding Saviour (Z. Chambless)"
        "Middlebury"
        "Pisgah"
        "Saints' Delight (F. Price)"

Wood, Dale (cont.)

"Sons of Sorrow"
"Wondrous Love (American)"
Pastoral on "Forest Green"--------------------------------Flammer

Wuensch, Karl   German

Einfache Orgelvorspiele (ed. H. Weber)--------------C. Kaiser (1959)
"Aus tiefer Not (Strassburg)"
"Jesu, meine Zuversicht"
"O Gottessohn voll ewiger Gewalt"

Wyton, Alec   English   1921-

Christ in the Wilderness--------------------------------H. W. Gray
Partita on "Heinlein"
Mixture IV--Flammer
2 American Folk Preludes:
"Land of Rest (Early American)"
"Pleading Saviour (Plymouth)"
Music for Lent (4 Chorale Preludes)------------------------Flammer
"Aberystwyth"
"Batty"
"Remember (Ravenscroft)"
"Spanish Hymn"
Preludes for Christian Praise-------------------- Sacred Music Press
"Hanson Place"
"Marching to Zion"
"Pilot"
"Sweet Hour"
Preludes on Contemporary Hymns--------------------------- Augsburg
"A Stable Lamp Is Lighted"
"Great God, Our Source (G. M. Cartford)"
"Holy Manna (Moore)"
"Look Now He Stands (C. Schalk)"
"Now the Silence (C. Schalk)"
"O God of Every Nation (D. Wood)"
"Restoration"
"Rhosymedre"
"Saints' Delight"
"This Night Did God Become a Child (K. Westerburg)"
Resurrection Suite (3 early carols)------------------------- Flammer
"Christ ist erstanden (Folk)"
"O Filii et Filiae"
This Joyful Eastertide ("Vruechten")

Young, Carlton R.

Intonation for Easter--------------------------------------- Hope
"Easter Hymn"
"Shaker Tune"

Young, Gordon E.   American   1919-

6 Pieces for 11 O'clock Worship-------------------------------WORD

Young, Gordon E. (cont.)

  "Maryton"
  "Munich" (2)
  "Old 100th"
  "Pax Tecum"
  "St. Anne"
  "Webb"
 7 Hymn Voluntaries for the Church Organist---------------Th. Presser
  "Ein feste Burg"
  "Kremser"
  "Martyn"
  "Nyland"
  "Olivet"
  "Vom Himmel hoch"
  "Wer nur den lieben (Neumark)"
 10 Christmas Organ Voluntaries on Familiar Carols-------Th. Presser
  "Adeste Fideles"
  "Antioch (Handel)"
  "Christmas (Handel)"
  "First Nowell"
  "Froehlich soll mein Herze"
  "Mendelssohn"
  "Mueller"
  "Stille Nacht"
  "Three Kings"
  "Veni Emmanuel"
 14 Pieces for Organ----------------------------Sacred Music Press
  Easter Chant ("O Filii et Filiae")
  Noël ("Stille Nacht")
  Prelude on "Deo Gracias (English)"
  Prelude on "Dundee"
  Prelude on "Guidance (Brackett)"
  Toccata on "Boylston (Mason)"
  Toccata and Variations on "Hyfrydol"
A Christmas Suite---Augsburg
  Fanfare on "Adeste Fideles"
  Gigue on "In Dulci Jubilo"
  Pastorale on "Nunc Dimittis (Genevan)"
  Prelude on "God Rest You Merry"
Chorale Preludes on 7 Hymn Tunes------------------------ Flammer
  "Crusaders Hymn" ("Schoenster Herr Jesu")
  "Dominus Regit Me"
  "Evan (Havergal)"
  "Hanover"
  "Hymn to Joy (Beethoven)"
  "Mercy (Gottschalk)"
  "Tallis Canon"
Collage for Organ--- Flammer
  Fanfare on "Austrian Hymn"
  March on "Martyrdom"
  Prelude on "St. Agnes"
  Postlude on "In Babilone"
  Postlude on "Lasst uns erfreuen"
Organ Music--- Broadman
  "Austrian Hymn"
  "Easter Hymn"

Young, Gordon E. (cont.)

    "Festal Song"
    "Olivet"
    "Palestrina"
    "St. Agnes"
    "St. Catherine"
Noël Joyeux (from Noël Preludes)---------------------------Flammer
    "Adeste Fideles"
    "Divinum Mysterium"
    "Greensleeves"
    "In Dulci Jubilo"
    "Tempus Adest Floridum"
Perspectives-- Flammer
    Prelude on a Bourgeois Tune ("Freu dich sehr")
    Prelude on "St. Thomas (Williams)"
    Postlude on "Old 100"
Preludes on Hymn Tunes-------------------------------------- Hope
    "Beatitudo"
    "Boylston"
    "Crusaders Hymn"
    "Darwall's 148th"
    "Diademata"
    "Hamburg"
    "Italian Hymn"
    "Manoah"
Sacred Organ Folio, Vol. 3 ---------------------------------- Lorenz
    "Marion"
Voluntaries for the Christian Year, Vol. 2 ------------------- Abingdon
    "Regent Square"

Zabel, Albert J.   Contemporary

All Glory, Laud and Honor (Organ and Handbells)-------------Flammer
    "Herzliebster Jesu"
    "In Dulci Jubilo"
    "Lasst uns erfreuen"
    "Lobe den Herren, den"
    "St. Theodulph"
    "Warum sollt ich"
Sacred Organ Folio, Vol. 4 ---------------------------------- Lorenz
    2 Communion Interludes:
        "Dominus Regit Me"
        "Hamburg"
    Interlude on "Bangor"

Zachara, Franciszek   1898-

   3 Organ Chorales --G. Schirmer

Zachau, Friedrich Wilhelm   German   1663-1713

   Seasonal Chorale Preludes (Manuals) (ed. Trevor)--------------Oxford
     Book I: add-
       "Allein Gott in der"
       "Jesu, meine Freude"

Zachau, Friedrich Wilhelm (cont.)

    Book II: add-
    "Christ lag in Todesbanden"
  Seasonal Chorale Preludes (Pedals)(ed. Trevor)----------------- Oxford
    Book I: add-
    "An Wasserfluessen"
    "Durch Adams Fall"

Zercher, J. Randall   American   Contemporary

  Hymn Preludes for the Mennonite Hymnal --------------Goshen College
    "Union"

Zipp, Friedrich   German   1914-

  Einfache Orgelvorspiele (ed. H. Weber)--------------------- C. Kaiser
    "Der du bist drei in Einigkeit"
    "Ich dank dir schon durch deinen Sohn"
    "Ich hab' mein Sach (Cassel)"
    "Nun freut Euch, lieben (Nuernberg)"
    "O Welt, ich muss dich"
    "Schwing dich auf (Crueger)"
    "Straf' mich nicht"
    "Such wer da will (Stobaeus)"
    "Tut mir auf"
    "Von Gott will ich nicht (Erfurt)"

TUNE NAME INDEX

A Babe Lies in the Cradle (Corner)

    Means, C.

A la venue de Noël (French)

    *

    Charpentier, M. A.   LeBègue, N. A. (3)
    Corrette, M.   Raison, A.
    Dandrieu, J. F.

A Minuit (Noël)

    *

    Dandrieu, J. F. (2)
    Raison, A.

    Variants:
    Mes bonnes gens attendez-moi
    Noël Lorraine

    Lasceux, G.

A Solis Ortus Cardine (Plainsong-
Mode 3)
See: Christum, wir sollen
loben schon

A Stable Lamp is Lighted
(P. Tollefson)

    Wyton, A.

Aa hjertens ve
See: O Traurigkeit

Aar och vaenner flykta

    Tune not found

    Runbaeck, A.

Aat dig, O Gud, som allt foermaar
See: Herzlich lieb hab' ich dich

Abbey (Scotch)

    *

    Bevan, G. J.

112

Aberystwyth (Parry)   *

    Hustad, D.   Thalben-Ball, G.
    Hutson, W.   Thomas, P. L.
    Moyer, J. H.   Wyton, A.
    Powell, R. J.

Abridge (Smith)   *

    Thalben-Ball, G.

Ach bleib bei uns (Calvisius)   *

    Krapf, G.

Ach bleib mit deiner Gnade   *
  (Vulpius)

    Paulson, G. (2)

  Variants:
  Christus, der ist mein Leben

    Gore, R. T.   Thompson, R. (2)
    Neubauer, H.   Walther, J. G.
    Raphael, G.

  Med straalekrans om tinde
  (Vulpius)

    Bangert, E.
    Steenberg, P.

  O Gud, det aer min glaedje
  (Vulpius)

    Hedwall, L.
    Olsson, T. V.

Ach Gott, erhoer mein Seufzen   *
  (Erfurt)

    Gore, R. T.

Ach Gott, tu dich erbarmen
  (Franck)   Z 141

    Gore, R. T.

Ach Gott und Herr (Schein)   *

    Gore, R. T.
    Paulson, G. (2)

  Variants:
  Ack Herre Gud (Schein)

Ach Gott und Herr (cont.)

Variants: (cont.)
Akk Herre Gud (Schein)

Haarklou, J.
Winter-Hjelm, O.

Min synd, O Gud

Aahlen, W.   Paulson, G.
Andersson, R.

Upplys vaar sjael

Nyvall, J.

Ach Gott vom Himmel (Erfurt)   *

Bornefeld, H.   Krapf, G.
Ehrlinger, F.   Mozart, W. A.
Gore, R. T.   Pachelbel, J.
Gwinner, V.   Praetorius, H.
Kauffmann, G. F.   Sweelinck, J. P.
Klenz, W. (2)   Telemann, G. P. (2)

Variant:
Vaer troestig, Sion

Winter-Hjelm, O.

Ach Gott, wie lang (Strassburg
 1525) (Psalm 13)
See also: Mensch, willst du
leben

                          Z 4439

Klenz, W.

Ach Gott, wie manches Herzeleid
 (Leipzig)

                          Z 2588

Gore, R. T.

Ach Gott, wie manches Herzeleid
See: Breslau

Ach Herr, mich armen Suender
See: Herzlich tut mich
verlangen

Ach Jesu mein (St. Gallen)

Faessler, G.

Ach lieben Christen, seid getrost

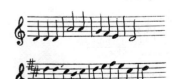

Gore, R. T.

Ach, was ist doch unser Leben
(Dretzel)
                                    Z 4909
    Gore, R. T.

Ach, was soll ich, Suender,   *
    machen (Altdorf)

    Gore, R. T.

Ach, wie fluechtig
    See: Ach, wie nichtig (Franck)

Ach, wie nichtig (Franck)   *

    Variant:
    Ach, wie fluechtig

        Boehm, G.   Ehrlinger, F.
        Eder, H.

Ach, wir armen Suender (German)   *

    Variants:
    O du armer Judas

        David, J. N.

    O wir armen Suender

        Gebhard, H.   Rohwer, J.
        Gore, R. T.   Telemann, G. P. (2)

Ack, att i synd vi slumra bort
    See: Pax (Swedish)

Ack bliv hos oss (Swedish)
    See: Pax (Swedish)

Ack Herre Gud (Schein)
    See: Ach Gott und Herr (Schein)

Ack, hjaertans ve
    See: O Traurigkeit

Ack jordens barn, vaar tid
    (Ericson--1917)

    Runbaeck, A.

Ack laatom oss lova och bedja
    vaar Gud
    See: Den signade dag
    (Thomissoen)

Ack, saella aero de
    See: Auf meinen lieben Gott
    (Regnart)

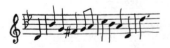

Ack vaermeland, du skoena
(Swedish Folk Song)

    Cundick, R.

Ad Te Clamamus (Plainsong)

    Schlick, A.

Ad Te Levavi (Mode 8)

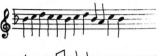

    Jong, M. De

Adam fut un pauvre homme
  See: Noël - Qu' Adam fut

Adelaide (Stebbins)   *

    Hustad, D.

    Variant:
Have Thine Own Way

    Purvis, R.

Adeste Fideles (Wade's)   *

    Balderston, M.   Metzger, H. A.
    Broughton, E.   Quignard, R.
    Fleury, A.   Saxton, S. E.
    Gigout, E.   Videroe, F.
    Lynn, G. A.   Young, G. E. (3)
    McKinney, H. D. (2)

Adoro Te Devote (Plainsong)   *

    Boëly, A. P. F.   Rowley, A.
    Browne, C. F.   Schehl, J. A.
    Jones, R. W.

Adrian Michelle (D. N. Johnson)

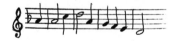

    Johnson, D. N.

Aelskar barnet modersfamnen
  (Schop)
  See: Jesu, du mein liebstes
Leben

Aen vaarder och foeder
  See: Hvad ljus oefver (Jespersoen)

Aera ske Gud, som fraan sin Tron
(Andersdotter)

    Bjarnegaard, G.

Aera ske Herren
See: Lobe den Herren, den
Maechtigen

Agincourt Song
          Hymn
See: Deo Gracias (English)

Agnus Dei
(Compare with O Lamm Gottes)

     Ahrens, J.

Agnus Dei (Liturgy)   *

     Nilsson, T.

     Variant:
     Christe, du Lamm Gottes

          Pepping, E.

Ak Fader, lad dit Ord (Lindeman)   *
Akk

          Haarklou, J.

Akk Herre Gud (Schein)
See: Ach Gott und Herr (Schein)

Akk, visste du (Lindeman)   *

     Islandsmoen, S.

Albano (Novello)

     Rowley, A.
     Thiman, E.

Albany (Jeffery)   *

     McKinney, H. D.

Aldrig er jeg uden vaade (Horn)   *

     Bangert, E.

     Variant:
     Wir glauben an Gott den Vater

Alene Gud i himmerik
See: Allein Gott in der Hoeh'

Alford (Dykes)   *

     McKinney, H. D.

All' Ehr' und Lob (Strassburg)   *

    Ore, C. W.

All Morgen ist ganz frisch   *
(Walther)

    Krapf, G.

All Saints New (Cutler)   *

    McKinney, H. D.

All the World (McCutchan)

    Owens, S. B.

Alla Herrens vaegar (Weman--1938)

    Hedwall, L.
    Olson, D.

Alle Menschen muessen sterben
(Dretzel)
                     Z 6781

    Gore, R. T.

Alle Menschen muessen sterben   *
(Mueller)

    Ehrlinger, F.   Krause, P.
    Klenz, W.   Telemann, G. P. (2)

    Variant:
    Jesu, meines Lebens Leben
    (Mueller)

        Pasquet, J.
        Wilson, R.

Alle Menschen muessen sterben   *
(Wessnitzer)

    Variants:
    Glad jag staedse

        Rosenquist, C. E.

    Herren Gud i alla tider

        Olson, D.

    Jesu er mitt liv i live
    (Wessnitzer)

        Bangert, E.
        Emborg, J. L.

Alle Menschen muessen sterben (cont.)

Jesu, meines Lebens Leben (Wessnitzer)

Hamm, W.

Snabbt som blixten de foersvinna

Berg, G.
Runbaeck, A.

Tvivlan ur min sjael

Lagergren, A.   Paulson, G.
Norrman, R.   Rosenquist, C. E.
Olson, D.

Alle Menschen muessen sterben
   (German--Bach)
See: Jesu, der du meine Seele (Bach)

Allein Gott in der Hoeh' (Plainsong)   *

Bornefeld, H.   Scheidt, G.
Dueben, A.   Scheidt, S.
Gantner, A.   Schildt, M. (2)
Gebhardi, L. E.   Schwartz, P.
Gore, R. T.   Sweelinck, J. P.
Hasse, P.   Telemann, G. P. (3)
Langlais, J. F.   Walther, J. G.
Lynn, G. A.   Wilson, R.
Ore, C. W.   Zachau, F. W.
Powell, R. J.

Variants:
Alene Gud i himmerik

Bangert, E.   Winter-Hjelm, O.
Haarklou, J.

Allena Gud i himmelrik

Johansson, S. E.   Olson, D.

O Helge And, goer sjaelen from

Olson, D.

Allein nach dir, Herr Jesu Christ
                              Z 8544
   Gore, R. T.

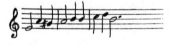

Allein zu dir (Wittenberg)   *

Bornefeld, H. (2)   Kauffmann, G. F.
Brown, R.   Lagergren, A.
Ehrlinger, F.   Pepping, E.
Gore, R. T.   Sweelinck, J. P. (2)

Allein zu dir (cont.)

Variants:
Tig dig allena

    Andersson, R.   Runbaeck, A.
    Olson, D.   Winter-Hjelm, O.

Till dig allena

    Bangert, E.

Alleluia, Dulce Carmen (Webbe)   *

    Manz, P.

Variant:
Dulce Carmen

    Powell, R. J.

Allena Gud i himmelrik
See: Allein Gott in der Hoeh'

Allenthalben wo ich gehe (Nuernberg)
                         Z 1337
    Gore, R. T.

Alles ist an Gottes Segen (Koenig-
Kuhnau)   *

    Beck, T.
    Ehrlinger, F.

Allez dans la paix
    Compare Christus Resurrexit

    Chauvin, D.

Allt maenskoslaektet (Waldis)
See: O Gud, ditt rike ingen ser

Allt vad vi paa jorden aega
(Nodermann--1911)

    *Norrman, R.
    *Runbaeck, A.

Alma Redemptoris Mater (Plainsong)   *

    Falcinelli, R.
    Peeters, F.

Als Jesus Christus in der Nacht
(Crueger)
                        Z 258
    *Fischer, I.

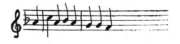

Also heilig ist der Tag
                    Z 7149 (2nd part)
        Senfl, L.

Amazing Grace (American)   *

        Burkhart, C.   Hustad, D.
        Gehring, P.   Martin, G. M.

    Variant:
    New Britain

        Held, W.

America (Carey)   *

        Chauvin, D.
        McKinney, H. D.

    Variant:
    God Save the Queen

        Whitford, H.

American Folk Hymn (tune not
    identified)

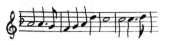

        McKay, G. F.

Amsterdam (Nares)   *

        McKinney, H. D.

An Wasserfluessen Babylon   *
    (Dachstein)

        Brown, R.   Paulson, G.
        Gore, R. T.   Zachau, F. W.
        Klenz, W.

    Variants:
    Det gaar ett tyst

        Andersson, R.

    Ein Laemmlein geht (Dachstein)

        Krapf, G.
        Neubauer, H.

    Her ser jeg (Strassburg)

        Bangert, E.
        Runbaeck, A.

    Song C (Dutch)

        Asma, F.

Anamma from de dyra naadeorden
    See: En syndig man, som laag

Ande, full av naade
    See: Brunnquell aller Guter
    (Crueger)

Andernach (French Psalm)   *

    Variant:
    Herr Jesu Christ, wahr Mensch
    und Gott (French Psalm)

        Gore, R. T.

Angel's Song (Gibbons)
    See: Song 34 (Gibbons)

Angelus (Joseph)   *

        Powell, R. J.
        Wilson, R.

Angelus Autem Domini   Tune not found

        Olsson, O. E.

Annunciation Carol (Provencal)

        Smith, G.

Antigua Carol

        Smith, G.

Antioch (Handel)   *

        *Hustad, D.   Young, G. E.
        McKinney, H. D.

Antioch (F. C. Wood)

        Hustad, D.
        Wood, D.

Apostlene sad i Jerusalem (Lindeman)   *
                satt

        Haarklou, J.
        Steenberg, P.

Ar-Hyd-Y-Nos (Welsh)   *

        Hutson, W.

Arden (Thalben-Ball)

        Thalben-Ball, G.

Arise (Southern Hymn Tune)   *

    Hustad, D.

Arlington (Arne)   *

    Bock, F.

Arnsberg
   See: Wunderbarer Koenig (Neander)

Asperges Me (Kyrial)   *

    Browne, C. F.   Vyverman, J.
    Huybrechts, L.

Att bedja aer ej
   See: Psalm 12 (Geneva)

Att bedja Gud han sjaelv
   See: Vater Unser (Leipzig)

Att tacka dig, O Gud, mig laer
(Waldis)

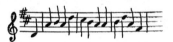

    Olson, D.
    Runbaeck, A.

Auch jetzt macht Gott (Koch)

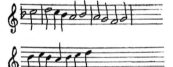

    Stearns, P. P. (2)

Audi Benigne Conditor

    Carleton, N.

Audi Benigne Conditor (Mode 2)   *

    Hulse, C. Van

Auf, auf, ihr Reichsgenossen (Selle)   *

    Stockmeier, W.

Auf, auf, mein Herz (Crueger)   *

    Ehrlinger, F.

Auf diesen Tag (Old Church)   *

    Ehrlinger, F.

Auf, ihr Hirten (German)

    McKinney, H. D.

Auf, ihr Hirten (Tyrolean)

    Schroeder, H.

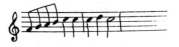

*

Auf meinen lieben Gott (Regnart)

    Bornefeld, H.   Lagergren, A. (2)
    Buxtehude, D.   Maurer, O.
    Ehrlinger, F.   Paulson, G. (2)
    Gore, R. T.

Variants:
Ack saella aero de

    Berg, G.

Fryd dig, du Kristi Brud (Regnart)

    Bangert, E.   Soederholm, V.
    Emborg, J. L.   Winter-Hjelm, O.
    Runbaeck, A.

Glaed dig, du Kristi Brud
(Tune variant)

    Aahlen, W.   Paulson, G.
    Bjarnegaard, G.

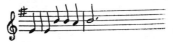

Jag vill i denna stund

    Olson, D.

Wo soll ich fliehen hin (Regnart)

    Gore, R. T.
    Stout, A.

Aughton (Bradbury)

    Diemer, E. L.

Variant:
He Leadeth Me

    Baumgartner, H. L.

Aurea Luce (Tone 3)

    Fasolo, G. B.

*

Aurelia (Wesley)

    Hilty, E. J.
    McKinney, H. D.

Aus der Tiefe (Herbst)   *

Variant:
Heinlein

    Johnson, D. N.
    Wyton, A.

Aus meines Herzens Grunde (Hamburg)   *

    Bach, J. C.   Gore, R. T.
    Bornefeld, H.   Manz, P.
    Ehrlinger, F.

Variants:
Den tro som Jesum favner

    Bangert, E.   Winter-Hjelm, O.
    Steenberg, P.

Jag lever och upphoejer

    Edlund, L.

Aus tiefer Not (Phrygian)   *

    Bloch, W.   Langlais, J. F.
    Bornefeld, H. (2)   Panel, L.
    *Brown, R.   Paulson, G. (2)
    *Duchow, M.   Pepping, E.
    Ehrlinger, F.   Rohwer, J.
    Gore, R. T.   Segond, P.
    Kluge, M.   Thompson, R.
    Kuhnau, J.   Videroe, F.
    Lagergren, A.   *Wiemer, W.

Variants:
Av djupets Noed (Phrygian)
  dypest

    Bangert, E.   Olsson, T. V.
    Haarklou, J.   Winter-Hjelm, O.
    Nilsson, T.

Aus tiefer Not (Strassburg)   *

    Kauffmann, G. F.
    Wuensch, K.

Variants:
Herr, wie du willst (Strassburg)

    Barlow, W.

O Hellig Aand (Strassburg)

    Bangert, E.   Winter-Hjelm, O.
    Moeller, S. O.

Aus tiefer Not (cont.)

   O Jesu Krist, som mandom tog

      Norrman, R.

Austrian Hymn (Haydn)   *

      Ellsasser, R.   Whitford, H.
      McKinney, H. D.   Young, G. E. (2)

Av djupets Noed (Phrygian)
  dypest
   See: Aus tiefer Not (Phrygian)

Av helig laengtan hjaertat slaar
   See: Uppfaren aer vaar Herre
   Krist

Av himlens hoejd
   See: Vom Himmel hoch

Av hjaertat haver jag dig kaer
   (German--1577)
   See: Herzlich lieb hab' ich dich
   (Schmid)

Av hoeiheten oprunnen er
   See: Wie schoen leuchtet

Ave Maria (Arcadelt)

      Elmore, R.
      Liszt, F.   Schehl, J. A.

Ave Maria klare
   See: Narenza (Cologne)

Ave Maris Stella (Lourdes)

      Gigout, E.

Ave Maris Stella (Mode 1)   *

      Bermudo, J.   *Joulain, J.
      Dandrieu, J. F.   Jullien, G.
      Falcinelli, R.   Langlais, J. F.
      Frescobaldi, G.   *St. Martin, L. de
      Hofhaymer, P.   Wideen, I.

Ave Regina Caelorum (Solesmes-   *
   Mode 6)

      Falcinelli, R.

Avon
   See: Martyrdom

Avondlied
See: Die Tugend wird durch's
(Halle)

Avondzang (Old Dutch)   *

Variant:
Song L (Dutch)

    Asma, F.

Awake Thou Wintry Earth (Dutch)   *

Variants:
This Joyful Eastertide

Vruechten (Dutch Carol)

    Brandon, G.   Wyton, A.
    Thalben-Ball, G.

Away in a Manger (Murray)
See: Mueller

Azmon (Glaeser)   *

    Frank, R.
    Jordahl, R.

Bangor (Tans'ur)   *

    Zabel, A. J.

Variant:
Den kaerlek du till

    Norrman, R.
    Welander, W.

Battle Hymn of the Republic (Steffe)   *

    Quinn, J.

Batty
See: Ringe recht (Kuhnau)

Beatitudo (Dykes)   *

    Young, G. E.

Bedford (Wheall)   *

    Thalben-Ball, G.

Beecher (Zundel)   *

    Hustad, D.

Befall i Herrens haender
   See: Old 130th

Befiehl du deine Wege (Gesius)   *

     Pepping, E.

Behaall oss Herre, vid det hopp
                              ord
   See: Erhalt uns, Herr (Klug)

Behaall oss vid ditt rena ord
   See: Pax (Swedish)

Bei stiller Nacht (Koeln)

     Faessler, G.

Belgrave (Horsley)

     Thalben-Ball, G.

Bellwoods (Hopkirk)

     Thalben-Ball, G.

Bemerton (Filitz)   *

     Wilson, R.

   Variant:
   Carlisle

     Thalben-Ball, G.

Benedic Anima Mea (Goss)   *

   Variants:
   Lauda Anima

     Hustad, D.
     Thiman, E.

   Praise My Soul

     Thalben-Ball, G.

Benediction (Hopkins)
   See: Ellers (Hopkins)

Beproeva mig, min Gud
   See: O Gott, du frommer Gott
   (Hannover)

Beredd mig haall, Herre Jesu Krist
   See: Eja, mitt hjaerta

Bereden vaeg foer Herran
   See: Messiah (Swedish)

Berijming van den 12 artikelen des
   geloofs (Credo)

     Asma, F.

Besançon Carol (French)   *

    Variants:
    Chantons, bargiés, Noué, Noué

    Shepherds Shake Off

      McKinney, H. D.

Bethany (Mason)   *

     Stearns, P. P.

Beulah Land (Sweney)

     Purvis, R.

Binchester (Croft)

     Clokey, J. W.

Bis hierher hat mich Gott
   See: Elbing (Sohren)

Bishopthorpe (Clark)   *

     Thalben-Ball, G.

Bleeding Saviour (Z. Chambless)

     Wood, D.

Blomstertid (Swedish Psalm)   *

     Paulson, G. (5)

    Variants:
    Den blomstertid nu kommer

      Damm, S.   Runbaeck, A.
      Hedwall, L. (2)   Thyrestam, G.

    Gud vare tack och aera

      Soederholm, V.

    Jeg vil mig Herren love (Swedish
    Psalm)

      Jader, J.   Runbaeck, A.

Blomstertid (cont.)

   Som spridda saedeskornen

     Olson, D.

   Vid evighetens brunnar

     Lindroth, H.

Blott en dag (Ahnfelt)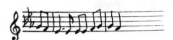

     Paulson, G. (3)

Bohemian Brethren   *

     Hemmer, E.

   Variant:
   Mit Freuden zart

      Videroe, F.
      Werner, F. E. H.

Bonar (Brunk)

     Burkhart, C. (3)

Bone Pastor (Mode 7)

     Heiller, A.

Bound for the Promised Land
(Southern Harmony)

     Moyer, J. H.

Boylston (Mason)   *

     Young, G. E. (2)

Bremen
   See: Wer nur den lieben (Neumark)

Breslau (Leipzig)   *

     Thalben-Ball, G.

   Variant:
   Ach Gott, wie manches Herzeleid

     Merkel, G.

Brich den Hungrigen dein Brot
(1953)

     Haeussler, G.

Brich uns, Herr (Micheelsen)   *

    Micheelsen, H. F.

Bring a Torch (French)   *

    Ellsasser, R.   McKinney, H. D.
    Hovdesven, E. A.

Bromsgrove (Dyer)   *

    Thalben-Ball, G.

Brother James' Air (Bain)   *

    Ellsasser, R.

   Variant:
   Marosa

    Martin, G. M.

Brunnquell aller Guter (Crueger)   *

    Paulson, G.

   Variant:
   Ande, full av naade

    Lundell, C.

Bryd frem, mit hjertes (Lindeman)   *

    Haarklou, J.

Bryd frem, mit hjertes (Zinck)   *
Bryt

    Bangert, E.
    Haarklou, J. (2)

Bryn Calfaria (Owen)   *

    Powell, W.

Buckland (Haynes)   *

    Thalben-Ball, G.

Caerlleon (Welsh)

    Clokey, J. W.

Caerllyngoed (Welsh)

    Hughes, E. J.

Caithness (Scotch)   *

     Thalben-Ball, G.

Cannock (Stanton)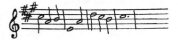

     Thalben-Ball, G.

Capel (English)   *

     Thalben-Ball, G.

Capetown (Filitz)   *

     Thalben-Ball, G.

Carey's
   See: Surrey (Carey)

Carlisle
   See: Bemerton (Filitz)

Carol (Willis)   *

     Corina, J.   Lynn, G. A.
     Ellsasser, R.   Schmutz, A. D.

Carol Melody
   See: Den die Hirten

Caswall (Lockhart)   *

     Thalben-Ball, G.

Celestia (Danish)   *

     Held, W.

   Variant:
   Dejlig er den Himmel blaa (Danish)

     Emborg, J. L.

Chantons, bargiés, Noué, Noué
   (French)
   See: Besançon Carol (French)

Chartres (French)   *

     Lynn, G. A.

   Variants:
   Noël - Nous voici dans la Ville

     Franck, C.

Chartres (cont.)

Noël - Or dites nous, Marie
        nous dites,

Balbastre, C.	Guilmant, A.
Charpentier, M. A.	LeBègue, N. A.
Dandrieu, J. F.	Raison, A.
Dandrieu, P.	

Chester (Billings)   *

Brandon, G.

Christ, der du bist der helle Tag   *
    (Bohemian)

Variant:
Christe, du bist der helle Tag

Gore, R. T.	Weiss, E.
Schwartz, G. von	Wiemer, W.

Christ is Born   *

Variant:
Noël - Le Messie vient de naître

Guilmant, A.

Christ ist erstanden (Folk)
    See: Christus Resurrexit (Plainsong)

Christ ist erstanden von dem Tod
    (Strassburg 1537)
                            Z 1703
        Klenz, W.

Christ lag in Todesbanden (Walther)
    See: Christus Resurrexit
    (Plainsong)

Christ, unser Herr, zum Jordan   *
    (Walther)

Bornefeld, H.	Stearns, P. P.
Gore, R. T.	

Variant:
Ic sie die Morgensterne

Roelstraete, H.

Christe, der du bist Tag und Licht   *
    (Old Church)

Gore, R. T.
Timme, T.

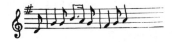

Christum, wir sollen loben schon   *

    Bender, J.   Praetorius, J.
    Boehm, G.

Variants:
A Solis Ortus Cardine (Plainsong-
Mode 3)

    Grigny, N. de
    Lesur, D.

Crudelis Herodes

    Lesur, D.

Fra Himlen hoeit jeg kommer

    Steenberg, P.

Christus, der ist mein Leben
   See: Ach bleib mit deiner Gnade
(Vulpius)

Christus, der uns selig macht   *
   (Ancient German)

    Ehrlinger, F.   Kauffmann, G. F.
    Hambraeus, B.   Telemann, G. P. (2)

Variant:
Soerg, O kjaere Fader

    Hovland, E.
    Winter-Hjelm, O.

Christus ist erstanden
   See: Christus Resurrexit
(Plainsong)

Christus Resurrexit (Plainsong)   *

Variants:
Christ ist erstanden (Folk)

    Anonymous (Buxheimer) (2)   Klenz, W. (3)
    *Baur, J.   Walcha, H.
    Eder, H.   Wilson, R.
    Ehrlinger, F.   Wyton, A.
    Fischer, J. K. F.

Christ lag in Todesbanden (Walther)

    Barlow, W.   Stevens, H.
    Boehm, G.   Telemann, G. P. (3)
    Klenz, W.   Zachau, F. W.

Christus Resurrexit (Plainsong) (cont.)

Christus ist erstanden

Albrechtsberger, J. G.

Den Herre Krist i doedens Baand

Baden, C.
Haarklou, J. (2)

Church Triumphant (Elliott)

Thalben-Ball, G.

Cleansing Fountain (Early American-
Mason)

*

Thiman, E.

Coelestis Urbs Jerusalem (Mode 8)

*

*Lesur, D.

Collingwood (Bate)

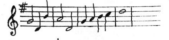

Thalben-Ball, G.

Come, Come, Ye Saints (English)

*

Blanchard, W. G.
Johannesen, G.

Come, Shepherds, Awake

*

Variant:
Noël - Allons, Pasteurs

Guilmant, A.

Comes the Snow (English)

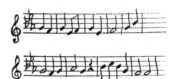

Ellsasser, R.

Communion (Brackett)

Stearns, P. P.

Conditor Alme Siderum
See: Creator Alme Siderum
(Mode 4)

Congleton (M. Wise--1684)

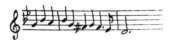

Johnson, D. N.

Consolation (Lindeman)   *

   Variant:
   Naar mit oeie (Lindeman)

      Cappelen, C.   Winter-Hjelm, O.
      Steenberg, P.

Consolation (Webbe)   *

      Stearns, P. P.

   Variant:
   Consolator

      Stearns, P. P.

Consolation (Wyeth)
   See: Morning Song (Wyeth)

Consolator
   See: Consolation (Webbe)

Copenhagen (Zinck)   *

   Variants:
   Jag vet paa vem jag tror

      Melin, H.

   Jeg vil mig Herren love (Zinck)

      Bangert, E.   Runbaeck, A.
      Nielsen, L.

Coronation (Holden)   *

      Frank, R.   Spong, J.
      McKinney, H. D.   Videroe, F.

Covenanters Tune (Scotch)   *

   Variant:
   Pisgah

      Hustad, D.
      Wood, D.

Coventry Carol (English)   *

      Cundick, R.
      Southbridge, J.

Cradle Hymn (Harmonia Sacra)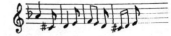

      Powell, R. J.

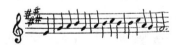

Cushman (Turner)

    Burns, W. K.

Cwm Rhondda (Hughes)   *

    Hustad, D.
    Wetherill, E. H.

Da Christus geboren war (Bohemian)   *

    Ehrlinger, F.
    Kluge, M.

Variants:
Frykt mit barn

    Bangert, E.
    Winter-Hjelm, O.

Singen wir aus Herzens Grund
(Horn)

    Gore, R. T.

Da Jesu an dem Kreuze stund   *

    Eder, H.   Fischer, J. K. F.
    Faessler, G.   Schmidt-Arzberg, G.

Da nun das Jahr
  See: Vexilla Regis (German)

Da Pacem Domine   *

    Bornefeld, H.
    Sweelinck, J. P. (2)

Dank sei Gott in der Hoehe (Gesius)   *

Variant:
Geduld die soll'n wir haben

    Johnson, D. N.

Danket dem Herren, denn er ist sehr
  freundlich (Klug)
                Z 13

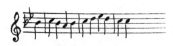

    Gore, R. T.

Dankt den Herrn
  See: Old 107th

Darwall's 148th   *

    Thalben-Ball, G.
    Young, G. E.

Das alte Jahr (Steuerlein)   *

      Klenz, W.
      Scheller, H.

Das neugebor'ne Kindelein (Vulpius)   *

      Bunjes, P.

Das walt Gott, Vater (Vetter)   *

      *Fischer, I.

Das walt mein Gott (Vopelius)   *

      Gore, R. T.

De herdar vaktade deras hjord
  See: Der Tag, der ist so
  freudenreich (Wittenberg)

De herlige himlar (Wideen)   *

  Variants:
  Det ringer till vila

      Rosenquist, C. E.

  I prektige himler

      Videroe, F.

De Profundis (Calvin)
  See: Psalm 129 (Calvin)

Deck the Halls (Welsh)   *

      Ellsasser, R.
      McKinney, H. D.

Decus Morum (Tone 8)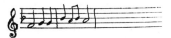

      Fasolo, G. B.

Deep River (Spiritual)   *

      Warner, R.

Dein Koenig kommt in niedern (Zahn)   *

      Hoegner, F.

Dein Wort, O Herr (Dessler--1704)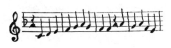

      Vogt, E.

Deinem Heiland, deinem Lehrer
See: Lauda Sion Salvatorem
(German--Salzburg)

Dejlig er den Himmel blaa (Danish)
See: Celestia (Danish)

Dejlig er jorden
See: Schoenster Herr Jesu
(Silesian)

Delight (Christian Psalmist)

   Brandon, G.

Den blomstertid nu kommer
See: Blomstertid (Swedish Psalm)

Den dag du gav oss Gud (Rung)
See: O lad din aand (Rung)

Den die Hirten lobten sehr (Latin)   *

   Variants:
   Carol Melody

      Stearns, P. P.

   Jesus Kristus aer vaar haelsa

      Olson, D.

   Kommt und lasst uns Christum ehren

      Bornefeld, H.

   Quem Pastores

      Johnson, D. N.

Den haerlighet och aera
See: Nun lob', mein Seel (Kugelman)

Den Herre Krist i doedens Baand
See: Christus Resurrexit (Plainsong)

Den kaerlek du till
See: Bangor (Tans'ur)

Den korta stund jag vandrar haer
See: O Jesu Christ, du hoechstes
Gut (Crueger)

Den ljusa dag framgaangen aer (Kingo)
    lyse   forgangen
  See: Vergangen ist der lichte Tag
(Danish)

Den signade dag (Thomissoen)   *

    *Hedwall, L.   Paulson, G. (3)
    *Hultin, L.   Sandvold, A.
    Olson, D.

    Variants:
    Ack laatom oss lova och bedja

      Andersson, R.

    Me hoeyrer stundom (Thomissoen)

      Olson, D.
      Runbaeck, A.

Den signede dag (Weyse)   *

    Bangert, E.   Haarklou, J.
    Emborg, J. L.   *Lindroth, H.

Den sjael som Gud (Zinck)   *

    Variant:
    Du hoeie fryd for rene sjele (Zinck)

      Haarklou, J.

Den store hvite flokk (Lindeman)   *

      Haarklou, J.

Den store hvite flokk (Norwegian)   *

    *Alnaes, E.   McKay, G. F.
    Burnham, C.

Den tro som Jesum favner
  See: Aus meines Herzens Grunde

Denne er dagen (Vulpius)
  See: Lobet den Herren, ihr
Heiden (Vulpius)

Dennis (Naegel)   *

    McKinney, H. D.

Deo Gracias (English)   *

    Miles, G.
    Young, G. E.

Deo Gracias (English) (cont.)

   Variant:
Agincourt Song
        Hymn

      Meek, K.
      Swann, F. L.

Deo Gratias (Latin)   *

      Schehl, J. A.

Der du bist Drei in Einigkeit   *
   (Plainsong)

      Gore, R. T.   Zipp, F.
      Hoegner, F.

Der Herr ist mein getreuer Hirt
   (Wittenberg)
   See: Psalm 23 (Bourgeois)

Der Mange skal komme (Stockholm)
   See: Stockholm

Der Tag bricht an (Vulpius)   *

      Gwinner, V. (2)
      Hoegner, F.

Der Tag, der ist so freudenreich   *
   (Wittenberg)

      Fischer, J. K. F.
      Werner, F. E. H.

   Variants:
De herdar vaktade

      Wikander, D.

   En jungfru foedde ett

      Norrman, R.

   O lue fra Guds (Weisse)

      Haarklou, J.
      Winter-Hjelm, O.

Der Tag hat sich geneiget

      Kluge, M.

Der Tag ist nun vergangen (Ahle)
                  Z 5476
      Gebhard, H.

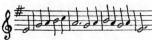

Der Tag ist seiner Hoehe nah (Werner)   *

      Werner, F. E. H.

Der Tag mit seinem Lichte (Ebeling)
                     Z 7511
      Werner, F. E. H.

Des Tages Glanz erloschen ist

      Micheelsen, H. F.

Det aer en ros
   See: Es ist ein Ros'

Det er saa yndigt (Weyse)   *

      Matthison-Hansen, G.
      Sandvold, A.

Det gaar ett tyst
   See: An Wasserfluessen Babylon

Det ringer till vila (Wideen)
   See: De herlige himlar (Wideen)

Det spirar i Guds oertagaard   Tune not found

      Skoeld, Y.

Detroit (Kentucky Harmony)

      Burnham, C.

Dett finns ett ord
   See: O hjelp mig, Gud (Waldis)

Deus Tuorum Militum (Latin - Mode 8)   *

   Variant:
   Jesu Corona Virginum (Mode 8)

      Vallambrosa, A. de

Diadem (Eller)   *

      Wetherill, E. H.

Diademata (Elvey)   *

      Pethel, J.   Young, G. E.
      Videroe, F.

Die gueld'ne Sonne (Ebeling)   *

      Marx, K.

Die helle Sonn' leucht' jetzt (Vulpius)   *

    Hoegner, F.
    Krapf, G.

Die Kirche ist ein altes Haus   *
(Lindeman)

    Paulson, G.

Variants:
Ewig steht fest

    Geilsdorf, P.
    Schmidt-Arzberg, G.

Gammal aer kyrken

    Egebjer, L.
    Paulson, G.

Kirken den er et gammelt hus

Aamodt, T.	Manz, P.
Bangert, E.	Nielsen, L.
Karlsen, R.	Pedersen, G.
Krapf, G.	Videroe, F.

Die Sonn' hat sich
    See: Psalm 8 (Geneva)

Die Stimme eines Engels ruft   *

Variant:
En fridens aengel

    Egebjer, L.

Die Tugend wird durch's Kreuz   *
(Halle)

    Lagergren, A.

Variants:
Avondlied

    Asma, F.

I maenskors barn, som alla aegen
(German)

    Olsson, T. V.

O du, som gav ditt liv foer faaren

    Andersson, R.

Dies Irae, Dies Illa (Plainsong)   *

     Guinaldo, N.

Dies sind die heil'gen Zehn Gebot   *
(Erfurt)

     Sweelinck, J. P.

  Variant:
In Gottes Namen fahren wir

     Vogt, E.

Dieses ist der Tag der Wonne
(Dretzel)   Z 3706
See also Hjaelp mig, Jesu

     Paulson, G.

  Variants:
Herre, var de trognas styrka

     Soerenson, T.

  Lova vill jag Herran

     Soerenson, T.

Dig, Helge Ande, bedja vi
  See: Soldau (Wittenberg)

Dig, Jesu, vare evigt pris
  See: Elbing

Dig klad i helighetens skrud   Tune not found

     Runbaeck, A.

Dig, ljusens Fader
  See: Stoerl I

Dig, min Jesu, nu jag skaader
(Albert)
  See: Vilken kaerlek oss bevisad

Dig skall ditt Sion sjunga se
  See: Old 100th

Dig skall min sjael
  See: Winchester New (Crasselius)

Dig vare lov och pris
  See: Ter Sanctus

Din dyre Ihukommelse (Gesius)
  See: Lasst uns zum Kreuze (Danish)

Din klara sol gaar
See: Stoerl I

Din spira, Jesu, straeckes ut
See: Nun freut Euch, lieben (Klug)

Dir, dir, Jehova (Halle)
See: Winchester New

Ditt namn, O Gud, jag lova vill
See: Praise (Swedish)

Ditt verk aer stort
See: Ich dank dir schon durch
(Praetorius)

Divinum Mysterium (Plainsong)   *

    Arnatt, R.   Held, W.
    Bock, F.   Southbridge, J.
    Casner, M.   Young, G. E.
    Corina, J.

Dix (Kocher)   *

    Brandon, G.   Papale, H.
    Curry, W. L.   Speller, F. N.
    Frank, R.   Stearns, P. P.

Domine Non Sum Dignus   Tune not found

    Schehl, J. A.

Dominus Dixit   *

    Gantner, A.

Dominus Regit Me (Dykes)   *

    McKinney, H. D.   Young, G. E.
    Thalben-Ball, G.   Zabel, A. J.

Dominus Sanctus (Pierre)
See: Steh auf in deiner Macht
(Psalm 68 - Pierre)

Dover (Williams)   *

    Plettner, A.

Down Ampney (Vaughan-Williams)   *

    Bender, J.   Johnston, H.
    Brandon, G.

Du bar ditt kors
See: So geh'st du nun (Darmstadt)

Du Friedefuerst (Gesius)   *

    Gore, R. T.

Du gaar, Guds lamm (Decius)
See: O Lamm Gottes, unschuldig

Du grosser Schmerzensmann (Vopelius)   *

    Kluge, M.
    Stockmeier, W.

Du hoeie fryd for rene sjele (Zinck)
See: Den sjael som Gud (Zinck)

Du kom till oss av himlen ned
See: Jesu, din Ihukommelse
(Gesius)

Du Lebensbrot, Herr Jesu Christ
(Sohren)
See: Elbing (Sohren)

Du livets broed, O Jesu Krist
See: Elbing (Sohren)

Du, meine Seele, singe (Ebeling)   *

    Bornefeld, H.
    Stockmeier, W.

Du, O schoenes Weltgebaeude (Crueger)   *

    Variant:
    Jesu, er mitt liv i live (Crueger)

    Winter-Hjelm, O.

Du oeppnar, O evige Fader (Lindberg)

    Paulson, G.
    Olson, D.

Du sanna vintraed, Jesu kaer
See: Herzlich lieb hab' ich dich
(Schmid)

Du Schoepfer aller Wesen (1934)

    Hamm, W.

Du segern oss foerkunnar
See: Herr Christ, der einig Gottes
Sohn (Erfurt)

Du som gaar ud fra (Lindeman)   *

    Haarklou, J.   Steenberg, P.

Du som haerlig staellde (Svensk
1675)

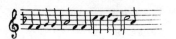

    Rosenquist, C. E.

Du som var den minstes vaen
   See: Liebster Jesu (Ahle)

Du som veien er og livet (Lindeman)   *

   Variant:
   Dyre bord som Jesus dekker
   (Lindeman)

    Enger, E.

Du tunga, soemn
   See: In dich hab' ich (Nuernberg)

Du vaere lovet, Jesus Krist (Walther)
   See: Gelobet seist du (Walther)

Du Volk, das du getaufet bist
   (Ebeling)
               Z 4676

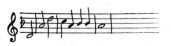

    Gebhard, H.

Duke Street (Hatton)   *

    Brandon, G.   McKinney, H. D.
    Held, W.   Powell, R. J.
    Martin, G. M.   Reichert, J. A.

Dulce Carmen
   See: Alleluia, Dulce Carmen
   (Webbe)

Dundee (Scotch)   *

    Bielawa, H.   Thalben-Ball, G.
    Hutson, W.   Young, G. E.

Dunfermline (Scotch)   *

    Thalben-Ball, G.

Dunlap's Creek (Christian Psalmist)

    Brandon, G.

Durch Adams Fall   *

    Bornefeld, H.   Praetorius, J.
    Klenz, W.   Raphael, G.
    Langlais, J. F.   Sweelinck, J. P.
    Pachelbel, J.   Telemann, G. P. (2)
    Paulson, G.   Zachau, F. W.

Durch Adams Fall (cont.)

Variant:
O Gud, vaar Broder Abels

Berg, G.
Soederholm, V.

Dwelling in Beulah Land

Purvis, R.

Dyre bord som Jesus dekker
(Lindeman)
See: Du som veien er og livet
(Lindeman)

Easter Glory (Lindeman)
See: Fred til bod (Lindeman)

Easter Hymn
See: Lyra Davidica

Ebeling (Bonn)   *

Variant:
Warum sollt ich mich denn graemen

Hovdesven, E. A.   Weiss, E.
Johnson, D. N.   Zabel, A. J.
Post, P.

See also: Tiden flyr: naer vill
du boerja

Ecce Advenit   *

Gantner, A.

Ecce Novum Gaudium   Tune not found

Forsberg, R.

Ecce Panis Angelorum (Plainsong-   *
Mode 8)

Dubois, T.

Eere zij God

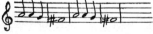

Asma, F.

Eg veit i himmerick (Folk Tune)   *

Kjellsby, E.   Sandvold, A.
Moseng, S.

Eia Ergo Advocata (Plainsong)

    Schlick, A.

Eia Martyr Stephane (15th Century
   English)

    Drayton, P.

Ein feste Burg (Luther)   *

    Bornefeld, H.   Maurer, O.
    Ellsasser, R.   Mueller, C. F.
    Gore, R. T.   Neubauer, H.
    Hustad, D.   Paulson, G. (2)
    Kauffmann, G. F.   Pethel, J.
    Krapf, G.   Stearns, P. P.
    Lagergren, A.   Ulrich, E. J.
    Langlais, J. F.   Videroe, F.
    Liszt, F.   Walther, J. G.
    Manz, P.   Young, G. E.

    Variants:
    Song 96 (Dutch)

        Asma, F.

    Vaar Gud aer oss

        Andersson, R.   Paulson, G.
        Melin, H.   Schoenberg, S. G.

    Vaar Gud han er saa

        Hovland, E.   Winter-Hjelm, O.
        Sandvold, A.

Ein Laemmlein geht (Dachstein)
    See: An Wasserfluessen Babylon

Einer ist Koenig (Darmstadt)   *

    Variant:
    Jesu hilf siegen (Darmstadt)

        Geilsdorf, P.

Eins ist Not (Crueger)
    See: Ratisbon (Crueger)

Eisenach
    See: Mach's mit mir, Gott (Schein)

Eja, mitt hjaerta   *

    Johansson, S. E.

Eja, mitt hjaerta (cont.)

Variants:
Beredd mig haall, Herre Jesu
Krist

Lindberg, K.

I hoppet sig min fraelsa

Andersson, R.

Som faagelen vid ljusan dag

Lindroth, H.

El cant dels Ocells (Spanish)

Guinaldo, N.

El Decembre (Spanish)

Guinaldo, N.

El tre pastorets (Spanish)

Guinaldo, N.

*

Elbing (Sohren)

Variants:
Bis hierher hat mich Gott

Pepping, E.

Dig, Jesu, vare evigt pris

Olson, D.

Du Lebensbrot, Herr Jesu Christ
(Sohren)

Schmidt-Arzberg, G.

Du livets broed, O Jesu Krist

Olson, D.

Ellers (Hopkins)   *

Held, W.   Stearns, P. P.
McKinney, H. D.

Variant:
Benediction

Stearns, P. P.

152

Elton (Mason)

    Bingham, S.

En dalande dag, en flyktig stund
(Wikander--1934)

    Rosenquist, C. E.
    Wikander, D.

En dunkel oertagaard jag vet
(Berglund)

    Hedwall, L.
    Lindstroem, M.

    Variant:
    Mitt vittne vare Gud

    Aahlen, W.

En fridens aengel
    See: Die Stimme eines Engels

En gaang doe, och sedan domen
    See: Freu dich sehr

En herrdag i hoejden (Swedish Folk)

    Bond, A.
    Damm, S.   Norrman, R.

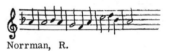

En jungfru foedde ett
    See: Der Tag, der ist so
    freudenreich

En stjaerna gick paa (French)
    Derived from Puer Natus in
    Bethlehem

    Olson, D.

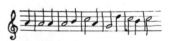

En syndig man, som laag (Svensk
1646)

    Edlund, L.

    Variants:
    Anamma from de dyra

    Carlman, G.

    Boenhoer mig, Gud (in Index)

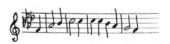

En vaenlig groenskas rika draekt
    See: Was Gott tut
(Gastorius)

Enchiridion (Erfurt)
    Compare with Old 80th (Scotch)

    Johnson, D. N.

Er weckt mich alle Morgen (1940)

        Genzmer, H.
        Hoegner, F.

Erbarm' dich mein (Walther)   *

        Bornefeld, H.   Krebs, J. L.
        Gore, R. T.   Sweelinck, J. P. (2)

Erfreut euch in Gott (1544)

        Klenz, W.

Erhalt uns, Herr, bei deinem Wort   *
    (Klug)

        Bielawa, H.   Thompson, R.
        Gore, R. T.   Weiss, E. (2)
        Ore, C. W.   Wilson, R.

    Variants:
    Behaall oss Herre, vid det hopp

        Runbaeck, A.

    Spires

        Huybrechts, A. J.

Ermunt're dich (Schop)   *

        Wilson, R.

Erschienen ist der herrlich Tag   *
    (Herman)

        Maurer, O.   Thompson, R.
        Neubauer, H.   Walther, J. G.
        Telemann, G. P. (2)

    Variant:
    Wir danken dir, Herr Jesu Christ,
    dass du von Tod (Fischer)

        Buxtehude, D.

Erstanden ist der heilig Christ (Triller)
                    heil'ge   Z 288
    Descant to Surrexit Christus Hodie

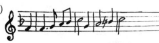

        Dueben, A. (2)
        Walther, J. G.

Erstanden ist der heil'ge Christ
heilig
See: Surrexit Christus Hodie

Es flog ein Taeublein weisse (German
Folk)

    Schroeder, H.

Variant:
Und unser lieben Frauen (Beuttner)

    Eder, H.

Es geht daher des Tages Schein   *
(Bohemian)

    Neubauer, H.

Es glaenzet der Christen (Freyling-   *
hausen)

    Neubauer, H.

Es ist das Heil (Wittenberg)   *

    Ehrlinger, F.   Paulson, G.
    Gebhardi, L. E.   Sweelinck, J. P.
    Neubauer, H.   Videroe, F.

Variants:
Gud har av sin barmhaertighet

    Norrman, R.
    Rosenquist, C. E.

Guds Soenn, er kommet

    Bangert, E.
    Winter-Hjelm, O.

I Herrens namn

    *Johansson, S. E.

Mitt fasta hopp till Herren

    Olson, D.

Es ist ein Ros' (Praetorius)   *
Reis

    Bartelink, B.   Paulson, G.
    Fronmueller, F.   Stearns, P. P. (2)
    Gantner, A.   Vretblad, P.
    McKinney, H. D.

Es ist ein Ros' (cont.)

   Variant:
Det aer en ros

     Paulson, G.

Es ist genug (Muehlhausen)   *

     Stearns, P. P.

Es ist gewisslich (Klug)
  See: Nun freut Euch (Klug)

Es ist kein Tag (Meyer)   *

   Variant:
Meyer

     Thalben-Ball, G.

Es jamm're, wer nicht glaubt   *
(Hirschberg)

     Neubauer, H.

Es kommt ein Schiff (Andernach)   *

     Bloch, W.   Neubauer, H.
     Kropfreiter, A. F.

Es liegt ein Schloss
  See: Op al den ting (Freiburg)

Es mag sein (1940)

     Geilsdorf, P.

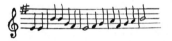

Es sind doch selig
  See: O Mensch, bewein (Strassburg)

Es spricht der Unweisen Mund   *
(Walther)

     Gore, R. T.
     Sweelinck, J. P.

Es steh'n vor Gottes Throne (Burck)   *

     Gore, R. T.

Es sungen drei Engel (Mainz)   *

     Eder, H.
     Hambraeus, B.

Es wird schon gleich dunkel

    Schroeder, H.

Es woll' uns Gott g'naedig sein (Strassburg)   *
  wolle Gott uns

    Gore, R. T.   Lagergren, A.
    Klenz, W.   Pachelbel, J.

    Variants:
    O Fader vaar, barmhaertig, god

      Hedwall, L.
      Melin, H.

    Psalm 67 (Strassburg)
    See also: In dich hab' ich gehoffet
    (Strassburg)

Estans assis aux rives (Goudimel)   Tune not found

    Girod, M. L.

Et barn er foedt (Lindeman)   *

    Cappelen, C.   Haarklou, J.
    *Egebjer, L.

Et barn er foedt
  See: Puer Natus In Bethlehem
  (Old German)

Et Incarnatus Est

    Ahrens, J.

Et Resurrexit   Tune not found

    Leighton, K.

Et trofast hjerte (Praetorius)   *

    Winter-Hjelm, O.

Ett klarligt ljus av dina bud
  See: Praise (Swedish)

Ett spel om en vaag som till Himla
  baar

    Bond, A.

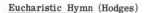

Eucharistic Hymn (Hodges)   *

    Mead, E. G.

Euraclydon (G. W. Torrance)

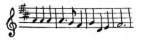

    Blake, G.

Evan (Havergal)   *

    Clokey, J. W.   McKinney, H. D.
    Gustafson, D.   Young, G. E.

Even Me (Bradbury)

  Variant:
  Heer, ik hoor

    Asma, F.

Eventide (Monk)   *

    McKinney, H. D.   Stearns, P. P. (2)
    Schehl, J. A.   Thalben-Ball, G.

Ewig steht fest
  See: Die Kirche ist ein (Lindeman)

Ewing   *

    Stearns, P. P. (2)
    Thalben-Ball, G.

Expectation (Berggreen)
  See: Taenk naer en gaang
  (Berggreen)

Exultet Luminum (Plainsong)

    Fasolo, G. B.

Fader, du vars hjaerta (Lindberg)

    Kullnes, A.
    Paulson, G.

Fader, jag i detta namn
  See: Jesu, allt mitt goda aer
  (Arrhenius)

Farrant (Tye)   *

    Hovdesven, E. A.

Fest soll mein Taufbund (Faber)   *

  Variant:
  Jesus, My Lord, My God, My All

    Campbell-Watson, F.
    Schehl, J. A.

Festal Song (Walter)   *

    Young, G. E.

First Nowell   *

    Balderston, M.   McKinney, H. D.
    Curry, W. L.   Sifler, P. J.
    Ellsasser, R.   Young, G. E.
    Held, W.

Fitzwilliam (English)

    Thalben-Ball, G.

Flemming   *

    Wetherill, E. H.

Foer alla helgon
    See: Pro Omnibus Sanctis (Barnby)

Foer mig sitt liv
    See: Nun freut Euch (Nuernberg)

Foerden skull, Jesu (Folk Tune)

    Olson, D.

Foergaeves all den omsorg (Waldis)
    See: O Gud, ditt rike ingen ser

Foerlossningen
    See: Herr Christ, der einig (Erfurt)

Folkefrelsar (Sletten)   *

    Enger, E.
    Islandsmoen, S.

Folkefrelser (1524)
    See: Nun komm, der Heiden Heiland

Fons Bonitans   *

    Variants:
    Herre Gud, Fader, du vaar
    (10th Century)

    Winter-Hjelm, O.

    Pater Noster (Liturgical)

    Langlais, J. F.   Reboulat, A.
    Plé-Caussade, S.

Forest Green (English)   *

  Barlow, W.   Wood, D.
  Held, W.

Fortem Virili Pectore (Plainsong)

  Fasolo, G. B.

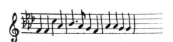

Fortunatus (Sullivan)   *

  Feibel, F.

Foundation (Early American)   *

  Hustad, D.   Moyer, J. H.
  Martin, G. M.   Southbridge, J.

Fra Himlen hoeit jeg kommer
 See: Christum, wir sollen

Fra Himlen hoejt kom
 See: Vom Himmel hoch

Fraan Gud vill jag ej vika
 See: Von Gott will ich nicht
 (Erfurt)

Fraelsta vaerld! (Swedish)

  Lagergren, A.
  Paulson, G.

 Variant:
 Kommen alla, som arbeten

  Rosenquist, C. E.

Fragrance   *

 Variant:
 What Is This Lovely Fragrance?

  Walter, S.

Franconia (Koenig-Havergal)   *

  Hunt, W.
  Thalben-Ball, G.

Franzen (Thomissoen)   *
 Compare Hilf Gott, dass mir's
 gelinge (Thomissoen)

  Paulson, G.

Franzen (cont.)

Variant:
O Jesu, aen de dina (Thomissoen)

    Olson, D.
    Soerenson, T.

Fred til Bod (Lindeman)   *

Variant:
Easter Glory (Lindeman)

    Cassler, G. W.

Freiburg
See: Op al den ting (Freiburg)

Freu dich Erd' und Sternenzelt
See: Salvator Natus (Bohemian)

Freu dich sehr (Bourgeois)   *

    Boehm, G.   Pasquet, J.
    Duchow, M.   Paulson, G. (3)
    Lagergren, A. (2)   Young, G. E.
    Manz, P.

Variants:
En gaang doe, och sedan domen

    Aahlen, W.
    Runbaeck, A. (2)

Geneva 42

    Parker, A.

Ingen herde kan saa

    Rosenquist, C. E. (2)

Jesu, dine dype vunder

    Bangert, E.   Rosenquist, C. E.
    Castegren, N.   Steenberg, P.
    Emborg, J. L.   Winter-Hjelm, O.
    Moeller, S. O.

Jesu, djupa saaren dina

    Andersson, R.

Psalm 42 (Geneva)

    Clokey, J. W.

Freu dich sehr (cont.)

   Saasom hjoeten traeget

      Castegren, N.

   Song 50 (Dutch)

      Asma, F.

   Vad kan dock min sjael foernoeja

      *Castegren, N.

   Wie der Hirsch

      Klenz, W.

   Wie nach einer Wasserquelle

      Gore, R. T.
      Sweelinck, J. P.

Freuen wir uns alle (Weisse)

                       Z 1176

      Krapf, G.

Freut Euch, ihr lieben Christen all
(Gesius)

                              *

      Vogt, E.

Frisch auf, mein Seel' (Dresden
1608)

      Gore, R. T.

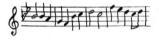

Froehlich soll mein Herze (Crueger)

                              *

      Johnson, D. N.   Wiemer, W.
      Marx, K.   Young, G. E.
      Peeters, E.

Froehlich wir nun all fangen an
(Strassburg)

                              *

      Bornefeld, H.   Weiss, E.
      Kammeier, H.

Fryd dig, du Kristi Brud (Regnart)
  See: Auf meinen lieben Gott
  (Regnart)

Frykt mit barn
  See: Da Christus geboren
  (Bohemian)

Fulda
   See: Germany (Beethoven)

Gaa varsamt, min Kristen
   See: Min lodd falt mig (Norsk
   Folk)

Gammal aer kyrken
   See: Die Kirche ist ein altes Haus

Gammal dalakoral (Name not found)

     Lindberg, O. F.

Gammal faebodpsalm (Swedish)
(Name not found)

     Lindberg, O. F.

Gardiner
   See: Germany (Beethoven)

Gaudeamus (Gregorian)   *

     Hens, C.

Gaudeamus Pariter (Horn)   *

     Groom, L.   Videroe, F.
     Johnson, D. N.

Geduld die soll'n wir haben
   See: Dank sei Gott in der Hoehe
   (Gesius)

Gegruesst seid, Jesu Wunden, mir
   See: Herz und Herz vereint
   (Gregor 167th)

Gelobet sei der Herr, der Gott
   Israels (Wittenberg)

     Gore, R. T.

Gelobet seist du (Walther)   *

     Buttstedt, J. H.   Krapf, G.
     Buxtehude, D.   Manz, P.
     Klenz, W.   Paulson, G.

     Variants:
     Du vaere lovet, Jesus Krist
     (Walther)

       Haarklou, J.
       Runbaeck, A.

Gelobet seist du (cont.)

   Lov vare dig, O Jesu Krist

     Olson, D.

Gelobt sei Gott (Vulpius)   *

     Barlow, W.   Kluge, M.
     Brandon, G.

   Variant:
   Vulpius

     Thalben-Ball, G.

Gen Himmel aufgefahren ist (Franck)   *

     Bornefeld, H.   Gore, R. T.
     Eder, H.   Teutsch, W.

Geneva 42
   See: Freu dich sehr

Geneva 124
   See: Old 124th

Gerald (Spohr)

     Stearns, P. P.

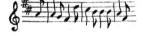

Germany (Beethoven)   *

     Frank, R.

   Variants:
   Fulda

     Thalben-Ball, G.

   Gardiner

     Hutson, W.
     Powell, R. J.

Gerontius (Dykes)   *

     McKinney, H. D.

Gesu Bambino (Yon)

     McKinney, H. D.

Giardini   *

   Variants:
   Italian Hymn

Giardini (cont.)

    Curry, W. L.   Young, G. E.
    McKinney, H. D.

Moscow

    Thalben-Ball, G.

Gib Fried, O frommer, treuer Gott
(Schneegass)
                  Z 7571
    Gore, R. T.

Giv att ditt ord oss lysa maa
    See: Pax (Swedish)

Gjoer doeren hoei
    See: Old 100th

Glad jag staedse vill bekaenna
    See: Alle Menschen muessen
    sterben (Wessnitzer)

Glade Jul, dejlige Jul
    See: Stille Nacht

Gladelig vil vi halleluja (Lindeman)   *

    Kjeldaas, A.

Glaed dig, du helga kristenhet (Weman-
1939)

    Hedwall, L.   Soederholm, V.
    Olson, D.

Glaed dig, du Kristi Brud (Tune
variant)
    See: Auf meinen lieben Gott
    (Regnart)

Gloaming (Stainer)   *

    Stearns, P. P.

Gloria (French Noël)
    See: Les anges dans nos

Gloria In Excelsis Deo (Mode 8)   *

    Ahrens, J.

Gloria Orbis Factor

    Langlais, J. F.

God, Father, Praise and Glory   *
  (Mainz)

    Hulse, C. Van

God Rest Ye Merry (English)   *
           You

    Held, W.   Young, G. E.
    McKinney, H. D.

God Save the Queen
  See: America (Carey)

Goer porten hoeg (Swedish)

    Berg, G.
    Nyvall, J.   Paulson, G.
                             Runbaeck, A. (2)

Goer porten hoeg
  See: Old 100th

Good King Wenceslas
  See: Tempus Adest Floridum

Gopsal (Handel)

    Thalben-Ball, G.
    Willcocks, D.

Gordon (Gordon)   *

    Frank, R.
    Hustad, D.

Goshen (Yoder)

    Burkhart, C.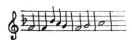

Gott, der Vater, wohn uns bei   *
  (Wittenberg)

    Gore, R. T.   Telemann, G. P. (2)
    Manz, P.   Werner, F. E. H.

  Variant:
  Gud, trefaldig, statt oss bi (German)

    Olsson, O. E.

Gott des Himmels (Alberti)   *

    Gore, R. T.   Scheller, H.
    Paulson, G.   Thompson, R.

  Variants:
  Hela vaerlden froejdes Herren

Gott des Himmels (cont.)

Jesu, du min froejd
        fryd

   Soerenson, T.

Jesu, laat mig staedse boerja
(Albert)

   Carlman, G.
   Olson, D.

Gott hat das Evangelium (Alberus)   *

   Gore, R. T.

Gott, Heil'ger Schoepfer aller Stern
See: Creator Alme Siderum
(Mode 4)

Gott ist mein Heil, mein Huelf und   *
   trost

   Gore, R. T.

Gott ist mein Licht
See: Psalm 27 (Geneva)

Gott sei Dank durch alle Welt (Halle)   *

   Thalben-Ball, G.

Gott sei gelobet (Walther)   *

   Gore, R. T.   Pfiffner, E.
   Pepping, E.   Scheidemann, H.

   Variant:
   Gud vare lovad

   Nilsson, T.

Gott sorgt fuer dich   *

   Schneidt, H. M.

Gott, Vater, der du deine Sonn'   *
   (Herman)

   Gore, R. T.

Gott will's machen (Steiner)   *

   Thalben-Ball, G.

Gottes Sohn ist kommen (Weisse)   *

     Neubauer, H.
     Schwartz, P.

Gottlob, es geht nunmehr   *

     Stearns, P. P. (2)

Grace Church (Pleyel)   *

     McKinney, H. D.

Grates Nunc Omnes   Z 8620

     Praetorius, J.

     Variant:
Lobet Gott, O lieben Christen
(Weisse)

Gratitude (Herr)

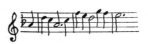

     Burkhart, C.

Great God   *

     Variant:
Noël - Grand Dieu

     Guilmant, A.

Great God, Our Source (G. M. Cart-
    ford)

     Wyton, A.

Green Fields (Sacred Harp)

     Hustad, D.

Greenland (Haydn)   *

     Feibel, F.

Greensleeves (English)   *

     Canning, T.   McKinney, H. D.
     Curry, W. L.   Roper, E. S.
     Diemer, E. L.   Young, G. E.

Grosser Gott, wir loben dich   *

     Thomas, B.
     Walter, S.

Grosser Gott, wir loben dich (cont.)

    Variants:
    Hursley

      Gantner, A.   Pethel, J.
      Maekelberghe, A.

    Te Deum (Vienna)

      Manz, P.

Gud aer haer tillstaedes (German)
    See: Tysk

Gud ej sitt tryckta barn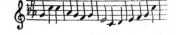

    Lagergren, A.

Gud er naadig (Lindeman)   *

    Kjeldaas, A.

Gud har av sin barmhaertighet
    See: Es ist das Heil (Wittenberg)

Gud laater sina trogna haer
    See: Nun freut Euch (Klug)

Gud, laer mig dock besinna
    See: Old 130th

Gud skal all ting (Crueger)
    See: Jesu, meine Freude

Gud, trefaldig, statt oss bi
    See: Gott, der Vater, wohn uns bei

Gud, vaar loesta tunga (O. Lind-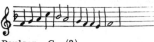
    stroem--1937)

      Olson, D.   Paulson, G. (2)
      Olsson, T. V.

Gud vaelsigna dessa hjaertan (Svensk
    1697)

      Runbaeck, A.

Gud vare lovad
    See: Gott sei gelobet (Walther)

Gud vare tack och aera
    See: Blomstertid (Swedish)

Guds rena lamm
    See: O Lamm Gottes (Decius)

Guds Soenn, er kommet
  See: Es ist das Heil

Guidance (Brackett)   *

     Stearns, P. P.
     Young, G. E.

Gwalchmai (Jones)   *

     Paxton, D.
     Thalben-Ball, G.

Haerlig aer jorden
  See: Schoenster Herr Jesu

Hamburg (Mason)   *

     Bijster, J.   Ulrich, E. J.
     Hutson, W.   Young, G. E.
     McKinney, H. D.   Zabel, A. J.
     Pisk, P. A.

Han lever! O min Ande, kaenn
  (Haeffner)

     Berg, G.

Hanover (Croft)   *

     Clokey, J. W.   Young, G. E.
     Thalben-Ball, G.

Hanson Place (Lowry)
  See: Shall We Gather at the River

Harts (Milgrove)

     Thalben-Ball, G.

Hast du denn, Jesu
  See: Lobe den Herren, den

Hav i ditt minne Jesus Krist
  See: In dich hab' ich gehoffet
  (Nuernberg)

Have Thine Own Way
  See: Adelaide (Stebbins)

He Leadeth Me
  See: Aughton

Heer, ik hoor
  See: Even Me (Bradbury)

Heil'ger Geist, du Troester mein   *
  (Crueger)

    Gebhard, H.   Micheelsen, H. F.
    Kluge, M.

Heilige Namen   *

    Gantner, A.

Heinlein
  See: Aus der Tiefe

Hela vaerlden froejdes Herran
  (Swedish)
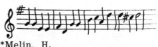
    *Hedwall, L.   *Melin, H.
    Jobs, A.   Paulson, G. (2)

Hela vaerlden froejdes Herren
  See: Gott des Himmels (Alberti)

Helig, helig, helig (Dykes)
  See: Nicaea (Dykes)

Helige Ande, laat din roest
  See: Lobet den Herrn, ihr Heiden
  all (Vulpius)

Helige Ande, laat nu ske
  See: Lobet den Herrn, ihr
  Heiden all (Vulpius)

Helige Ande, sanningens Ande
  (Scandelli)
  See: Lobet den Herren, denn er
  ist sehr (Scandelli)

Helige, som bor i ljuset
  See: Wachet auf

Hell morgonstjaerna, mild och ren
  See: Wie schoen leuchtet

Hemelvaartslied
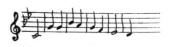
    Asma, F.

Hendon (Malan)   *

    Hamill, P.

Her ser jeg (Strassburg)
  See: An Wasserfluessen (Dachstein)

Herald Angels
  See: Mendelssohn

Herongate (English)

    Thalben-Ball, G.

Herr Christ, der du die Deinen
  liebst (1531)

    Haffner, W.

Herr Christ, der einig Gottes Sohn
(Erfurt)

    Kauffmann, G. F.   Schildt, M. (2)
    Lorentz, J.   Sweelinck, J. P.
    Paulson, G.   Telemann, G. P. (2)
    Scheidt, S.   Walther, J. G.

    Variants:
    Du segern oss foerkunnar

        Olson, D.
        Paulson, G.

    Foerlossningen

        Andersson, R.   Olsson, O. E.
        Lagergren, A. (4)

    O naadens sol og sete (Erfurt)

        Olson, D.   Wikander, D.
        Runbaeck, A.

Herr erhoere meine Klagen (Psalm
77)
  See: Psalm 86 (Geneva)

Herr Gott, dich loben alle wir
  See: Old 100th

Herr Gott, dich loben wir (Babst)

    Gore, R. T.
    Praetorius, J.

Herr Gott, erhalt uns fuer und fuer
  (Burck)
                    Z 443

    Gore, R. T.

Herr Gott, wann du dein Volk (Waldis)
  See: Hur froejdar sig i templets
  famn (Waldis)

Herr hoere doch auf meine Rede
  (Geneva 1542)
  See: Psalm 5 (Geneva)

*

*

Herr, ich habe missgehandelt   *
 (Crueger)

    Schwartz, P.
    Thompson, R.

Variant:
Herre, jeg har handlet ille
 (Crueger)

    Emborg, J. L.
    Winter-Hjelm, O.

Herr Jesu Christ, dich zu uns wend   *
 (Gotha)

    Boehm, G.   Parker, A.
    Gebhardi, L. E.   Schack, D. A.
    Geilsdorf, P.   Skaalen, P. A.
    Klenz, W.   Telemann, G. P. (4)
    Manz, P.

Variant:
O Herre Krist, dig til oss vend

    Bangert, E.
    Winter-Hjelm, O.

Herr Jesu Christ, du hoechstes Gut   *
 (Goerlitz)

    Bornefeld, H. (2)   Haffner, W.
    Gore, R. T.

Variant:
Herr Jesu, deine Angst und Pein
 (Goerlitz)

    Micheelsen, H. F.

Herr Jesu Christ, ich weiss gar
 wohl (Hof)
                  Z 4525
    Gore, R. T.

Herr Jesu Christ, meins Lebens
 Licht (Calvisius)

    Gore, R. T.

Herr Jesu Christ, meins Lebens
 Licht (Nuernberg)   *

Variant:
O Jesu Christe, wahres Licht
 (Nuernberg)

    Seiler, G.

Herr Jesu Christ, wahr Mensch und
    Gott (French Psalm)
    See: Andernach (French Psalm)

Herr Jesu, deine Angst und Pein
    (Goerlitz)
    See: Herr Jesu Christ, du
    hoechstes Gut (Goerlitz)

Herr, nun lass in Friede (Bohemian)   *

        Haffner, W.

Herr, send herab nun deinen Sohn
    See: Creator Alme Siderum

Herr, straf' mich nicht (Crueger)   *

        *Duchow, M.
        Klenz, W.

Herr und Aeltster (Moravian)   *

        Variant:
        Slotzang

            Asma, F.

Herr, wie du willst (Strassburg)
    See: Aus tiefer Not (Strassburg)

Herre dig i naad foerbarma (Koenig)
        i din naad
                            Z 6726
        Norrman, R.   Olsson, O. E.
        Nyvall, J.   Runbaeck, A.

Herre, du et hjem (Solheim)   *

        Steenberg, P.

Herre Gud, ditt dyre navn (Norwegian   *
    Folk Tune)

        Drischner, M.   Moseng, S.
        Hovland, E.   Pedersen, G.

Herre Gud, ditt dyre navn (Steenberg)   *

        Steenberg, P.

Herre Gud, Fader, du vaar (10th
    Century)
    See: Fons Bonitans

Herre, jag vil bida (O. Lindberg-
    1937)

Herre, jag vil bida (cont.)

    Franzen, B.
    Paulson, G.

Herre, jeg har handlet ille (Crueger)
    See: Herr, ich habe missgehandelt
    (Crueger)

Herre, jeg hjertelig oensker (Folk)   *

    Sandvold, A.

Herre, signe du och raade
    See: Werde munter (Schop)

Herre, var de trognas styrka
    See: Dieses ist der Tag der
    Wonne (Dretzel)

Herren aer min herde god

    Egebjer, L.
    Runbaeck, A.

    Variant:
    Wennerberg I

Herren Gud i alla tider
    See: Alle Menschen (Wessnitzer)

Herz und Herz vereint (Gregor 167th)
                    Z 6738
    Variant:
    Gegruesst seid, Jesu Wunden, mir

    Faessler, G.

Herz und Herz vereint zusammen
(Basel)
    See: O du Liebe meiner Liebe
    (Herrnhag-Ebeling)

Herzlich lieb hab' ich dich (Schmid)   *

    Alberti, J. F.   Reda, S.
    Ehrlinger, F.   Schildt, M. (2)
    Gore, R. T.   Sweelinck, J. P. (2)

    Variants:
    Aat, dig, O Gud, som allt

    Andersson, R.

    Av hjaertat haver jag dig kaer
    (German 1577)

    Kullnes, A.   Lundell, C.

Herzlich lieb hab' ich dich (cont.)

   Du sanna vintraed, Jesu kaer

     Olson, D.

Herzlich tut mich erfreuen (German)   *

     Block, W.
     Johnson, D. N.

Herzlich tut mich verlangen (Hassler)   *

     Buxtehude, D.   Lagergren, A.
     Gebhard, H.   Paulson, G.
     Kauffmann, G. F.   Stearns, P. P.

     Variants:
     Ach Herr, mich armen Suender

     Buxtehude, D.   Telemann, G. P. (2)
     Gore, R. T.

     Nu hjertelig jeg langes
                mig lenges

     Bangert, E.
     Winter-Hjelm, O.

   O Haupt voll Blut

     Allgen, C. L.   Faessler, G. (2)
     Brown, R.   Klenz, W.
     Duchow, M.   Peeters, F.
     Eder, H.

   O huvud, blodigt saarat

     Hellden, D.
     Janáček, B.

   O Sacred Head

     Bielawa, H.   Smart, D.
     Diemer, E. L.

   Passion Chorale

     Bock, F.   Johnson, D. N.
     Hustad, D.   Long, P. C.

   Song 32 (Dutch)

     Asma, F.

   Song 43 (Dutch)

     Asma, F.

Herzliebster Jesu (Crueger)   *

        Berruyer, G.   Kauffmann, G. F.
        Beverst, G. E.   Kluge, M.
        Bloch, W.   Manz, P.
        Bornefeld, H.   Russell, O. N.
        Clokey, J. W.   Schehl, J. A.
        Edmundson, G.   Videroe, F.
        Gebhardi, L. E.   Wilson, R.
        Gore, R. T.   Zabel, A. J.
        Johnson, D. N.

    Variants:
    Var aer den vaen, som oeverallt

        Olson, D.

    Vreden din avvend (Crueger)

        Bangert, E.

Het Kruis

        Asma, F.

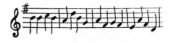

Heut triumphieret Gottes Sohn   *
    (Gesius)

        Vogt, E.

Hilf Gott, dass mir's gelinge   *
    (Dresden)

    Variant:
    Wenn meine Suend' mich kraenken
    (Leipzig)

        Weiss, E.

Hilf Gott, dass mir's gelinge   *
    (Thomissoen)
    Compare with Franzen

    Variant:
    Naar mig min synd

        Winter-Hjelm, O.

Hilf, Herr Jesu, lass gelingen (Schop)   *

        Vogt, E.

Hilf, Herr Jesu, lass gelingen
    (Kocher)
    See: Werde Licht, du Volk
    (Kocher)

Himmelriket aer naera (G. Nordquist)
   See: Jesus fraan Nasaret (Nordquist)

Himmelriket liknas vid tio jungfrur   Tune not found

      Lundborg, G.

Hit, O Jesu, samloms vi (Briegel)
   See: Liebster Jesu (Crueger?)

Hjaelp mig, Jesu, troget vandra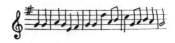
   (Swedish)
   Variant of Dieses ist der Tag
   (Dretzel)

      Lagergren, A.   *Runbaeck, A.
      *Rosenquist, C. E.

Hjaelp mig, min Gud, ack fraels
   See: O hjelp mig, Gud (Waldis)

Hjerte, loeft din gledes vinger   *
   (Steenberg)

      Baden, C.   Thorkildsen, J.
      Skottner, F.

Hoechster Priester (Basel)   *

      Paulson, G.

   Variant:
   Lova Herren Gud, min sjael

      Norrman, R.

Hoega Majestaet vi alla
   See: Wie schoen leuchtet

Hoer, Gud, aennu sin naad
   See: Winchester New (Wach auf du
   Geist - Halle)

Hoeyr kor Kyrkjeklokka (Norse Folk)   *

   Variant:
   Kjaerlighet er lysets kilde (Norse
   Folk)

      Drischner, M.
      Pedersen, G.

Holland (1609)

   Variant:
   Members of One Mystic Body

      Schwarz-Schilling, R.

Holly and the Ivy (English)   *

    Ellsasser, R.

Holy Manna (Moore)   *

    Held, W.   Wyton, A.
    Hustad, D.

Hos Gud er idel glede (Norse Folk   *
   Tune)

    Braein, E.   Islandsmoen, S.
    Enger, E.   Nystedt, K.

Hosanna Filio David   *

    Joulain, J.
    Langlais, J. F.

Hosianna David's Sohne (1653)

    Vogt, E.

Hostis Herodes Impie (Plainsong-
   Mode 3)

    Diruta, G.
    Fasolo, G. B.

Hur froejdar sig i templets famn
   (Waldis)
                   Z 4473
    Andersson, R.
    Carlman, G.

    Variant:
    Herr Gott, wann du dein Volk
    (Waldis)

Hur kan och skall jag dig
   See: O Gott, du frommer Gott
   (Hannover)

Hursley
   See: Grosser Gott, wir loben dich

Huru laenge skall mitt hjaerta (Crueger)
   See: Schmuecke dich

Hvad kan oss komme (Klug)
   See: Nun freut Euch (Klug)

Hvad ljus oefver (Jespersoen)   *

    Variant:
    Aen vaarder och foeder

    Runbaeck, A.

Hvad ljus oefver (cont.)

  Vad ljus oever griften

      Andersson, R. (2)   Paulson, G.
      Olson, D. (2)   Rosenquist, C. E.
      Olsson, O. E.   Runbaeck, A. (2)

Hvad roest, hvad ljuvlig roest
(Aahlstroem)

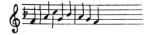

      Egebjer, L.
      Paulson, G.

  Variants:
  St. James (Stockholm)

  Vad roest, vad ljuvlig roest
  (Aahlstroem)

      Paulson, G.
      Olson, D.

Hvem aer den stora (Lewenhaupt)

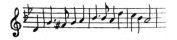

      Egebjer, L.

Hvo ene lader (Neumark)
  See: Wer nur den lieben Gott
  (Neumark)

Hvor er det godt aa lande (Norsk)   *

      Enger, E.
      Skottner, F.

Hyfrydol (Pritchard)   *

      Diemer, E. L.   Near, G.
      Held, W.   Schack, D. A.
      Hutchison, W.   Thalben-Ball, G.
      Hutson, W.   Young, G. E.
      Lynn, G. A.

Hymn to Joy (Beethoven)   *

      Ellsasser, R.   Young, G. E.
      Hustad, D.

I dag om Herrens roest
  See: I denna verdens sorger
  (Swedish Psalm - Haeffner)

I denna ljuva sommartid (Soederblom)   *

      Aahlen, W.   Hedwall, L.
      Andersson, R.   Lundborg, G.

I denna ljuva sommartid (cont.)

    Norrman, R.
    Paulson, G. (2)

  Variant:
  Laer mig du skog

    Runbaeck, A.

I denna verdens sorger (Swedish   *
  Psalm - Haeffner)

    Rosenquist, C. E.

  Variants:
  I dag om Herrens roest

    Andersson, R.   Runbaeck, A.
    Lagergren, A.

  I levernets bekymmer saenkt

    Rosenquist, C. E.

I Herrens namn
  See: Es ist das Heil

I himmelen (Norwegian)   *

    Kjellsby, E.   Skottner, F.
    Moseng, S.

I himmelen, i himmelen (Swedish)
  See: Laurinus (Swedish)

I hoppet sig min fraelsa
  See: Eja, mitt hjaerta

I Jesu navn (Kingo)   *

    Bangert, E.
    Winter-Hjelm, O.

I Kristne som toer (Geneva)
  See: Psalm 6 (Geneva - Marot)

I levernets bekymmer saenkt
  See: I denna verdens sorger
  (Swedish Psalm - Haeffner)

I maenskors barn, som alla aegen
  (German)
  See: Die Tugend wird durch's
  (Halle)

I moerker sjoenko
  See: Psalm 8 (Geneva)

I naad och sanning bland
    See: Wie schoen leuchtet

I Need Thee Every Hour
    See: Need (Lowry)

I oester stiger solen opp (Lindberg)

        Norrman, R.
        Paulson, G.

I prektige himler (Wideen)
    See: De herlige himlar

I Saw Three Ships   *

        McKinney, H. D.

Iam Moesta (Luther)   *

        Paulson, G.

    Variants:
    Med sorgen og klagen

        Bangert, E.   Olson, D.
        Emborg, J. L.   Winter-Hjelm, O.

    Nu tystne de klagande ljuden

        Aahlen, W.

    O Gud, foer de tragna Martyrer

        Runbaeck, A.

Ic sie die Morgensterne
    See: Christ, unser Herr, zum
    Jordan (Walther)

Ich dank dir, lieber Herre (Bohemian)   *

        Gore, R. T.

    Variant:
    Lob Gott getrost mit singen
    (Bohemian)

        Geilsdorf, P.
        Kammeier, H.

Ich dank dir schon durch deinen Sohn   *
    (Praetorius)

        Barlow, W.   Zipp, F.
        Gore, R. T.

Ich dank dir schon durch deinen Sohn (cont.)

   Variants:
Ditt verk aer stort

      Andersson, R.

   Lov, pris, och aera (German)

Ich erhebe mein Gemuethe (Psalm
  25 - Geneva 1551)

      Klenz, W.

Ich hab' mein Sach (Cassel)   *

      Zipp, F.

Ich ruf' zu dir, Herr Jesu Christ   *
(Klug)

      Bornefeld, H.   Neubauer, H.
      Kauffmann, G. F.   Pepping, E.
      Kluge, M.   Sweelinck, J. P. (2)
      Luebeck, V.   Telemann, G. P. (2)

   Variants:
Jeg raaber Herre Jesu Krist
(Wittenberg)

      Lagergren, A.

   O Jesu, som har elsket mig

      Olson, D.   Winter-Hjelm, O.
      Runbaeck, A.

   Saa hoegt har Gud, oss till stor
froejd

      Bjarnegaard, G.

   Till dig jag ropar

      Aahlen, W.
      Andersson, R.

Ich sehe dich, O Jesu, schweigen   *

   Faessler, G.

Ich weiss' an wen ich glaube (Schuetz)   *

   Variant:
Ich weiss' woran ich glaube

      Schneidt, H. M.

Ich weiss' ein Bluemlein huebsch
  und fein (Dresden)
                                    Z 1681

    Gore, R. T. (2)

Ich weiss' ein leiblich Engelspiel   *
  (Strassburg)

    Reda, S.

Ich weiss', mein Gott, dass all   *
  mein Thun (Schein)

    Weiss, E.

Ich weiss' woran ich glaube
  See: Ich weiss' an wen ich glaube
  (Schuetz)

Ich will, so lang ich lebe (Schuetz)   *

    Vogt, E.

Ich wollt, dass ich daheime waer   *
  (Strassburg)

    Johns, D.   Weiss, E.
    Rohwer, J.

Ihr Hirten erwacht (Paderborn)   *

    Schroeder, H.

Ihr Kinderlein kommet (Schulz)   *

    McKinney, H. D.

Ihr Knecht des Herrn
  See: Old 100th

Ihr lieben Christen, freut Euch nun
  (Herman)
  See: O Heilige Dreifaltigkeit

Ihr Menschenkinder .
  See: Old 100th

Il est né, le divin enfant (French)   *

    Chauvin, D.
    Parisot, O.

Illsley (Bishop)

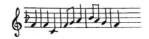

    Thalben-Ball, G.

Im Frieden dein (Dachstein)   *

    Pepping, E.

In Babilone (Dutch)   *

    Johnson, D. N.
    Young, G. E.

In dich hab' ich gehoffet (Leipzig)   *

    Bach, J. C.

In dich hab' ich gehoffet (Nuernberg)   *

    Gore, R. T.   Paulson, G.
    Klenz, W.   Pepping, E.
    Lagergren, A.

    Variants:
    Du tunga soemn

      Paulson, G.

    Hav i ditt minne Jesus Krist

      Johansson, S. E.

    In Te Domine Speravi

      *Baumgartner, H. L.
      Huber, K.

    Paa dig jag hoppas (German)

      Aahlen, W.

In dich hab' ich gehoffet (Strassburg)
                     Z 1706
    Compare with Es woll' uns Gott

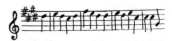

    Gore, R. T.

In dich hab' ich gehoffet (Zuerich)   *

    Scheidemann, H.

In Dir ist Freude (Gastoldi)   *

    Micheelsen, H. F.

In Dulci Jubilo   *

    Allgen, C. L. (2)   Gantner, A.
    Buxtehude, D.   Held, W.
    Crane, R. E.   Johnson, D. N.
    Dobson, C.   Karlsen, R.
    Eder, H.   Klenz, W.
    Forsberg, R.   Lagergren, A.

In Dulci Jubilo (cont.)

Manz, P.
Mareschall, S.
McKinney, H. D.
Paulson, G. (2)
Pethel, J.
Rohlig, H.

Runbaeck, A.
Schroeder, H.
Thorkildsen, J.
Videroe, F.
Young, G. E. (2)
Zabel, A. J.

Variants:
Jeg synger Julekvad

Kjellsby, E.

Statt upp, O Sion

Norrman, R.

In God and Love We Trust

Polifrone, J.

Tune not identified

In Gottes Namen fahren wir
See: Dies sind die heil'gen Zehn
Gebot

In stiller Nacht (German Folk)

Schroeder, H.

In Te Domine Speravi
See: In dich hab' ich (Nuernberg)

Infant King (Basque)
See: Noël Angevin

Ingen herde kan saa leta
See: Freu dich sehr

Ingen vinner frem til den (Norse Folk
Tune)   *

Drischner, M.
Forsberg, R.
Hambraeus, B.
Kjellsby, E.

Moseng, S.
Nielsen, L.
Pedersen, G.

Innsbruck (Isaac)   *

Hovdesven, E. A.
Paulson, G.

Variants:
Nu hviler mark og enge

Bangert, E.
Emborg, J. L.
Winter-Hjelm, O.

Innsbruck (cont.)

   Nu vilar hela jorden

      Hedwall, L.
      Norrman, R.

   Nun ruhen alle Waelder

      Drayton, P.   Gore, R. T.
      Fischer, I.

   O Welt, ich muss dich lassen

      Micheelsen, H. F.   Schilling, H. L.
      Ore, C. W.   Zipp, F.

   O Welt, sieh hier dein Leben

      Mourant, W.

Intercessor (Parry)

      Thalben-Ball, G.

Irby (Gauntlett)   *

      Thalben-Ball, G.

Irwinton (Sacred Harp)
   See: Resignation (U.S. Southern)

Ist Gott fuer mich (Augsburg)   *

      Bornefeld, H.
      Stockmeier, W.

Iste Confessor (Rouen)
   See: Rouen (Poitiers)

Italian Hymn
   See: Giardini

Ite Missa Est (Gregorian)   *

      Ahrens, J.   Hofhaymer, P.
      Doyen, H.   Pikéthy, T. K.

Itzt komm' ich als ein armer Gast
   See: Nun freut Euch, lieben (Klug)

Jag gaar mot doeden (Gotha)

      Aahlen, W.
      Jonsson, J.   Runbaeck, A.

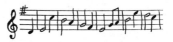
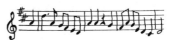
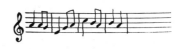

Jeg ser dig, O Guds Lam (Norsk   *
   Folk)

   Baden, C.   Nielsen, L.
   Karlsen, R.

Jeg synger Julekvad
   See: In Dulci Jubilo

Jeg vet mig en soevn (Schein)
   See: Mach's mit mir, Gott (Schein)

Jeg vil mig Herren love (Thomissoen)   *

   Carlman, G.

   Variant:
   Min vilotimma ljuder

   Bjarnegaard, G.   Runbaeck, A.
   Bond, A.   Soerenson, T.

Jeg vil mig Herren love (Swedish
   Psalm)
   See: Blomstertid

Jeg vil mig Herren love (Norse Folk
   Tune)
   See: Mitt hjerte alltid vanker

Jeg vil mig Herren love (Zinck)
   See: Copenhagen (Zinck)

Jeg ville lova och prisa   *

   Variant:
   Som harpoklangen foersvinner

   Berg, G.

Jerusalem, du hochgebaute (Franck)   *

   Gebhardi, L. E.
   Weiss, E.

Jervaulx Abbey (French)   *

   Variant:
   Wie lieblich ist das Haus

   Klenz, W.

Jesus, aer min haegnad
   See: Jesu, meine Freude (Crueger)

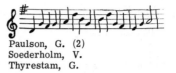

Jesu, din Ihukommelse (Gesius)   *

    Paulson, G.

Variants:
Du kom till oss av himlen ned

    Aahlen, W.

Saell den som haver Jesus kaer

    Olson, D.

Vaar Herres Jesu Kristi doed
    Herras

    Norrman, R.   Paulson, G.
    Olson, D.

Jesu, din soete forening (Norse Folk)   *

    Enger, E.
    Kjellsby, E.

Jesu, din soete forening (Koenig)
    See: Sollt mich die Liebe (Koenig)

Jesu, dine dype vunder
    See: Freu dich sehr

Jesu, djupa saaren dina
    See: Freu dich sehr

Jesu, du bist allzu schoene

    Boehm, G.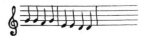

Jesu, du dig sjaelv uppvaeckte
(Swedish)
    See: Kriste, som ditt ursprung

Jesu, du mein liebstes Leben (Schop)
                    Z 7891
    Variant:
    Aelskar barnet modersfamnen

    Olsson, T. V.

Jesu, du min froejd
           fryd
    See: Gott des Himmels (Alberti)

Jesu, du mitt liv, min haelsa
(Svensk--1676)

    Lagergren, A.   Paulson, G.
    Norrman, R.   Rosenquist, C. E.

Jesu, du mitt liv, min haelsa (cont.)

Variant:
Jesu, dig i djupa noeden

Welander, W.

Jesu, du som sjaelen spisar (Svensk
1691 - Arrhenius)

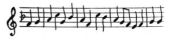

Hedwall, L.
Runbaeck, A.

Jesu er mitt haap
See: Jesu, meine Zuversicht

Jesu er mitt liv i live (Crueger)
See: Du, O schoenes Weltgebaeude

Jesu er mitt liv i live (Wessnitzer)
See: Alle Menschen (Wessnitzer)

Jesu foer vaerlden (Ekstroem)

Paulson, G.

Jesus fraan Nasaret (Nordquist)   *

Hedwall, L.
Paulson, G. (2)

Variant:
Himmelriket aer naera (G. Nordquist)

Olson, D.

Jesu Frelser
See: Liebster Jesu (Ahle)

Jesu, geh voran
See: Seelenbraeutigam (Drese)

Jesu, hast du mein vergessen
See: Vilken kaerlek oss bevisad
(Albert)

Jesu hilf siegen (Darmstadt)
See: Einer ist Koenig (Darmstadt)

Jesu i det hoeie troner (Lindeman)   *

Steenberg, P.

Jesu, Kreuz, Leiden und Pein (Vulpius)
See: Jesu, Leiden, Pein und Tod

Jesus Kristus aer vaar haelsa
    See: Den die Hirten

Jesu, laat mig staedse boerja (Albert)
    See: Gott des Himmels

Jesu, laer mig raett betaenka (Albert)
    See: Vilken kaerlek oss bevisad

Jesu, Leiden, Pein und Tod (Vulpius)   *

    Walther, J. G.

    Variants:
    Jesu, Kreuz, Leiden und Pein
    (Vulpius)

        Hamm, W.

    Jesu, meiner Seele Licht (Vulpius)

        Maurer, O.

Jesu, meine Freude (Crueger)   *

    Binkerd, G.   Miles, R. H.
    Clokey, J. W.   Schack, D. A.
    Diemer, E. L.   Telemann, G. P. (2)
    Fischer, I.   Wiemer, W.
    Hamm, W.   Wilson, R.
    Lagergren, A.   Zachau, F. W.
    Manz, P.

    Variants:
    Gud skal all ting (Crueger)

        Bangert, E.   Winter-Hjelm, O.
        Nyvall, J.

    Jesus, aer min haegnad

        Anjou, H.   Sjoegren, A., Jr.
        Berg, G.   Soederholm, V.
        Nyvall, J.

    Jesus, You Are My Life

        Loewe, A. L.

    Meine Seel' ist stille

        Kaminski, H.

Jesu, meine Zuversicht (Crueger)   *

    Brown, R.   Thompson, R. (3)
    Clokey, J. W.   Wuensch, K.
    Schwartz, G. von

Jesu, meine Zuversicht (cont.)

Variants:
Jesu er mitt haap

Winter-Hjelm, O.

Song 62 (Dutch)

Asma, F. (2)

Jesu, meiner Seele Licht (Vulpius)
See: Jesu, Leiden, Pein und Tod
(Vulpius)

Jesu, meines Herzens Freud (Ahle)   *

Gore, R. T.

Jesu, meines Lebens Leben (Mueller)
See: Alle Menschen muessen
sterben (Mueller)

Jesu, meines Lebens Leben (Wessnitzer)
See: Alle Menschen muessen
sterben (Wessnitzer)

Jesus, My Lord, My God, My All
See: Fest soll mein Taufbund

Jesu, Redemptor Omnium (Sarum)
See: Christe, Redemptor Omnium
(Sarum)

Jesu Tibi Vivo (Jesu, Dir leb ich)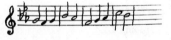
(Plainchant)

Schehl, J. A.

Jesu, wollest uns weisen (Schneegass)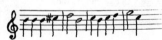
                              Z 8557
Scheidemann, H.

Jesus, You Are My Life
See: Jesu, meine Freude

Jesu, zu dir rufen wir   *

Faessler, G.

Joanna (Welsh)   *

Variant:
St. Denio

Hutson, W.   Speller, F. N.
Moyer, J. H.   Thalben-Ball, G.

Jordan (Sacred Harp)

    Johnson, D. N.

Jordan's Banks (Sacred Harp)

    Hustad, D.

Joseph est bien marié (Noël)   *

    Dandrieu, J. F.   Guilmant, A.
    Gigout, E.   Raison, A.

Joseph, lieber Joseph mein (Klug)   *

    Means, C.

  Variants:
  Singen wir mit Froehlichkeit

    Schroeder, H.

  Var kristtrogen froejde sig

    Berg, G.   Olson, D.
    Norrman, R.

Joshua Fit the Battle of Jericho   *

    Sowande, F.

Jubilate Deo

    Gantner, A.

Judas Maccabeus (Handel)   *

    Groom, L.

Julsaanger (Title not found)

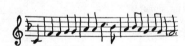

    Vretblad, P.

Kaerlek av hoejden
  See: Lobet den Herren, alle die
  ihn (Crueger)

Kedron
  See: Thou Man of Griefs (Dare)

Keine Schoenheit hat die Welt (Joseph)
                 Z 1199
    Hulse, C. Van

Keinen hat Gott verlassen (Crueger)   *

    Gore, R. T.

Kom hjerte, ta ditt regnebrett
  See: Mein' Seel' erhebt den Herren
  (Strassburg)

Komm, Gott Schoepfer, Heil'ger Geist
  (Klug)
  See: Veni Creator Spiritus (Sarum-
  Mode 8)

Komm, Heiliger Geist, erfuell die
  Herzen
  See: Veni, Sancte Spiritus (Old
  Church)

Komm, Heiliger Geist, Herre Gott   *
  (Walther)

    Armsdorff, A.   Manz, P.
    Barlow, W.   Micheelsen, H. F.
    Geilsdorf, P.   Scheidemann, H.
    Gore, R. T.   Telemann, G. P. (2)
    Klenz, W.

    Variants:
    Kom, Helge Ande, Herre Gud

      Olsson, O. E.   Runbaeck, A.
      Rosenquist, C. E.

    Kom, Hellige Aand, Herre Gud
    (Walther)

      Bangert, E.   Winter-Hjelm, O.
      Runbaeck, A.

Komm Heiliger Geist mit deiner
  G'nad
  See: O Jesulein suess (Cologne)

Komm, O komm, du Geist (J. C.
  Bach)
  See: St. Leonard (Meiningen)

Komm, Seele (J. W. Franck)

    Mader, C.

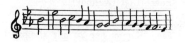

Kommen alla, som arbeten
  See: Fraelsta vaerld

Kommet, ihr Hirten (Bohemian)   *

    McKinney, H. D.
    Seiler, G.

Kriste, som ditt ursprung leder (cont.)

   Vaenligt oever jorden (Svensk)

      Olsson, T. V.
      Rosenquist, C. E.

Kyrie (Lutheran 1528)

    Guinaldo, N.

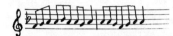

Kyrie Cum Jubilo

    Merulo, C.

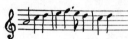

Kyrie Dicta De Angelis (Kyrial)

    Browne, C. F.

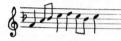

Kyrie: Eucharistia

    Cassler, G. W.

Kyrie, Gott, Vater in Ewigkeit

    Langlais, J. F.

                                        *

Kyrie: Herr erbarme dich

    Rohwer, J.

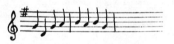

Kyrie (Ite Missa Est)

    Hays, R. W.

                                        *

Kyrie Orbis Factor

      Fasolo, G. B.
      Langlais, J. F.

                                        *

Ladywell (Ferguson)

    Thalben-Ball, G.

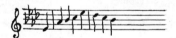

Laer mig du skog
  See: I denna ljuva sommartid
  (Soederblom)

Laetare
  Compare with Wachet auf

    *Faessler, G.

Lancashire (Smart)

                                      *

      Elmore, R.   Mueller, C. F.
      McKinney, H. D.

Land of Rest (Early American)   *

    Proulx, R.
    Wyton, A.

Langran   *

    McKinney, H. D.

Lass mich dein sein und bleiben
(Bohemian)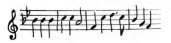

    Gore, R. T.

Lasset uns mit Jesu ziehen (Bolze)   *

    Beck, T.

Lasst uns das Kindlein gruessen
  See: Lasst uns das Kindlein wiegen

Lasst uns das Kindlein wiegen (Folk   *
Tune)

    Gantner, A.
    Schroeder, H.

    Variant:
    Lasst uns das Kindlein gruessen

Lasst uns erfreuen (Cologne)   *

    Beverst, G. E.   Lynn, G. A.
    Bielawa, H.   McKinney, H. D.
    Brandon, G.   Ore, C. W.
    Cassler, G. W.   Schack, D. A.
    Clarke, F. R. C.   Thalben-Ball, G.
    Curry, W. L.   Young, G. E.
    Hustad, D.   Zabel, A. J.

Lasst uns zum Kreuze (Danish)   *

    Lindorff-Larsen, E.

    Variants:
    Din dyre Ihukommelse (Gesius)

      Cappelen, C. (2)

    Mein' Seel', O Herr, muss loben
    dich (Gesius)

      Schneidt, H. M.

Lauda Anima
  See: Benedic Anima Mea (Goss)

Lauda Sion (Plainsong - Mode 7)   *

    DuBois, T.   Heiller, A.
    *Grunenwald, J. J.

Lauda Sion Salvatorem (German-
  Salzburg)

    Schehl, J. A.

  Variant:
Deinem Heiland, deinem Lehrer

Laudes Domini (Barnby)   *

    Lynn, G. A.

Laurinus (Swedish)   *

  Variant:
I himmelen (Swedish)

    Andersson, R.   Paulson, G. (2)
    *Hedwall, L.   *Soederholm, V.
    *Olson, D. (2)

Laus Deo
See: Redhead 46

Lead Me to Calvary (Kirkpatrick)

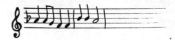

    Bock, F.

Lennox (Edson)   *

    *Jenkins, J. W.

Leoni (Hebrew)   *

    Curry, W. L.   Videroe, F.
    Hutson, W.

Les Anges dans nos (French Carol)   *

    Gigout, E.   Parisot, O.
    McKinney, H. D.   Roques, L.

  Variants:
Gloria (French Noël)

    Lynn, G. A.
    Sifler, P. J.

  Westminster Carol

    Arnatt, R.
    Corina, J.

Les Commandemens
  See: <u>Wenn wir in hoechsten</u>
<u>Noethen</u> (Bourgeois)

Let Us Break Bread Together (Negro
  Spiritual)

    Brandon, G.
    Warner, R.

Let Us Sing Loudly (Noël)   *

  Variant:
  Noël - Chantons, je vous prie

    Dandrieu, J. F.
    Guilmant, A.

Liebster Jesu (Ahle)   *

    Manz, P.   Thompson, R.
    Paulson, G.   Walther, J. G.
    Richardson, H. A.   Weiss, E.
    Stearns, P. P. (2)   Wetherill, E. H.
    Thalben-Ball, G.   Wilson, R.

  Variants:
  Du som var den minstes vaen

    Johansson, S. E.

  Jesu Frelser

    Castegren, N.   Winter-Hjelm, O.
    Emborg, J. L.

Liebster Jesu (Crueger?)   *

    Lagergren, A. (3)
    Paulson, G.

  Variants:
  Hit, O Jesu, samloms vi (Briegel)

    Hedwall, L. (2)   Runbaeck, A.
    Norrman, R.   Soederholm, V.
    Olson, D.   Soerenson, T.

  O du haerlighetens sken

    Carlman, G.

Liksom vandraren (Finnish)

    Salonen, S.

Livets ande, kom fraan ovan
  See: Jesus aer min vaen den
  (Dueben)

Llanfair (Williams)   *

    Cassler, G. W.
    Thalben-Ball, G.

Llangoedmor (Welsh)

    Clokey, J. W.

Llangollen (Welsh)   *

    Clokey, J. W.

Lob Gott getrost mit Singen (Bohemian)
  See: Ich dank dir, lieber Herre

Lob sei dem Allmaechtigen (Crueger)   *

    Lagergren, A.
    Paulson, G.

    Variant:
    Vaart paaskalamm, O Jesu Krist

    Runbaeck, A.

Lob sei Gott in des Himmels Thron   *
  (Erfurt)

    Gore, R. T.

Lobe den Herren, den Maechtigen   *
  (Stralsund)

    Beverst, G. E.   Stearns, P. P.
    Jong, M. de   Webber, W. S. L.
    McKinney, H. D.   Zabel, A. J.
    Paulson, G.

    Variants:
    Aera ske Herren

    Melin, H.   Runbaeck, A.
    Norrman, R.

    Hast du denn, Jesu

    Gore, R. T.

    Lover den Herre

    Cappelen, C.
    Winter-Hjelm, O.

Lobe den Herren, O meine Seele *
  (Freylinghausen)

    Manz, P.
    Werner, F. E. H.

Lobet den Herren, alle die ihn *
  (Crueger)

    Clokey, J. W.   Schwartz, G. von
    Paulson, G. (3)

  Variants:
  Kaerlek av hoejden

    Nyvall, J.
    Olsson, T. V.

  Lobet den Herren, denn er ist sehr
  (Crueger)

    Gore, R. T.

  Oblation

    Grieb, H. C.

  Saliga de som ifraan vaerldens
  oeden

    Runbaeck, A.

Lobet den Herren, denn er ist *
  (Scandelli)

    Scheidemann, H.

  Variant:
  Helige Ande, sanningens Ande
  (Scandelli)

    Berg, G.   Runbaeck, A. (2)
    Paulson, G.

Lobet den Herren, denn er ist sehr
  (Crueger)
  See: Lobet den Herren, alle die
  ihn (Crueger)

Lobet den Herrn, ihr Heiden all *
  (Vulpius)

    Paulson, G.
    Schack, D. A. (2)

  Variants:
  Denne er dagen (Vulpius)

Lobet den Herrn, ihr Heiden all (cont.)

   Helige Ande, laat din roest

      Nyvall, J.

   Helige Ande, laat nu ske

      Andersson, R.

   Sjaa han gjeng (Vulpius)

      Bangert, E.   Runbaeck, A.
      Olson, D.

Lobet Gott, O lieben Christen (Weisse)
  See: Grates Nunc Omnes

Lobt den Herrn
  See: Psalm 136 (Pierre)

Lobt Gott, ihr Christen (Herman)   *

      Gebhardi, L. E. (2)   Pasquet, J.
      Hamm, W.   Walther, J. G.
      Kauffmann, G. F.

   Variant:
   Op alle som paa Jorden (Herman)

      Bangert, E.

Lobt Gott, ihr frommen Christen   *
  (Old German)

      Hamm, W.

Lofzang van Maria   *

   Variant:
   Song B (Dutch)

      Asma, F.

London New (Scotch)   *

      Powell, R. J.
      Thalben-Ball, G.

Look Now He Stands (C. Schalk)

      Wyton, A.

Lord, I Want to Be a Christian
  (Negro Spiritual)

      Warner, R.

Lord Is My Shepherd (Bourgeois)
   See: Psalm 23 (Bourgeois)

Louez le Seigneur (Psalm 147,
   French 1562)

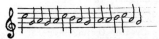

    Klenz, W.

Lourdes Pilgrim Hymn (French)   *

    Koert, H. Van

Louvan (Taylor)

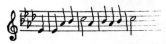

    McKinney, H. D.

Lov, pris och aera (German)
   See: Ich dank dir schon (Praetorius)

Lov vare dig, O Jesu Krist
   See: Gelobet seist du (Walther)

Lova Herren Gud, min sjael
   See: Hoechster Priester (Basel)

Lova vill jag Herran
   See: Dieses ist der Tag (Dretzel)

Lovad, vare Herran, vaara (Svensk)

    Olson, D.

Love Divine (Stainer)   *

    Thalben-Ball, G.

Lovely Infant   *

   Variant:
   Schoenstes Kindlein

    Schehl, J. A.

Lover den Herre
   See: Lobe den Herren, den
   Maechtigen

Lover Gud i himmelshoejd (Lagergren)

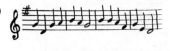

    Egebjer, L.
    Rosenberg, H.

Lovet vaere du (Folk Tune)   *

   Variant:
   Kjaere Guds barn (Folk)

Lovet vaere du (cont.)

    Bangert, E.
    Matthison-Hansen, G.

Lucis Creator Optime (Angers)   *

    Geoffroy, J. N.

Lucis Creator Optime (Mode 8)   *

    Alain, J.

Lucis Creator Optime (Sarum - Mode 8)   *

Variant:
O Fader, stor i makt

    Runbaeck, A.

Lyft, min sjael, ur jordegruset
See: Werde munter

Lyons (Haydn)   *

    Bielawa, H.   McKinney, H. D.
    Hovdesven, E. A.   Videroe, F.

Lyra Davidica   *

    Feibel, F.   Johnston, E. F.
    Goemanne, N.   Smart, D.
    Hegedus, A.

Variant:
Easter Hymn

    Lovelace, A. C.   Young, C. R.
    Lynn, G. A.   Young, G. E.
    McKinney, H. D.

Mache dich, mein Geist (Dresden)   *

    Walther, J. G.

Variant:
Straf' mich nicht

    Gebhardi, L. E.
    Zipp, F.

Mach's mit mir, Gott (Schein)   *

    Gebhardi, L. E.   Paulson, G.
    Gore, R. T.   Schneidt, H. M.
    Johnson, D. N.   Walther, J. G.

Mach's mit mir, Gott (cont.)

Variants:
Eisenach

   Near, G.   Thalben-Ball, G.
   Pasquet, J.

Jeg vet mig en soevn (Schein)

   Haarklou, J.
   Nyvall, J.

Mitt vittne vare Gud

   Runbaeck, A.

Till haerlighetens land igen

   Aahlen, W.
   Olsson, O. E.

Macht hoch die Tuer (Freylinghausen)   *

   Johnson, D. N.   Wiemer, W.
   Schneidt, H. M.

Madrid (Carr)   *

Variant:
Spanish Hymn

   Curry, W. L.   Wetherill, E. H.
   Hustad, D.   Wyton, A.

Mag' ich Unglueck (Klug)   *

   Gore, R. T.

Variant:
Jag hoeja vill till Gud min saang

   Allgen, C. L.
   Thyrestam, G.

Magnificat (one on each Tone)

   Dandrieu, J. F. (6 Tones)   Pachelbel, J.
   Guilain (Freinsberg)   Praetorius, H.
   LeBègue, N. A.   Scheidemann, H.

Magnificat (Tone 1)   *

   Schildt, M.

Magnificat (Tone 6?)

   Langlais, J. F.

Magnificat (Tone 8)   *

    Scheidt, S.

Magnificat Germanicae
   See: Meine Seele erhebet (Klug)

Manoah (Rossini)   *

    Young, G. E.

Marching (Shaw)

    Thalben-Ball, G.

Marching to Zion (Lowry)

    Wyton, A.

Maria durch den Dornwald ging   *
           ein

    Eder, H.
    Grimes, T.

Maria, jung und zart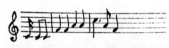

    Thalben-Ball, G.

Marion (Messiter)   *

    McKinney, H. D.
    Young, G. E.

Marosa
   See: Brother James' Air (Bain)

Marseillaise (French National Anthem)

    Whitford, H.

Martyn (Marsh)   *

    Young, G. E.

Martyrdom (Wilson)   *

    Diemer, E. L.   Thalben-Ball, G.
    Miles, R. H.   Young, G. E.
    Powell, R. J.

    Variant:
    Avon

    Frank, R.
    Gustafson, D.

Martyrs (Wesley) *

    Thalben-Ball, G.

Maryton (Smith) *

    Frank, R.
    Young, G. E.

Materna (Ward) *

    McKinney, H. D.   Smith, L.
    Purvis, R.   Whitford, H.

Me hoeyrer stundom (Thomissoen)
   See: Den signade dag (Thomissoen)

Mear (Southern Harmony) *

    Brandon, G.

Med Jesus vil jeg fara (Norse Folk) *

    Drischner, M.
    Nystedt, K.

Med pelarstoder tolv
   See: Nun danket alle Gott (Crueger)

Med Sorgen og Klagen
   See: Iam Moesta

Med straalekrans om tinde (Lindeman) *

    Skottner, F.

Med straalekrans om tinde (Vulpius)
   See: Ach bleib mit deiner

Med tacksam roest och tacksam sjael
   See: Stoerl I

Mein Gott, warum verlaesst du mich
   See: Psalm 22 (Geneva - Marot)

Mein' Seel' erhebt den Herren (Strassburg) *

    Klenz, W.

    Variant:
   Kom hjerte, ta ditt regnebrett

    Winter-Hjelm, O.

Mein' Seel', O Herr, muss loben dich
   (Gesius)
   See: Lasst uns zum Kreuze (Danish)

Mein Wallfahrt ich vollendet hab'
(Cramer)
                          Z 5704a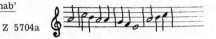
     Gore, R. T.

Meine Hoffnung (Neander)   *

     Thalben-Ball, G.

Meine Seel' ist stille
     See: Jesu, meine Freude (Crueger)

Meine Seele erhebet den Herren (Klug)   *
(Tonus Peregrinus)

     Gore, R. T.   Thompson, R. (3)
     Langlais, J. F.   Walther, J. G.

     Variant:
     Magnificat Germanicae

     Praetorius, J.

Meinen Jesum lass ich nicht (Ulich)   *

     Bloch, W.

Melcombe (Webbe)   *

     Thalben-Ball, G.
     Thiman, E.

Members of One Mystic Body
     See: Holland (1609)

Mendebras (German)   *

     McKinney, H. D.

Mendelssohn   *

     Mueller, C. F.
     Young, G. E.

     Variant:
     Herald Angels

     McKinney, H. D.

Mendip (English Traditional)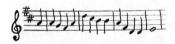

     Thalben-Ball, G.

Mendon (German)   *

     Powell, R. J.
     Wetherill, E. H.

Mensch, willst du leben (Walther)   *

    Buxtehude, D.   Scheidemann, H.
    Gore, R. T.

Mentzer
    See: O dass ich tausend (Koenig)

Mercy (Gottschalk)   *

    Hustad, D.
    Young, G. E.

Merrial (Barnby)   *

    McKinney, H. D.

Mes bonnes gens attendez-moi
    See: A Minuit

Messiah (Swedish)   *

    Paulson, G. (2)

    Variant:
    Bereden vaeg foer Herran

      Aahlen, W.   Joelson, A. G.
      Andersson, R.   Olsson, O. E.
      Carlman, G.   Rosenquist, C. E.

Metzler's Redhead
    See: Redhead 66 (Metzler)

Meyer
    See: Es ist kein Tag (Meyer)

Middlebury

    Wood, D.

Midt i livet
    See: Mitten wir im Leben (Walther)

Miles Lane (Shrubsole)   *

    Thalben-Ball, G.

Min Fraelsare (Swedish)

    Norrman, R.

Min glede i min Gud (Kingo)   *

    Winter-Hjelm, O.

Min hoegsta skatt
  See: O Jesu Christ, du hoechstes
  Gut (Crueger)

Min lodd falt mig (Norsk Folk Tune)   *

    Drischner, M.

    Variant:
    Gaa varsamt, min Kristen

    Runbaeck, A.

Min sjael, ditt hopp till Herran
  See: Old 130th

Min sjael, du maaste (Swedish Folk)   *

    Janáček, B.   Wikander, D.
    Norrman, R.

Min sjael, min sjael, lov Herren   *
  (Lindeman)

    Aamodt, T.

Min sjael och sinne
  See: Wer nur den lieben (Neumark)

Min sjael skall lova Herren (Kugelmann)
  See: Nun lob', mein Seel (Kugelmann)

Min sjel, min sjel, lov Herren
  (Kugelmann)
  See: Nun lob', mein Seel (Kugel-
  mann)

Min sjel og aand (Thomissoen)   *

    Winter-Hjelm, O.

Min synd, O Gud
  See: Ach Gott und Herr (Schein)

Min vilotimma ljuder (Thomissoen)
  See: Jeg vil mig Herren love
  (Thomissoen)

Missionary Hymn (Mason)   *

    Stearns, P. P. (2)

Mit Freuden zart
  See: Bohemian Brethren

Mit Fried' und Freud' (Wittenberg)   *

    Bach, J. C.   Klenz, W.
    Bornefeld, H.

Mitt fasta hopp till Herren
  See: Es ist das Heil

Mitt hjerte alltid vanker (Norse Folk   *
Mit   Tune)

    Variant:
    Jeg vil mig Herren love (Norse Folk
    Tune)

      Islandsmoen, S.

Mitt vittne vare Gud
  See: En dunkel oertagaard

Mitt vittne vare Gud
  See: Mach's mit mir, Gott

Mitten wir im Leben (Walther)   *

    Gore, R. T.   Schneidt, H. M.
    Rohwer, J.

    Variant:
    Midt i livet

      Winter-Hjelm, O.

Monkland (Antes)   *

    Thalben-Ball, G.

Monksgate (English)   *

    Thalben-Ball, G.

Morecambe (Atkinson)   *

    Elmore, R.

Morgen kommt der Weihnachtsmann
  (German)

    McKinney, H. D.

Morgenglanz der Ewigkeit (Freyling-   *
  hausen)

    Geilsdorf, P.   Schmidt-Arzberg, G.
    Genzmer, H.

Morning Hymn (Bartholemon)   *

    Thalben-Ball, G.

Morning Song (Wyeth)   *

  Variant:
  Consolation (Wyeth)

    Beck, T.   Moyer, J. H.
    Burkhart, C.

Morning Star (Harding)   *

    Russell, O. N.

Moscow
  See: Giardini

Mueller   *

    Hilf, R.   Young, G. E.
    Mueller, C. F.

  Variant:
  Away in a Manger

    Curry, W. L.
    McKinney, H. D.

Munich (Stoerl)
  See: O Gott, du frommer Gott
  (Stoerl)

My Shepherd Will Supply My Need
  See: Resignation (U.S. Southern)

Naar mig min synd
  See: Hilf Gott, dass mir's
  gelinge (Thomissoen)

Naar mit oeie (Lindeman)
  See: Consolation (Lindeman)

Naar vi i stoerste (Lyons)
  See: Wenn wir in hoechsten

Naer dombasuners straenga ljud
(Swedish)

    Runbaeck, A.

Naer ingen dager oegat skaadar
  See: Wer nur den lieben Gott

Naer juldags-morgon glimmer (German Folk Tune)

    Vretblad, P.

Naer mitt hjaerta maaste
  See: Kriste, som ditt ursprung
leder

Naer stormens lurar (Lindberg)

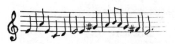

    Lindberg, O. F.
    Norrman, R.

Naer vaerldens hopp (Rhau - Vulpius)

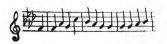

    Berg, G.
    Paulson, G.

Naer vaerldens hopp fortvinat stod
  See: O Jesu Krist, till dig
foervisst

Naglet til et kors (Zinck)   *

    Sandvold, A. (2)
    Winter-Hjelm, O.

Narenza (Cologne)   *

    Thalben-Ball, G.

  Variant:
  Ave Maria klare

    Fischer, J. K. F.

National Hymn (Warren)   *

    Brandon, G.

Nativity (Lahee)   *

    Thalben-Ball, G.

Neander
  See: Unser Herrscher (Neander)

Need (Lowry)   *

  Variant:
  I Need Thee Every Hour

    Hughes, R. J.

Netherlands (Valerius)   *

    Whitford, H.

Netherlands (cont.)

Variant:
Kremser

Groom, L.   Pethel, J.
Hughes, R. J.   Young, G. E.
McKinney, H. D.

Nettleton (Wyeth)   *

Burkhart, C.
Martin, G. M.

Neumark
See: Wer nur den lieben Gott
(Neumark)

New Britain
See: Amazing Grace (American)

Nicaea (Dykes)   *

McKinney, H. D.
Paulson, G. (2)

Variant:
Helig, helig, helig

Nyvall, J. (2)   Runbaeck, A.
Olson, D.

Nicht so traurig (Bach)   *

Clarke, F. R. C.

Noël   Tunes not found

Braequemond, M.   Hastings, E. H.
Collot, J.

Noël (Name not found)

Archer, J. S.

Noël (Name not found)

Dubois, T.

Noël (Name not found)

Langlais, J. F.

Noël (Name not found)

Langlais, J. F.

Tune not found

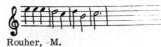

Rouher, M.

        *

        *

Noël - Bergers prenons nos chalu-
    meaux

    Guilmant, A.

Noël Brabançon

    Guilmant, A.

Noël - Cette journée   *

    Dandrieu, J. F.   Raison, A.
    LeBègue, N. A.

Noël - Chanson de St. Jacques

    Dandrieu, J. F.

Noël - Chant du Roi René (Provençal)

    Guilmant, A.

Noël - Chantans tous avoué (Bisontin)

    Rouher, M.

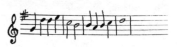

Noël - Chanton de Voix Hautaine
    (Lorraine)

    Dandrieu, J. F.

Noël - Chantons, je vous prie

    Dandrieu, J. F.

Noël - Chantons, je vous prie
    See: Let Us Sing Loudly

Noël - Chantons les louanges

    Guilmant, A.

Noël - Chrétien qui suivez l'Eglise   *

    Dandrieu, J. F.

Noël - Comment tu oses petite Rose

    Balbastre, C.

Noël de Saintonge

    Dandrieu, J. F.

Noël de Sts. Innocens

    Raison, A.

Noël - Divine Princesse

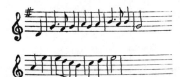

    Balbastre, C.

Noël - D'ou viens-tu bergère?
  (Languedocien)

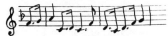

    Guilmant, A.

Noël Ecossais

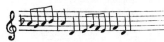

    Guilmant, A.

Noël - Ecoute, Michel, une chanson
  (Carcassonnais)

    Guilmant, A.

Noël - Entend ma voix fidèle

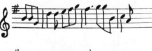

    Guilmant, A.

Noël Espagnol

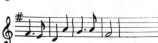

    Guilmant, A.

Noël - Fanne coraige, le diale â mor

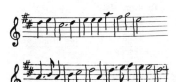

    Balbastre, C.

Noël Flamand

    Guilmant, A.

Noël - Grand Dieu
  See: Great God

Noël - Il fait bon aimer

    Dandrieu, J. F.

Noël - Il n'est rien de plus tendre

    Balbastre, C.
    Dandrieu, J. F.

Noël - Ile de France   *

  Variant:
  Nous sommes en voie

    Dandrieu, J. F.

Noël - Jacob que tu es habile

    Dandrieu, J. F.

Noël - Je me suis levé   *

    Dandrieu, J. F.
    Dornel, L. A.

Noël - Je rends graces à mon Dieu

    Balbastre, C.

Noël - Joseph, tu es bien joyeux

    Dandrieu, J. F.

Noël - Laissez paître vos bêtes
              paistre   bestes
    See: Venez Divin Messie (French
Noël)

Noël Languedocien   *

    Guilmant, A.

Noël - Le Messie vient de naître
    See: Christ Is Born

Noël - Le petit nouveau né

    LeBègue, N. A.

Noël - Le Roy des Cieux

    Dandrieu, J. F.

Noël - Lei Mage dius Jerusalem
    (Provençal)

    Rouher, M.

Noël - Les Bourgeoises de Chartres
    See: Noël - Tous les Bourgeois
    de Chartres

Noël Lorraine
    See: A Minuit (Noël)

Noël - Mais on san es allé Nau

    Dandrieu, J. F.

Noël - Marchons, marchons gaiement

    Dandrieu, J. F.

Noël - Michau qui causoit ce grand
    bruit

    Dandrieu, J. F.

Noël - Noei vén, j'aivon criai si for

      Balbastre, C.
      Guilmant, A.

Noël - Nous voici dans la Ville
  See: Chartres

Noël nouvelet   *

      Paxton, D.

Noël - Nuit sombre, ton ombre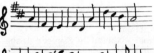

      Guilmant, A.

Noël - O Createur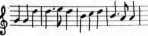

      Raison, A.

Noël - O Dieu! que n'etois je en vie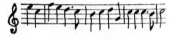

      Raison, A.

Noël - O jour ton divin flambeau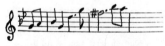

      Balbastre, C.
      Guilmant, A.

Noël - O nuit, hereuse nuit (Breton)

      Dandrieu, J. F.

Noël - Or dites nous, Marie
          nous dites,
  See: Chartres

Noël - Où s'en vont ces gais bergers   *

      Charpentier, M. A.   LeBègue, N. A. (2)
      Dandrieu, J. F.   Raison, A.

Noël - Pastre dei mountagne (Saboly)
  See: Shepherds of the Mountains

Noël Poitevin (au Saint Neau)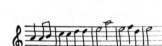

      Dandrieu, J. F.
      Raison, A.

Noël pour l'amour de Marie   *
(Au ciel d'hiver)

      Dandrieu, J. F.
      LeBègue, N. A. (2)

Noël - Promptement levez-vous mon
voisin (Bourguignon)

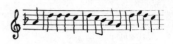

Rouher, M.

Noël - Qu' Adam fut   *

Variant:
Adam fut un pauvre homme

Dandrieu, J. F.

Noël - Quand Dieu naquit   *

Variant:
Noël - Quand le Sauveur Jesus
Christ

Dandrieu, J. F.

Noël - Quand je méveillai

Dandrieu, J. F.

Noël - Quand le Sauveur Jesus Christ
See: Noël - Quand Dieu naquit

Noël - Qué tu grô jan, quei folie

Balbastre, C.

Noël - Quel désordre dans la nature

Balbastre, C.

Noël - Qui a ce peu machuret

Balbastre, C.

Noël - Rangeans-nous tre tous
(Bisontin)

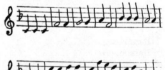

Rouher, M.

Noël - Reveillez-vous belle endormie
(Lorraine)

Rouher, M.

Noël - Savez-vous mon cher voisin

Dandrieu, J. F.

Noël - Si c'est pour ôter la vie

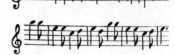

Balbastre, C.
Dandrieu, J. F.

Noël - Sortons de nos chaumières
   (Lorraine)

    Dandrieu, J. F.

Noël suisse   *

    Dandrieu, J. F.

Noël - Suivons les Rois dans l'étable
   (Lorraine)

    Rouher, M.

Noël - Tous les Bourgeois de Chartres   *

    Dandrieu, J. F.
    McKinney, H. D.

   Variant:
   Noël - Les Bourgeoises de Chartres

    LeBègue, N. A.
    Raison, A.

Noël - Un jour Dieu se résolut
   (Lorraine)

    Dandrieu, J. F.

Noël - Une Bergère jolie (Bourguignon)

    Dandrieu, J. F.

Noël - Une jeune pucelle
         vierge
  See: Von Gott will ich nicht
  (Erfurt)

Noël - Vé noei blaizôte

    Balbastre, C.
    Guilmant, A.

Noël - Voici le jour Solemnel (Bourgui-
      Voye   gnon)

    Dandrieu, J. F.
    Raison, A.   Rouher, M.

Nous allons, ma mie
  See: Noël - Ah, ma voisine

Nous sommes en voie
  See: Noël - Ile de France

Now the Silence (C. Schalk)

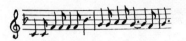

    Wyton, A.

Nu beder vi den Hellig Aand
   See: Soldau (Wittenberg)

Nu glaed dig, min ande
   See: Oss kristna boer (Swedish)

Nu haver denna dag (Esthonian)

    Runbaeck, A.

Nu hjertelig jeg lenges (Hassler)
   See: Herzlich tut mich verlangen

Nu hjertelig mig langes
           jeg
   See: Valet

Nu hviler mark og enge
   See: Innsbruck

Nu kjaere menige Kristenhet
   See: Nun freut Euch (Nuernberg)

Nu la oss takke Gud
   See: Nun danket alle Gott (Crueger)

Nu laemna vi stoftet aat graven   Tune not found

    Runbaeck, A.

Nu rinner solen op (Zinck)   *

    Bangert, E.   Winter-Hjelm, O.
    Skottner, F.

Nu segrar alla trognas hopp
   See: Wie schoen leuchtet

Nu sijt wellekomme
  zijt wellekome
  siyt wellecome
   See: Nun sei uns willkommen

Nu tacker Gud allt folk
   See: Nun danket alle Gott

Nu tystne de klagande ljuden
   See: Iam Moesta (Luther)

Nu vilar hela jorden
   See: Innsbruck

Nun bitten wir (Walther)
   See: Soldau (Wittenberg)

Nun freut Euch, lieben (cont.)

   Gud laater sina trogna haer

      Soederholm, V.

   Hvad kan oss komme (Klug)

      Bangert, E.
      Winter-Hjelm, O.

   Itzt komm' ich als ein armer Gast

      Gore, R. T.

Nun freut Euch, lieben (Nuernberg)   *

      Barlow, W.   Paulson, G.
      Busarow, D.   Sweelinck, J. P. (2)
      Gore, R. T.   Weckmann, M.
      Krapf, G.   Weiss, E.
      Manz, P.   Zipp, F.
      *Micheelsen, H. F.

      Variants:
      Foer mig sitt liv

        Soerenson, T.

   Nu kjaere menige Kristenhet

      Karlsen, K. M.   Runbaeck, A.
      Olson, D.   Winter-Hjelm, O.
      Rosenquist, C. E.

   Var man maa nu vael

      Norrman, R.
      Rosenquist, C. E. (2)

Nun gibt mein Jesu gute Nacht
(Eccard)
                Z 423
      Gore, R. T.

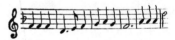

Nun haben wir den grossen Bund

      Schehl, J. A.

Nun jauchzt dem Herren (Hannover)   *

      Pepping, E.
      Schneidt, H. M.

Nun komm, der Heiden Heiland   *

      Buttstedt, J. H.   Herzogenberg, H. von
      David, J. N. (2)   Klenz, W. (2)

Nun komm, der Heiden Heiland (cont.)

    Manz, P.   Paulson, G.
    Maurer, O.   Schneidt, H. M.
    Ore, C. W.   Sweelinck, J. P.
    Paponaud, M.   Vetter, A. N.

Variants:
Folkefrelser (1524)

    Steenberg, P.

Vaerldens fraelsare kom haer

    Hedwall, L. (2)
    Olson, D.

Nun lasst uns den Leib (Stahl)   *

    Geilsdorf, P.
    Gore, R. T.

Nun lasst uns Gott (Selnecker)   *

    Geilsdorf, P.   Luebeck, V.
    Gore, R. T.   Pachelbel, J.

Variants:
Selnecker

    Powell, R. J.

Vak upp, min sjael, giv aera

    Paulson, G.

Nun lob', mein Seel (Kugelmann)   *

    Druckenmueller, G. W.   Paulson, G.
    Gore, R. T.   Pepping, E.
    Kauffmann, G. F.   Schneidt, H. M.
    Lagergren, A.

Variants:
Den haerlighet och aera

    Nyvall, J.

Min sjael skall lova Herren

    Olsson, O. E.
    Rosenquist, C. E.

Min sjel, min sjel, lov Herren
(Kugelmann)

    Bangert, E.   Runbaeck, A.
    Olson, D.   Steenberg, P.

Nun lob', mein Seel (cont.)

   Upp psaltare och harpa

      Andersson, R.
      Paulson, G.

Nun ruhen alle Waelder
   See: Innsbruck

Nun sei uns willkommen   *

      Stockmeier, W.

   Variant:
   Nu sijt wellecome

      Brabanter, J.

Nun sich der Tag (Krieger)   *

      Bornefeld, H.   Paulson, G.
      Fronmueller, F.   Thompson, R. (2)

   Variant:
   Saa gaar en dag aen fraan vaar tid

      Janáček, B.
      Soederholm, V.

Nun Dimittis (Genevan)
   See: Song of Symeon (Geneva)

Nyland (Finnish)   *

      Young, G. E.

O bliv hos mig (Steenberg)   *

      Karlsen, R.
      Kjeldaas, A.

O Bone Jesu

      Belli, P. G.

O Christe, Morgensterne (Gesius-   *
   Leipzig)

      Krapf, G.

O Christenheit, sei hoch erfreut   *
   (Micheelsen)

      Micheelsen, H. F.

O Come Emmanuel (German)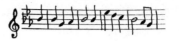

    Schehl, J. A.

O dass ich tausend (Dretzel)   *

      Ore, C. W.
      Schack, D. A.

O dass ich tausend (Koenig)   *

      Manz, P. (2)   Schmidt, W.
      Micheelsen, H. F.   Wilson, R.

    Variant:
    Mentzer

      Powell, R. J.

O du armer Judas
   See: Ach, wir armen Suender

O du haerlighetens sken
   See: Liebster Jesu (Crueger?)

O du Helge Ande, kom till oss in
   See: Veni Sancte Spiritus (Old
Church)

O du hochheilige Kreuze (Koeln)   *

    Eder, H.

O du Liebe meiner Liebe (Herrnhag-   *
Ebeling)

    Variant:
    Herz und Herz vereint zusammen
    (Basel)

    Vogt, E.

O du, mein Volk

    Faessler, G.

O du, min aedla skatt (Hannover)
   See: O Gott, du frommer Gott
(Hannover)

O du, som gav ditt liv foer faaren
   See: Die Tugend wird durch's
(Halle)

O du som ser, o du som vet (Wall-
1934)

    Runbaeck, A.

O du som skapat stjaernors haer   Tune not found

    Olson, D.

O Dulcis Maria (Plainsong)

    Schlick, A.

O Durchbrecher (Halle)   *

    Ehrlinger, F.
    Hoegner, F.

Variant:
Overmaade fuldt av naade (Freylinghausen)

    Cappelen, C.
    Winter-Hjelm, O.

O Ewigkeit, du Donnerwort (Schop)   *

    Thompson, R.

Variant:
Vak upp, bed Gud om kraft och mod

    Aahlen, W.
    Olsson, T. V.

O Fader, stor i makt
  See: Lucis Creator Optime (Sarum-
Mode 8)

O Fader vaar, barmhaertig, god
  See: Es woll' uns Gott g'naedig
sein (Strassburg)

O Fader vaar i Himmerik
  See: Vater Unser

O Fader vise   Tune not found

    Nilsson, G.

O Filii Et Filiae (French)   *

    Brandon, G.   Martin, G. M.
    Chaudeur, R.   Nees, S.
    Dandrieu, J. F. (3)   Peek, R.
    Dubois, T.   Pelz, W.
    Johnson, D. N.   Schehl, J. A.
    Langlais, J. F.   Walter, S.
    LeBègue, N. A.   Wyton, A.
    Lynn, G. A.   Young, G. E.

O glaeubig Herz (Praetorius)   *

    Bornefeld, H. (2)   Pepping, E.
    Gebhard, H.

O God, O Lord of Heaven and Earth
   (J. Bender)

    Bender, J.

O God of Every Nation (D. Wood)

    Wyton, A.

O Gott, du frommer Gott (Hannover)   *

    Gore, R. T.   Paulson, G.
    Lagergren, A.

  Variants:
  Beproeva mig, min Gud

    Soerenson, T.

  Hur kan och skall jag dig

    Olson, D.

  Jag vet paa vem jag tror

    *Andersson, R.   Soerenson, T.
    Soederholm, V.

  O du, min aedla skatt (Hannover)

    Olson, D.

  O Gud, du gode Gud (Hannover)

    Olson, D.
    Winter-Hjelm, O.

  Steadfast

    Powell, R. J.

O Gott, du frommer Gott (Stoerl)   *

    Manz, P.

  Variant:
  Munich (Stoerl)

    Brandon, G.   Videroe, F.
    Diemer, E. L.   Young, G. E. (2)
    McKinney, H. D.

O Gottessohn voll ewiger (1955)

  Wuensch, K.

O grosser Gott von Macht (Franck)   *
         Z 5105a
  Gore, R. T.

O Gud, all sannings kaella
 See: Old 130th

O Gud, det aer en hjaertans troest
 (Svensk)
 See: Praise (Swedish)

O Gud, det aer min glaedje (Vulpius)
 See: Ach bleib mit deiner

O Gud, ditt rike ingen ser (Waldis)
        Z 8097
  Andersson, R.
  Hedwall, L.
  Lagergren, A.   Paulson, G. (3)

  Variants:
  Allt maenskoskektet (Waldis)

   Aahlen, W.
   Runbaeck, A.

  Foergaeves all den omsorg (Waldis)

   Rosenquist, C. E.

O Gud, du gode Gud (Hannover)
 See: O Gott, du frommer Gott
 (Hannover)

O Gud, foer de tragna Martyrer
 See: Iam Moesta

O Gud, om allt mig saeger (von Rosén)

  Egebjer, L.

O Gud, som tiden vender (Erfurt)
 See: Von Gott will ich nicht
 (Erfurt)

O Gud, vaar Broder Abels
 See: Durch Adams Fall

O Gud, vaar hjaelp
 See: St. Anne

O Gud vors Lands (Sveinbjoeinsson)
 (Icelandic National Anthem)

  Stout, A.

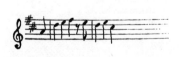

O Guds Lam uskyldig
    See: O Lamm Gottes unschuldig
(Decius)

O Haupt voll Blut
    See: Herzlich tut mich verlangen
(Hassler)

O Heiland, reiss (Rheinfels)   *

      Eder, H.
      Stockmeier, W.

O Heilige Dreifaltigkeit (Herman)   *

      Ore, C. W.

    Variants:
    Ihr lieben Christen, freut Euch nun
(Herman)

      Stockmeier, W.

    Steht auf, ihr lieben Kinderlein

      Hoegner, F.

O Heiliger Geist, du goettlich Feuer
(Vulpius)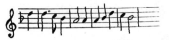
              Z 2027
      Gore, R. T.

O Heiliger Geist, O Heiliger Gott
    See: O Jesulein suess (Cologne)

O Helge And, goer sjaelen from
    See: Allein Gott in der Hoeh'

O Hellig Aand (Strassburg)
    See: Aus tiefer Not (Strassburg)

O Herre Gott, dein goettlich Wort   *
(Erfurt)

      Gebhard, H.
      Gore, R. T.

O Herre Gud, O aendelig (Crespin)
    See: Old 100th

O Herre Krist, dig til oss vend
    See: Herr Jesu Christ, dich zu
uns wend (Gotha)

O hjelp mig, Gud (Waldis)   *

      Videroe, F.

O hjelp mig, Gud (cont.)

   Variants:
   Dett finns ett ord

      Olsson, T. V.

   Hjaelp mig, min Gud, ack fraels

      Lagergren, A.
      Runbaeck, A.

   Saa snart aer det med

      Runbaeck, A.

O hjertenskjaere Jesus Krist
   See: Vater Unser

O Holy Night (Adam)   *

      McKinney, H. D.

O huvud, blodigt saarat
   See: Herzlich tut mich verlangen
   (Hassler)

O Jesu, aen de dina (Thomissoen)
   See: Franzen

O Jesu Christ, dein Krippelein   *
   (Crueger)

   Variant:
   Wir Christenleut (Crueger)

      Scheller, H.

O Jesu Christ, du hoechstes Gut   *
   (Crueger)

      Lagergren, A.
      Paulson, G. (2)

   Variants:
   Den korta stund jag vandrar haer

      Olsson, T. V.   Thyrestam, G.
      Rosenquist, C. E.

   Min hoegsta skatt

      Norrman, R.

   Si, Herrens ord aer rent

      Aahlen, W.
      Rosenquist, C. E.

O Jesu Christe, wahres Licht
  See: Herr Jesu Christ, meins
  Lebens Licht (Nuernberg)

O Jesu, du edle Gabe (Weberbeck)
                       Z 8740

    Gore, R. T.

O Jesu, for din pine (Kingo)   *

    Variants:
    Se hvor nu Jesus traeder (Kingo-
    Arrebo)

      Hovland, E.

    Se, vi gaa upp (Kingo)

      Emborg, J. L.
      Janáček, B.

O Jesu Krist, dig till oss vaend
  See: Wenn wir in hoechsten

O Jesu Krist, du naadens brunn (Ny-   *
  stad)

      Aahlen, W.

    Variant:
    Jag kommer, Gud, och soeker dig

      Olson, D.

O Jesu Krist, Guds ende son
  See: Praise (Swedish)

O Jesu Krist, som mandom tog
  See: Aus tiefer Not (Strassburg)

O Jesu Krist, till dig foervisst
  (von Rosén)

      Egebjer, L.
      Runbaeck, A.

    Variant:
    Naer vaerldens hopp

      Aahlen, W.   Melin, H.
      Castegren, N.   Runbaeck, A.
      Johansson, S. E.

O Jesu, naer jag haedan skall
  See: Wo Gott, der Herr, nicht
  bei uns (Wittenberg)

O Jesu, som har elsket mig
  See: Ich ruf' zu dir (Klug)

O Jesu, wie ist dein' Gestalt (Franck)
                                Z 8360

    Gore, R. T.

O Jesulein suess (Cologne)   *

  Variant:
  Komm Heiliger Geist mit deiner
  G'nad

    Albrechtsberger, J. G.
    Fischer, J. K. F.

  O Heiliger Geist, O Heiliger Gott

    Gore, R. T.

O Koenig, Jesu Christe (13th Century)   *

    Stockmeier, W.

O Kriste, du som ljuset aer
  See: Christe, der du bist Tag und
  Licht

O lad din aand (Rung)   *

    Bangert, E.

  Variant:
  Den dag du gav oss Gud (Rung)

    Egebjer, L.

O Lamm Gottes, unschuldig (Decius)   *

    Bloch, W.   Paulson, G. (2)
    Gebhard, H.   Telemann, G. P. (3)
    Lagergren, A. (4)   Walther, J. G.

  Variants:
  Christe, du Lamm Gottes (Decius)

    Ehrlinger, F.
    Manz, P.

  Du gaar, Guds lamm (Decius)

    Runbaeck, A.

  Guds rena lamm

    Edlund, L.   Paulson, G.
    Olson, D.   Wikander, D.

O Lamm Gottes, unschuldig (cont.)

   O Guds Lam uskyldig

     Olson, D.
     Runbaeck, A.

O Lebensbruennlein (Goerlitz)   *

     Schmidt-Arzberg, G.

O liv som blev taant (Aulen)

     Hedwall, L.
     Paulson, G.

O Lord with Wondrous Mystery   *
     in this Great
(Andriessen)

     Andriessen, H.

O lue fra Guds (Weisse)
See: Der Tag, der ist so (Wittenberg)

O Lux Beata Trinitas (Sarum - Mode 8)   *

     Plettner, A.   Sweelinck, J. P.
     *Siedel, M.

O maa vi noga maerka
See: Valet

O maenniska, glaed dig och prisa din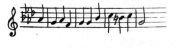
Gud (Swedish Folk Tune)

     Aahlen, W.

O Mensch, bewein (Strassburg)   *

   Variants:
   Es sind doch selig

     Schmidt-Arzberg, G.

   Jauchz' Erd', und Himmel

     Weiss, E.

   Old 113th

     Near, G.

   Psalm 36 (Geneva)

     Sweelinck, J. P.

O Mensch, bewein (cont.)

   Psalm 37 (Calvin 1539)

     Klenz, W.

O min Jesu, dit du gaatt
   See: Schwing dich auf (Crueger)

O naadens sol og sete (Erfurt)
   See: Herr Christ, der einig
   Gottes (Erfurt)

O Perfect Love
   See: Sandringham (Barnby)

O Pia (Plainsong)

     Schlick, A.

O Quam Suavis Est (Gregorian)   *

     Boulnois, M.

O Quanta Qualia   *

     Clarke, F. R. C.
     Ossewaarde, J.

O Quot Undis Lacrimarum   Tune not found

     Olsson, O. E.

O Sacrament Most Holy (Schehl)

     Schehl, J. A.

O Sacred Head
   See: Herzlich tut mich verlangen
   (Hassler)

O Sacrum Convivium

     Belli, P. G.

O Salutaris Hostia (Duquet)   *

     Jong, M. de
     Weegenhuise, J.

O Sanctissima
   See: Sicilian Mariners

O schlafe, lieblicher Jesu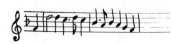

     Schroeder, H.

Old 100th (cont.)

Paulson, G.   Thompson, V. D.
Sister M. T.   Young, G. E. (2)
Thalben-Ball, G.

Variants:
Dig skall ditt Sion sjunga se

Olson, D.

Gjoer doeren hoei

Bangert, E.   Sandvold, A.
Emborg, J. L.

Goer porten hoeg

Herr Gott, dich loben alle wir

Gore, R. T.   Pachelbel, J.
Micheelsen, H. F.   Seiler, G.

Ihr Knecht des Herrn

Ihr Menschenkinder

O Herre Gud, O aendelig (Crespin)

Runbaeck, A.

Saa aelskade Gud vaerlden all

Norrman, R.

Old 104th (Ravenscroft)   *

Thalben-Ball, G.

Old 107th (Geneva)   *

Clokey, J. W.

Variant:
Dankt den Herrn

Klenz, W.

Old 113th
See: O Mensch, bewein (Strassburg)

Old 122nd (Bourgeois)   *

Variant:
Psalm 3 (Geneva)

Clokey, J. W.

Old 124th (Geneva)   *

    McKinney, H. D.
    Rowley, A.

Variants:
Geneva 124

    Withrow, S. S.

Toulon (Bourgeois)

    McKinney, H. D.

Old 130th (French)   *

    Lagergren, A.
    Paulson, G. (2)

Variants:
Befall i Herrens haender

    Carlman, G.   Runbaeck, A.
    Paulson, G.   Soedersten, G.

Gud, laer mig dock besinna

    Rosenquist, C. E.
    Runbaeck, A.

Min sjael, ditt hopp till Herran

    Aahlen, W.   Runbaeck, A. (2)
    Andersson, R.

O Gud, all sannings kaella

    *Soerenson, T.

Till dig, av hjaertens grunde
(French)

    Olson, D.
    Runbaeck, A.

Uverdig er jeg Herre

    Bangert, E.   Runbaeck, A.
    Carlman, G.   Winter-Hjelm, O.
    Olson, D.

Old 134th (Estes)   *

Variant:
St. Michael (Geneva)

    Thalben-Ball, G.
    Videroe, F.

Old Rugged Cross (Bennard)

Hustad, D.

Oldown (Harwood)   *

Stearns, P. P.

Olive's Brow (Bradbury)   *

Baumgartner, H. L.

Olivet (Mason)   *

Lynn, G. A.   Young, G. E. (2)
McKinney, H. D.

Om Kristus doeljes nu foer dig
   (Waldis)
   See: Was hilft's den Heiden
   (Waldis)

Om nogen til ondt (Norsk - Ehrenborg)   *

Drischner, M.

On freudt verzer   *

Hofhaymer, P.

Ons ist gheboren
   See: Puer Nobis Nascitur
   (Praetorius)

Onse Vader
   See: Vater Unser

Op al den ting (Freiburg)   *

Bangert, E.   Winter-Hjelm, O.
Emborg, J. L.

Variants:
Es liegt ein Schloss

Pasquet, J.

Freiburg

Hovdesven, E. A.
Johnson, D. N.

Op alle som paa Jorden (Crueger)
   See: Nun danket all' und bringet
   Ehr

Op alle som paa Jorden (Herman)
   See: Lobt Gott, ihr Christen
   (Herman)

Opstanden er den Herre Krist
   See: Surrexit Christus Hodie

Oriel (Ett)   *

   Thalben-Ball, G.

Ortonville (Hastings)   *

   Frank, R.

Oss kristna boer tro och besinna
   (Swedish)

   Aahlen, W.
   Lindroth, H.
   Norrman, R.   Rosenquist, C. E.

   Variant:
   Nu glaed dig, min ande

   Hedwall, L.

Overmaade fullt av naade (Freylinghausen)
   See: O Durchbrecher (Halle)

Oyigiyigi (Yoruba Folk)

   Sowande, F.

Paa dig jag hoppas (German)
   See: In dich hab' ich gehoffet
   (Nuernberg)

Paa Gud alene (Zinck)   *

   Bangert, E.   Winter-Hjelm, O.
   Hovland, E.

Paaskemorgen (Lindeman)   *

   Hovland, E.

Palestrina   *

   Young, G. E.

   Variant:
   Victory (Palestrina)

   Curry, W. L.   Johnson, D. N.
   Hustad, D.   McKinney, H. D.

Palisades (Sowerby)   *

    Arnatt, R.

Pange Lingua Gloriosa (Sarum-   *
  Mode 3)

    Bermudo, J.   Goller, F.
    Bielawa, H.   Rowley, A.
    Dufay, G.

Passion Chorale
  See: Herzlich tut mich verlangen
  (Hassler)

Pater Noster (Liturgical)
  See: Fons Bonitans

Pax (Swedish)   *

    Lagergren, A. (2)

    Variants:
    Ack, att i synd vi slumra bort

      Runbaeck, A.

    Ack bliv hos oss (Swedish)

      Andersson, R.
      Edlund, L.

    Behaall oss vid ditt rena ord

      Rosenquist, C. E.

    Giv att ditt ord oss lysa maa

      Olsson, L.

Pax Tecum (Caldbeck - Vincent)   *

    Young, G. E.

Peek (Peek)

    Braun, H. M.

Penitance (Lane)   *

    Lynn, G. A.

Pentecost (Byrd)   *

    McKinney, H. D.

Petra
  See: Redhead 76

Picardy (French)   *

Albrecht, M. B.	Hutchison, W.
Clokey, J. W.	Joubert, J.
Diemer, E. L.	Mueller, C. F.
Ellsasser, R.	Powell, R. J.
Fromm, H.	Thalben-Ball, G.
Held, W.	Wiebe, E.

Pilot (Gould)   *

Purvis, R.
Wyton, A.

Pisgah
See: Covenanters Tune

Pleading Saviour (Plymouth)   *

Diemer, E. L.
Wyton, A.

Pleasant Pastures (Bradbury)   *

Baumgartner, H. L.	Hughes, R. J.
Bock, F.	

Potsdam (Bach)   *

Videroe, F.

Praise (Swedish)   *

Lagergren, A. (3)
Paulson, G.

Variants:
Ditt namn, O Gud, jag lova vill

Andersson, R. (2)
Hedwall, L. (2)

Ett klarligt ljus av dina bud

Carlman, G.

O Gud, det aer en hjaertans troest
(Svensk)

Aahlen, W.
Olsson, T. V.

O Jesu Krist, Guds ende son

Olson, D.

Praise My Soul
See: Benedic Anima Mea (Goss)

Pro Omnibus Sanctis (Barnby)   *

    Paulson, G.

    Variant:
    Foer alla helgon

Pro Pace Et Principe (French)
(Based on Veni Redemptor)

    Hedwall, L.

Proles De Coelo Prodiit (Tone 5)

    Fasolo, G. B.

Psalm 3 (Calvin 1539)

    Klenz, W.

Psalm 3 (Geneva)
    See: Old 122nd (Bourgeois)

Psalm 5 (Geneva)   *

    Variant:
    Herr hoere doch auf meine Rede
    (Geneva 1542)

    Klenz, W.

Psalm 6 (Geneva - Marot)   *

    Variant:
    I Kristne som toer (Geneva)

    Winter-Hjelm, O.

Psalm 8 (Geneva)   *

    Variants:
    Die Sonn' hat sich

    Genzmer, H.

    I moerker sjoenko

    Andersson, R.
    Edlund, L.

    Wie herrlich gibst du, Herr

    Klenz, W.

Psalm 12 (Geneva)   *

    Variant:
    Att bedja aer ej

Psalm 28 (Geneva)   *

    Kousemaker, A.

Psalm 29 (Bourgeois)   *

    Kousemaker, A.

Psalm 30 (Geneva)   *

    Kousemaker, A.

Psalm 31 (Bourgeois)   *

    Klenz, W.

Psalm 32 (Calvin 1539)

    Klenz, W.

Psalm 36 (Geneva)
   See: O Mensch, bewein (Strassburg)

Psalm 37 (Calvin 1539)
   See: O Mensch, bewein (Strassburg)

Psalm 42 (Geneva)
   See: Freu dich sehr (Bourgeois)

Psalm 47 (Bourgeois)   *

    Klenz, W.

Psalm 50 (Calvin 1539)

    Klenz, W. (2)

Psalm 55 (Pierre)   *

    Klenz, W.

Psalm 60 (Dutch)
   See: Psalm 108 (Pierre)

Psalm 67 (Strassburg)
   See: Es woll' uns Gott g'naedig
   sein (Strassburg)

Psalm 74 (Geneva)   *

  Variant:
  Psalm 116 (de Beze)

    Sweelinck, J. P. (2)

Psalm 79 (Geneva)   *

    Klenz, W.

Psalm 81 (Pierre)   *

    Fisher, N. Z.

Psalm 86 (Geneva)   *

    Variant:
    Herr, erhoere meine Klagen
    (Psalm 77)

       Klenz, W.

Psalm 88 (Dutch--Pierre) (French
    1562)

       Klenz, W.

Psalm 89 (Pierre)   *

    Variant:
    Song 132 (Dutch)

       Asma, F.

Psalm 100 (Geneva)   *

    Variant:
    Song I (Dutch)

       Asma, F.

Psalm 105 (Pierre)   *

       Klenz, W.

Psalm 108 (Pierre)   *

    Variant:
    Psalm 60 (Dutch)

       Anonymous (Sweelinck School)

Psalm 116 (de Beze)
    See: Psalm 74 (Geneva)

Psalm 118 (Geneva)   *

       Asma, F.

    Variants:
    Jauchzt alle Lande, Gott zu Ehren

       Bornefeld, H.   Vogt, E.
       Stockmeier, W.

    Rendez à Dieu

       Englert, E.   Maekelberghe, A.

Psalm 122 (Geneva)   *

    Dragt, J.

Psalm 125 (Strassburg 1525)

    Klenz, W.

Psalm 129 (Calvin 1539)

    Klenz, W.

Variant:
De Profundis (Calvin)

Psalm 136 (Pierre)   *

    Clokey, J. W.

Variant:
Lobt den Herrn

    Klenz, W.

Psalm 137 (Bourgeois)   *

    Klenz, W.

Psalm 140 (Geneva)
See: Wenn wir in hoechsten

Psalm 148 (Dutch--Pierre) (French
1562)

    Klenz, W.

Psalm 149 (Pierre)

    *Cellier, A. E.

Puer Natus Est Nobis   *

    Jacob, Dom C.
    Verschraegen, G. (2)

Puer Natus Est Nobis
See: Puer Nobis Nascitur (Praetorius)

Puer Natus In Bethlehem (Old German)   *

    Buxtehude, D.
    Siefert, P.

Variant:
Et barn er foedt

    Haarklou, J.   Karlsen, R.

Puer Nobis Nascitur (Praetorius)   *

Bornefeld, H.   Hutson, W.
Dandrieu, J. F.   LeBègue, N. A.
Dandrieu, P. (2)   Ore, C. W.
Grimes, T.   Raison, A.
Guilmant, A.   Sweelinck, J. P.

Variants:
Ons ist gheboren

Sweelinck, J. P.

Puer Natus Est Nobis

*Gantner, A.
Goemanne, N.

Uns ist ein Kindlein heut' gebor'n

*Duchow, M.

Puritan Nativity Hymn (1602)

Smith, G.

Que li darem

Guinaldo, N.

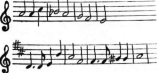

Quebec (Baker)   *

Sergisson, ?

Quem Pastores
See: Den die Hirten lobten sehr

Quem Vidistis Pastores

Belli, P. G.

Quietude (Green)

Hustad, D.

Quoy! ma voisine
See: Noël - Ah, ma voisine

Rachie (C. Roberts)

Powell, W.

Rathbun (Conkey)   *

McKinney, H. D.
Whitford, H.

Ratisbon (Crueger)   *

    Paulson, G.
    Thalben-Ball, G.

   Variant:
   Eins ist Not (Crueger)

    Neubauer, H.

Redhead 46   *

   Variant:
   Laus Deo

    Thalben-Ball, G.

Redhead 66 (Metzler)   *

   Variant:
   Metzler's Redhead

    Thalben-Ball, G.

Redhead 76   *

   Variant:
   Petra

    Wetherill, E. H.

Regent Square (Smart)   *

    Bock, F.   Thalben-Ball, G.
    Frank, R.   Videroe, F.
    McKinney, H. D.   Young, G. E.

Reges Tharsis

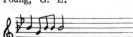

    Preston, T.
    Renauld, P.

Regina Caeli

    Hemmer, E.

Regina Coeli Laetare (Mode 6)   *

    Falcinelli, R.

Remember (Ravenscroft)

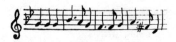

    Wyton, A.

Rendez à Dieu
  See: Psalm 118 (Geneva)

Resignation (U.S. Southern)   *

      Moyer, J. H.
      Videroe, F.

   Variants:
   Irwinton (Sacred Harp)

      Hustad, D.

   My Shepherd Will Supply My Need

Restoration (Southern Harmony)

      Held, W.
      Owens, S. B.   *Wyton, A.

Rhosymedre (Edwards)   *

      Wyton, A.

Rhyddid (Welsh)

      Clokey, J. W.
      Moyer, J. H.

Ridderholm
   See: Upp min tunga (Swedish)

Ringe recht, wenn Gottes Gnade   *
   (Kuhnau)

      Johnson, D. N.   Paulson, G.
      Neubauer, H.

   Variant:
   Batty

      Wyton, A.

Rockingham (Miller)   *

      Clokey, J. W.   Thalben-Ball, G.
      McKinney, H. D.   Wetherill, E. H.

Roept uit aan alle stranden

      Asma, F.

Rouen (Poitiers)   *

   Variant:
   Iste Confessor (Rouen)

      Clarke, F. R. C.
      Videroe, F.

Royal Proclamation (Christian Psalmist)

   Brandon, G.

Russian Hymn (Lwoff)   *

   McKinney, H. D.

Rutherford (Urhan)   *

   Stearns, P. P. (2)

Saa aelskade Gud vaerlden all
   See: Old 100th

Saa gaar en dag aen fraan vaar tid
   See: Nun sich der Tag (Krieger)

Saa hoegt har Gud, oss till stor froejd
   See: Ich ruf' zu dir (Klug)

Saa skoen gaar morgonstjaernan fram
   See: Wie schoen leuchtet

Saa snart aer det med
   See: O hjelp mig, Gud (Waldis)

Saasom hjorten traeget
   See: Freu dich sehr (Bourgeois)

Sacramentum Unitatis (Lloyd)   *

   Grieb, H. C.

Sacris Solemnis (Mode 4)   *

   Boulnois, M.   Langlais, J. F.
   *Girod, M. L.

Saeg mig den vaegen   Tune not found

   Soederholm, V.

Saell den som haver Jesus kaer
   See: Jesu, din Ihukommelse

St. Agnes (Dykes)   *

   Bock, F.   McKinney, H. D.
   Clokey, J. W.   Young, G. E. (2)

St. Anne (Croft)   *

   Beverst, G. E.   Mueller, C. F.
   Clokey, J. W.   Paulson, G.
   McKinney, H. D.   Thalben-Ball, G.

St. Anne (cont.)

    Young, G. E.

   Variant:
O Gud, vaar hjaelp

    Norrman, R.

St. Asaph (Bambridge)

    McKinney, H. D.

St. Bernard (Cologne)   *

    Powell, R. J.
    Thalben-Ball, G.

St. Catherine (Hemy)   *

    McKinney, H. D.
    Young, G. E.

St. Christopher (Maker)   *

    McKinney, H. D.   Southbridge, J.
    Mueller, C. F.

St. Clement (Scholefield)   *

    Grieb, H. C.
    Thalben-Ball, G.

St. Columba (Irish)   *

    Barlow, W.
    *Hunt, W.

St. Crispin (Elvey)   *

    McKinney, H. D.

St. Cross (Dykes)   *

    Beck, T.

St. Denio
  See: Joanna (Welsh)

St. Drostane (Dykes)   *

    Broughton, E.

St. Dunstan's (Douglas)   *

    Bock, F.

St. Elizabeth
  See: Schoenster Herr Jesu

St. Etheldreda (Turton)

    Thalben-Ball, G.

St. Ethelwald (Monk)   *

    Thalben-Ball, G.

St. Flavian (Day's)   *

    Clokey, J. W.

St. George's Windsor (Elvey)   *

      Quinn, J.
      Speller, F. N.

St. Gertrude (Sullivan)   *

      McKinney, H. D.

St. Hugh (Hopkins)   *

    Thalben-Ball, G.

St. James (Courteville)   *

    Thalben-Ball, G.

St. James (Stockholm)
  See: Hvad roest (Aahlstroem)

St. John (Welsh)

    Clokey, J. W.

St. Kevin (Sullivan)   *

      Feibel, F.   Lynn, G. A.
      Hovdesven, E. A.

St. Leonard (Meiningen)   *

    Thalben-Ball, G.

    Variants:
    Komm, O komm, du Geist (J. C.
    Bach)

      Drischner, M.

    Song 107 (Dutch--Bach)

      Asma, F.

St. Thomas (Williams)   *

    Videroe, F.
    Young, G. E.

Saints' Delight (F. Price)

    Wood, D.
    Wyton, A.

Salem (Christian Psalmist)

    Brandon, G.

Salig, salig, den som kaende
  See: Schmuecke dich

Saliga de som ifraan vaerldens oeden
  See: Lobet den Herren, alle die
  ihn

Saligheten er oss naer (Lindeman)   *

    Steenberg, P.

Salvator Natus (Bohemian)   *

    Variant:
    Freu dich Erd' und Sternenzelt

    Schroeder, H.

Salve Mater   *

    Schehl, J. A.

Salve Regina   *

    Falcinelli, R.
    *Rehm, P. O.   Schlick, A.

Salve Regina (Mode 1)   *

    Browne, C. F.   *Olsson, O. E.
    Caurroy, E. du   *Weitz, G.
    Liszt, F.

Salve Sancte Parens

    Belli, P. G.

Salzburg (Hintze)   *

    Lynn, G. A.
    Pasquet, J.

Sanctorum Meritis (Plainsong)

     Fasolo, G. B.

Sanctuary (Runyan)

     Hustad, D.

Sanctus

     Ahrens, J.

Sandon (Purday)

     Wetherill, E. H.

*

Sandringham (Barnby)

     Brandon, G.

*

     Variant:
     O Perfect Love

     Hustad, D.

Schaffe in mir, Gott (Witt)

     Neubauer, H.

*

Schlummerlied der Hirten

     Schroeder, H.

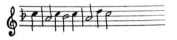

Schmuecke dich (Crueger)

*

Clokey, J. W.	Paulson, G. (2)
Gore, R. T.	Proctor, R. E.
Klenz, W.	Russell, O. N.
Lagergren, A. (2)	Schehl, J. A.
Manz, P. (2)	Schwartz, G. von
Micheelsen, H. F.	Stout, A.
Ore, C. W.	Telemann, G. P. (2)

     Variants:
     Huru laenge skall mitt hjaerta
     (Crueger)

        Paulson, G.
        Thyrestam, G.

     Salig, salig, den som kaende

        Runbaeck, A.

     Taenk paa honom som var frestad

        Runbaeck, A.

Schmuecke dich (cont.)

Upp min sjael, att korset baera

    Wikander, D.

Schoenster Herr Jesu (Silesian)   *

    Coates, D. M.   Peek, R.
    Hoeller, K.   Stow, D. G.
    Paulson, G.

Variants:
Crusaders Hymn

    Ellsasser, R.   Mueller, C. F.
    Frank, R.   Quinn, J.
    McKinney, H. D.   Young, G. E. (2)

Dejlig er jorden

    Haarklou, J.   Sandvold, A.
    Runbaeck, A.

Haerlig aer jorden

    Ahlberg, V.

St. Elizabeth

    Curry, W. L.

Schoenstes Kindlein
See: Lovely Infant

Schwing dich auf (Crueger)   *

    Paulson, G.
    Zipp, F.

Variant:
O min Jesu, dit du gaatt

    Carlman, G.   Norrman, R.
    Lindstroem, M.

Se hvor nu Jesus traeder (Kingo-
   Arrebo)
See: O Jesu, for din pine (Kingo)

Se Jesus aer ett troestrikt
See: Wenn wir in hoechsten
Noethen

Se kaerlet brast (Vretblad 1939)

    Ohlsson, S. O.

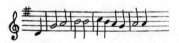

Se solens skjoenne (Norse Folk)   *

    Karlsen, R.
    Sandvold, A.

Se, vi gaa upp (Swedish)

    *Hallnaes, H.
    Nyvall, J.
    Paulson, G.   Rosenberg, G.

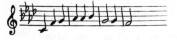

Se, vi gaa upp (Kingo)
  See: O Jesu, for din pine (Kingo)

Seelenbraeutigam (Drese)   *

    Near, G.   Wilson, R.
    Paulson, G.

  Variants:
  Jesu, geh voran

    Ehrlinger, F.

  Vaka, sjael, och bed

    Norrman, R.
    Olsson, T. V.

Sei gegruesset, Jesu guetig (Vopelius)   *

    Duchow, M.
    Gore, R. T. (2)

Sei gegruesset, sei gekuesset

    Faessler, G.

Sei Lob und Ehr (Crueger)
  See: Wach auf, mein Herz (Lyon)

Selnecker
  See: Nun lasst uns Gott (Selnecker)

Serenity (Wallace)   *

    Stearns, P. P. (2)

Shaker Tune
  See: Simple Gifts

Shall We Gather at the River? (Lowry)   *

  Variant:
  Hanson Place (Lowry)

    Wyton, A.

Sharon (Boyce)

    Thiman, E.

Shepherding (R. Hillert)

    Hillert, R.

Shepherds of the Mountains   *

    Variant:
    Noël - Pastre dei mountagne

        Guilmant, A.

Shepherds Shake Off
    See: Besançon Carol (French)

Si, Herrens ord aer rent
    See: O Jesu Christ, du hoechstes
    Gut (Crueger)

Si Jesu aer ett troestrikt
    See: Wenn wir in hoechsten
    Noethen

Sicilian Mariners   *

    Dub, G.   Paulson, G.
    McKinney, H. D.   Vretblad, P.

    Variant:
    O Sanctissima

    Dressler, J.   Smith, G.
    Schehl, J. A.

Sieh hier bin ich (Darmstadt)   *

    Variant:
    Jeg er rede til (Darmstadt)

    Thorkildsen, J.

Silent Night
    See: Stille Nacht

Simple Gifts (Shaker Hymn)

    Southbridge, J.

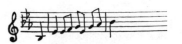

    Variant:
    Shaker Tune

    *Young, C. R.

Sine Nomine (Vaughan-Williams)   *

     Guinaldo, N.   Thatcher, H. R.
     Manz, P.

Singen wir aus Herzens Grund (Horn)
    See: Da Christus geboren
    (Bohemian)

Singen wir mit Froehlichkeit
    See: Joseph, lieber Joseph mein
    (Klug)

Sion klagar med stor smaerta
    See: Zion klagt mit Angst (Crueger)

Sions Vekter
    See: Wachet auf (Nicolai)

Sjaa han gjeng (Vulpius)
    See: Lobet den Herrn, ihr Heiden
    all

Skaader, skaader, nu haer alle
(Swedish)

     Rosenberg, G.
     Welander, W.   Wideen, I.

Slane (Irish)   *

     Hutchison, W.   Merritt, C.
     Iderstine, A. P. Van   Schwartz, P.

Slotzang
    See: Herr und Aeltster

Snabbt som blixten de foersvinna
    See: Alle Menschen (Wessnitzer)

Snow Lay on the Ground   *

     Sowerby, L.

So fuehrst du doch (Koenig) (Gregor's
   192nd)
                     Z 6196c
     Schmidt-Arzberg, G.

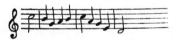

So geh'st du nun (Darmstadt)   *

     Paulson, G. (2)

    Variant:
    Du bar ditt kors

     Lindegren, J.   Rosenquist, C. E.
     Olson, D.

So nimm, denn, meine Haende   *
(Silcher)

    Beverst, G. E.
    Paulson, G.

So wuensch' ich euch ein gute Nacht
(Neusidler)
                Z 4405a
    Gore, R. T.

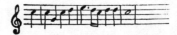

Social Band (Mennonite)

    Burkhart, C.

Soerg, O kjaere Fader (Lindeman)   *

    Hovland, E.

Soerg, O kjaere Fader
  See: Christus, der uns selig macht

Soldau (Wittenberg)   *

    Variants:
    Dig, Helge Ande, bedja vi

        Andersson, R.
        Egebjer, L.

    Nu beder vi den Hellig Aand

        Bangert, E.   Sandvold, A.
        Moeller, S. O.   Winter-Hjelm, O.

    Nun bitten wir (Walther)

        Bornefeld, H.   Krapf, G.
        Brunner, A.   Scheidemann, H.
        Eder, H.   Schneidt, H. M.
        Gore, R. T.

Solid Rock (Bradbury)   *

    Hustad, D.

Sollt ich meinem Gott (Schop)   *

    Kammeier, H.

    Variants:
    Song 76 (Dutch)

        Asma, F.

    Song 173 (Dutch)

        Asma, F.

Sollt mich die Liebe (Koenig)   *

    Variant:
Jesu, din soede forening (Koenig)
        soete

      Emborg, J. L.   Winter-Hjelm, O.
      Nielsen, L.

Som den gylne (Schop)
    See: Werde munter, mein Gemuete
(Schop)

Som faagelen vid ljusan dag
    See: Eja, mitt hjaerta

Som harpoklangen foersvinner
    See: Jeg ville lova och prise

Som spridda saedeskornen
    See: Blomstertid (Swedish Psalm)

Som toerstige hjoert monne (Linde-   *
    man)

      Aamodt, T.

Something For Jesus (Lowry)   *

      Miles, R. H.

Song 1 (Gibbons)   *

      Clokey, J. W.

Song 1 (Dutch)
    See: Valet (Teschner)

Song 4 (Gibbons)

      Clarke, F. R. C.

Song 13 (Gibbons)   *

      Clokey, J. W.
      Videroe, F.

Song 22 (Gibbons)   *

      Clokey, J. W.

Song 24 (Gibbons)   *

      Clokey, J. W.

Song 32 (Dutch)
    See: Herzlich tut mich verlangen

Song 34 (Gibbons)   *

   Variant:
   Angel's Song (Gibbons)

      Smith, G.
      Thalben-Ball, G.

Song 43 (Dutch)
   See: Herzlich tut mich verlangen

Song 50 (Dutch)
   See: Freu dich sehr (Bourgeois)

Song 58 (Dutch)   *

    Rippen, P.

Song 62 (Dutch)
   See: Jesu, meine Zuversicht

Song 67 (Gibbons)   *

    Clokey, J. W.
    Thalben-Ball, G. (2)

Song 76 (Dutch)
   See: Sollt ich meinem Gott (Schop)

Song 83 (Dutch--Bach)
   See: Kommt Seelen, dieser Tag
   (Bach)

Song 89 (Dutch)   *

    Asma, F.

Song 96 (Dutch)
   See: Ein feste Burg

Song 107 (Dutch--Bach)
   See: St. Leonard (Meiningen)

Song 132 (Dutch)
   See: Psalm 89 (Pierre)

Song 153 (Dutch--Huet)   *

    Asma, F.

Song 173 (Dutch)
   See: Sollt ich meinem Gott (Schop)

Song A (Dutch)
   See: Wenn wir in hoechsten

Song B (Dutch)
   See: Lofzang van Maria

Song C (Dutch)
See: An Wasserfluessen Babylon

Song D (Dutch)
See: Song of Symeon (Geneva)

Song E (Dutch)
See: Vater Unser

Song H (Dutch) (1560)

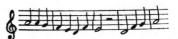

Asma, F.

Song I (Dutch)
See: Psalm 100 (Geneva)

Song L (Dutch)
See: Avondzang

Song of Symeon (Geneva)   *

Variants:
Nunc Dimittis (Genevan)

*Young, G. E.

Song D (Dutch)

Asma, F.

Song of the Rhine (German)

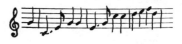

Whitford, H.

Sonne der Gerechtigkeit (Bohemian)   *

Gebhard, H.
Kluge, M.

Sons of Sorrow (Early American)

Wood, D.

Sorgen och glaedjen (Swedish Folk)

*Runbaeck, A.

Sorgen og gleden (Lindeman)   *

Hovland, E.

Southwell (Damon's)   *

Beck, T.

Spanish Hymn
See: Madrid (Carr)

Spires
    See: Erhalt uns, Herr (Klug)

Spiritus Sancti Gratia (Schein)
                              Z 370b
        Gore, R. T.

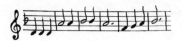

Stabat Mater Dolorosa (Mainz)   *

        Dandrieu, P.

Stabat Mater Dolorosa (Mode 1-   *
    Mechlin)

        Falcinelli, R.
        LeBêgue, N. A.

Statt upp, O Sion
    See: In Dulci Jubilo

Steadfast
    See: O Gott, du frommer Gott
    (Hannover)

Steal Away (Spiritual)   *

        Warner, R.

Steh' auf in deiner Macht (Psalm 68-
    Pierre)

        Klenz, W.

    Variant:
    Dominus Sanctus (Pierre)

Steht auf, ihr lieben Kinderlein
    See: O Heilige Dreifaltigkeit
    (Herman)

Stille Nacht (Gruber)   *

        Balderston, M.   Schehl, J. A.
        Lynn, G. A.   Sifler, P. J.
        McKinney, H. D.   Vretblad, P.
        Paulson, G. (2)   Young, G. E. (2)

    Variants:
    Glade Jul, dejlige Jul

        Haarklou, J.
        Thorkildsen, J.

    Silent Night

        Martin, G. M.   Pethel, J.
        Pedemonti, G.

Stockholm   *

    Paulson, G.

Variants:
Der Mange skal komme

    Haarklou, J.   Videroe, F.
    Rosenquist, C. E.

Vart flyr jag foer Gud

    Hedwall, L.   Olson, D.
    Janáček, B.   Rosenquist, C. E.

Stockport (Wainwright)   *

Variant:
Yorkshire

    Corina, J.

Stockton (Wright)

    Thalben-Ball, G.

Stoerl I   Z 211
                 also in 3
                     4

    Lagergren, A. (4)

Variants:
Dig, ljusens Fader

    Rosenquist, C. E.

Din klara sol gaar

    Andersson, R.   Paulson, G. (3)
    Lagergren, A.

Med tacksam roest och tacksam
sjael

    *Forsberg, R.

Stracathro (Hutcheson)   *

    Thalben-Ball, G.

Straf' mich nicht
    See: Mache dich, mein Geist
    (Dresden)

Stuttgart (Gotha)   *

    Eliot, D.   Pasquet, J.
    Lynn, G. A.   Thalben-Ball, G.

Such wer da will (Stobaeus)   *

    Zipp, F.

Surrexit Christus Hodie   *

  Variants:
  Erstanden ist der heil'ge Christ
                heilig

   *Neubauer, H.

  Opstanden er den Herre Krist

    Steenberg, P.

Surrey (Carey)   *

    Thalben-Ball, G.

  Variant:
  Carey's

    Powell, R. J.

Swedish Litany   *

    Hokanson, M.

Swedish Melody
  See: Tryggare kan ingen vara

Sweet Hour of Prayer (Bradbury)   *

    Wyton, A.

Sweet Rivers of Redeeming Love   *

    Hustad, D.

Taenk, naer en gaang (Berggreen)   *

  Variant:
  Expectation (Berggreen)

    Stearns, P. P. (2)

Taenk paa honom som var frestad
  See: Schmuecke dich

Tallis 1st Mode

    Clokey, J. W.

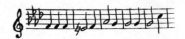

Tallis 3rd Mode   *

    Clokey, J. W.

Tallis 5th Mode

    Clokey, J. W.

Tallis Canon   *

    Clokey, J. W.   Young, G. E.
    Gustafson, D.

Tallis Ordinal   *

    Thalben-Ball, G.

Tantum Ergo (Novello)
    See: St. Thomas (Wade)

Te Deum (Vienna)
    See: Grosser Gott, wir loben dich

Te Deum Laudamus (Tone 3)   *

    Gantner, A.   St. Martin, L. de
    Pikéthy, T. K.

Te Lucis Ante Terminum (Sarum-   *
    Tone 8)

    *Siedel, M.

Tempus Adest Floridum   *

    Schultz, R.
    Young, G. E.

    Variant:
    Good King Wenceslas

    Ellsasser, R.

Ter Sanctus (Rostock)   *

    Lagergren, A.
    Paulson, G. (2)

    Variants:
    Dig vare lov och pris

    Andersson, R.   Olson, D.
    Hedwall, L.   Soederholm, V.

    Vi lova dig, O store Gud

    Egebjer, L.   Olson, D.
    Ek, G.   Olsson, O. E.
    Nyvall, J.   Soerenson, T.

Terra Beata
    See: Terra Patris (Sheppard)

Terra Patris (Sheppard)   *

   Variant:
   Terra Beata

      Curry, W. L.

They'll Know We Are Christians
(Scholtes)

      Bock, F.   Held, W.
      Gehring, P.

This Joyful Eastertide
   See: Awake Thou Wintry Earth
(Dutch)

This Night Did God Become a Child
(K. Westbury)

      Wyton, A.

Thou Man of Griefs (Dare)   *

   Variant:
   Kedron

      Johnson, D. N.

Three Kings of Orient (Hopkins)   *

      Balderston, M.   Spong, J.
      McKinney, H. D.   Young, G. E.

   Variant:
   We Three Kings

      Bock, F.   Guglielmi, A.
      Clifford, J.

Tiden flyr: naer vill du boerja
   (Becker) (Derived from Ebeling)
                 Z 6458
      Aahlen, W.
      Norrman, R.   Rosenquist, C. E.

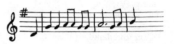

Tig dig allena
   See: Allein zu dir (Wittenberg)

Till den himmel, som bliv allas
   See: Vad kan dock min sjael
(Swedish)

Till dig allena
Til dig alene
   See: Allein zu dir (Wittenberg)

Till dig, av hjaertens grunde (French)
    See: Old 130th (French)

Till dig jag ropar
    See: Ich ruf' zu dir

Till haerlighetens land igen (Schein)
    See: Mach's mit mir, Gott (Schein)

Till himmelen, dit laengtar jag   Tune not found

        Lunden, L.
        Sventelius, H.

To God Be the Glory (Doane)

        Hustad, D.

To Jesus Christ, Our Sov'reign King
    (Peoples Mass Book)

        Fissinger, E.
        Quinn, J.

Ton-y-Botel (Williams)   *

        Ellsasser, R.   Videroe, F.
        Thalben-Ball, G.   Wetherill, E. H.

Toplady (Hastings)   *

        Hustad, D. (2)

Toulon (Bourgeois)
    See: Old 124th (Geneva)

Treurer Heiland, wir sind hier   *
    (Swiss Hymnal)

        Maurer, O.

Troestet, troestet (Micheelsen)   *

        Micheelsen, H. F.

Truro (Burney)   *

        Hovdesven, E. A.
        Klenz, W.

Tryggare kan ingen vara   *

        Powell, R. J.

    Variant:
    Swedish Melody

        Hovdesven, E. A.

Tu auf, tu auf, du schoenes Blut
   See: Tu auf, tu auf, O Sunderherz

Tu auf, tu auf, O Sunderherz   *

   Variant:
   Tu auf, tu auf, du schoenes Blut

     Faessler, G.

Tut mir auf die schoene Pforte
   See: Unser Herrscher (Neander)

Tvaa vaeldiga strida (Svensk 1640)

     Edlund, L.
     Schoenberg, S. G.

Tvang til tro (Steenberg)   *

     Hovland, E.

Tvivlan ur min sjael (Wessnitzer)
   See: Alle Menschen muessen
sterben (Wessnitzer)

Twelve Days of Christmas

     McKinney, H. D.

Tysk   *

   Variant:
   Gud aer haer tillstaedes

     Aahlen, W.

U, heilig Godslam
     Asma, F.

Ubi Caritas Et Amor (Plainsong - Mode 6)   *

     Lechat, J.

Uffingham (Clarke)
   See: St. Luke (Clarke)

Und unser lieben Frauen (Beuttner)
   See: Es flog ein Taeublein weisse

Unde Et Memores (Monk)   *

     Giorgi, P.

Underfulle Konge (Steenberg)   *

    Hovland, E.   Steenberg, P.
    Karlsen, R.

Union (Mennonite)

    Zercher, J. R.

University College (Gauntlett)   *

    Thalben-Ball, G.

Uns ist ein Kindlein heut' gebor'n
  See: Puer Nobis Nascitur (Praetorius)

Unser Herrscher (Neander)   *

    Feibel, F.

  Variants:
  Neander

    Thalben-Ball, G.

  Tut mir auf die schoene Pforte

    Zipp, F.

Upp min sjael, att korset baera
  See: Schmuecke dich

Upp min tunga (Swedish)   *

    Hedwall, L.   Runbaeck, A.
    Paulson, G.

  Variant:
  Ridderholm

Upp psaltare och harpa
  See: Nun lob', mein Seel (Kugelmann)

Uppfaren aer vaar Herre Krist
  (Swedish)   also in 3
                             4

    Norrman, R.
    Paulson, G.

  Variant:
  Av helig laengtan

    Olson, D.

Upplys vaar sjael
  See: Ach Gott und Herr (Schein)

Uverdig er jeg Herre
See: Old 130th (French)

Vaakn op, du som sover (Lindeman)   *

    Hovland, E.

Vaakn op og slaa
See: Winchester New (Crasselius)

Vaar blick mot helga berget gaar
(Olsson 1916)

    Allgen, C. L.   Olson, D.
    Nyvall, J.

Vaar Gud aer oss
See: Ein feste Burg

Vaar Gud han er saa
See: Ein feste Burg

Vaar Herras Jesu Kristi doed
    Herres
See: Jesu din Ihukommelse

Vaar kraft, O Gud, foeroka
See: Valet (Teschner)

Vaar raetta spis vid hemmets (Waldis)

    Runbaeck, A.

Vaara stunder ila (Wideen 1917)

    Runbaeck, A.

Vaart paaskalamm, O Jesu Krist
See: Lob sei dem Allmaechtigen
(Crueger)

Vad gott kan jag dock goera
See: Von Gott will ich nicht (Erfurt)

Vad kan dock min sjael (Swedish)

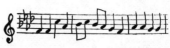

    Nyvall, J. (2)

    Variant:
Till den himmel, som bliv allas

    Wikander, D.

Vad kan dock min sjael foernoeja
See: Freu dich sehr (Bourgeois)

Vad ljus oever griften
See: Hvad ljus oefver (Jespersoen)

Vad min Gud vill
See: Was mein Gott will (French)

Vad roest, vad ljuvlig roest (Aahlstroem)
See: Hvad roest, hvad ljuvlig
roest (Aahlstroem)

Vaelsignet vare Jesu namn

Norrman, R.

Vaend av din vrede
See: Wend ab deinen Zorn

Vaenligt oever jorden (Svensk)
See: Kriste, som ditt ursprung
leder

Vaer troestig, Sion
See: Ach Gott vom Himmel (Erfurt)

Vaerldens fraelsare kom haer
See: Nun komm, der Heiden
Heiland

Vak upp, bed Gud om kraft och mod
See: O Ewigkeit, du (Schop)

Vak upp, min sjael, giv aera
See: Nun lasst uns Gott (Selnecker)

Vaka, sjael, och bed
See: Seelenbraeutigam

Vaken upp! en staemma bjuder
Vakna
See: Wachet auf

Valet (Teschner)   *

Drischner, M.   Paulson, G.
Gore, R. T.   Schehl, J. A.
Kauffmann, G. F.   Vogt, E.
Manz, P.

Variants:
Jag lyfter mina haender
Jeg

Aahlen, W. (2)   Norrman, R.
Carlman, G.   Runbaeck, A.
Franzen, B.   Soerenson, T.
Janáček, B.

Valet (cont.)

Nu hjertelig mig langes jeg

Bangert, E.   Runbaeck, A.
Olson, D.

O maa vi noga maerka

Soederholm, V.

St. Theodulph

Curry, W. L.   Russell, O. N.
Elmore, R.   Wilson, R.
Mueller, C. F.   Zabel, A. J.
Pethel, J.

Song 1 (Dutch)

Asma, F.

Vaar kraft, O Gud, foeroka

Runbaeck, A.

Var aer den vaen, som oeverallt
See: Herzliebster Jesu (Crueger)

Var haelsad, skoena morgonstund
See: Wie schoen leuchtet (Nicolai)

Var kristtrogen froejde sig
See: Joseph, lieber Joseph mein

Var man maa nu vael (Nuernberg)
See: Nun freut Euch (Nuernberg)

Varina (Root)   *

Elmore, R.

Vart flyr jag foer Gud
See: Stockholm

Vater Unser (Leipzig)   *

Bach, J. C.   Kauffmann, G. F. (2)
Barlow, W.   Krieger, J. (2)
Bender, J.   Lagergren, A.
Boehm, G. (2)   Langlais, J. F.
Bornefeld, H.   Linke, N.
Brunner, A.   Lorentz, J.
Buxtehude, D.   Pachelbel, J.
David, J. N.   Pepping, E.
Ehrlinger, F.   Rohwer, J.
Haigh, M.   Saxton, S. E.

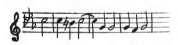

Veni Creator Spiritus (cont.)

Variants:
Kom, Helge Ande, Herre god

Hallnaes, H.
Soerenson, T.

Kom, Hellig Aand, med

Winter-Hjelm, O.

Komm, Gott Schoepfer, Heil'ger
Geist (Klug)

Barlow, W.
Manz, P.

Veni Emmanuel (Plainsong)   *

Curry, W. L.   Manz, P.
Eliot, D.   McKinney, H. D.
Ellsasser, R.   Mueller, C. F.
Groom, L.   Sifler, P. J.
Lehr, M. D.   Smart, D.
Lynn, G. A.   Young, G. E.
Maekelberghe, A.

Veni Sancte Spiritus (Dublin - Mode 1)   *

Pikéthy, T. K.

Veni Sancte Spiritus (Old Church)

Allgen, C. L. (2)

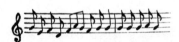

Variants:
Komm, Heiliger Geist, erfuell die   *
Herzen

Gore, R. T.

O du Helge Ande, kom till oss in   *

Veni Sancte Spiritus (Webbe)   *

Thalben-Ball, G.

Venid Niños (Spanish)

Guinaldo, N.

Verbum Supernum (Plainsong-   *
Mode 8)

Langlais, J. F.

Vergangen ist der lichte Tag (Danish)   *

  Variant:
  Den ljusa dag framgaangen aer (Kingo)
       lyse   forgangen

      Carlman, G.   Lundborg, G.
      Emborg, J. L.   Paulson, G. (2)
      Haarklou, J.   Rosenquist, C. E.
      Hedwall, L.

Verleih uns Frieden (Nuernberg)   *

      Bornefeld, H.   Weiss, E.
      Pepping, E.

Vernon (Mennonite)

      Burkhart, C.

Versuchet euch doch selbst
   See: Was frag' ich nach (Fritsch-
   Darmstadt)

Verzage nicht, O frommer Christ
                               Z 254
      Scheidt, S.

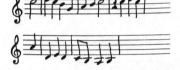

Vexilla Regis

      Dufay, G.

Vexilla Regis (German)   *

  Variant:
  Da nun das Jahr

      Gantner, A.

Vexilla Regis Prodeunt (Sarum-   *
   Mode 1)

      Bermudo, J.   Olsson, O. E.
      Broek, P. Van den   Peek, R.

Vi bedje dig, sann Gud och man
   See: Vi tacke dig, O Jesu god
   (Swedish)

Vi lova dig, O store Gud
   See: Ter Sanctus (Rostock)

Vi oenska nu vaar brudgum (Svensk
   1697)

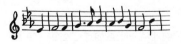

      Runbaeck, A.

Vi prise dig, O Fader kaer   Tune not found

    Hedwall, L.
    Kullnes, A.

Vi tacke dig, O Jesu god (Swedish)   *

    Andersson, R.   Paulson, G.
    Carlman, G.

    Variant:
    Vi bedje dig, sann Gud och man

    Aahlen, W.

Vi tror og troester (Walther)
See: Wir glauben all an einen
Gott, Schoepfer (Wittenberg)

Victimae Paschali Laudes (Gregorian-   *
Mode 1)

    Arnatt, R.   Doyen, H.
    Asola, M.   Erbach, C.
    *Demessieux, J.   Koert, H. Van
    Desprez, J.   Pineau, C.

Victory
See: Palestrina

Vid evighetens brunnar
See: Blomstertid (Swedish Psalm)

Vienna (Knecht)   *

    Thalben-Ball, G.

Vilken kaerlek oss bevisad (Albert)
                        Z 3567
    Aahlen, W.

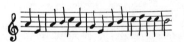

    Variants:
    Dig, min Jesu, nu jag skaader
    (Albert)

    Aahlen, W.

    Jesu, hast du mein vergessen

    Jesu, laer mig raett betaenka
    (Albert)

    Paulson, G.

Vom Himmel hoch da komm ich her   *
(Luther)

    Boehm, G.   Curry, W. L.

Vom Himmel hoch da komm ich her (cont.)

Gantner, A.
Held, W.
Johnson, D. N.
Klenz, W.
Lagergren, A. (4)

Paulson, G. (2)
Schack, D. A.
Walther, J. G.
Wilson, R.
Young, G. E.

Variants:
Av himlens hoejd

Aahlen, W.
Olsson, O. E.
Paulson, G.

Rosenberg, G.
Runbaeck, A.
Soederholm, V.

Fra Himlen hoejt kom

Bangert, E.
Winter-Hjelm, O.

Von Gott will ich nicht lassen (Crueger)   *

Variants:
Crueger

Thalben-Ball, G.

Fraan Gud vill jeg ej vika

Von Gott will ich nicht lassen (Erfurt)   *

Gore, R. T.
Kauffmann, G. F.
Lagergren, A.

Walther, J. G.
Zipp, F.

Variants:
Fraan Gud vill jag ej vika

Hedwall, L.
Paulson, G.

Noël - Une jeune pucelle
                  vierge

Charpentier, M. A.
Dandrieu, J. F.
Dandrieu, P.

LeBègue, N. A.
Raison, A.

O Gud, som tiden vender (Erfurt)

Olson, D.
Winter-Hjelm, O.

Vad gott kan jag dock goera

Aahlen, W.

Vous qui désirez (French Noël)   *

    Corrette, M.   Raison, A. (2)
    Dandrieu, J. F.

Vreden din avvend (Crueger)
  See: Herzliebster Jesu

Vruechten (Dutch Carol)
  See: Awake Thou Wintry Earth

Vulpius
  See: Gelobt sei Gott (Vulpius)

W zlobié leży (Polish Carol)   *

    Variant:
    Noël - Accourez bergers (Polish)

      Guilmant, A.

Wach auf, mein Herz (Lyon)   *

    Variant:
    Sei Lob und Ehr (Crueger)

      Fronmueller, F.
      Micheelsen, H. F.

Wach auf, wach auf, du deutsches   *
Land

    Altman, L.

Wachet auf (Nicolai)   *

    Bloch, W.   Linke, N.
    Bornefeld, H.   Manz, P.
    Eliot, D.   Paulson, G.
    Finkbeiner, R.   Rohwer, J.
    Krapf, G.   Walther, J. G.
    Lagergren, A. (4)

    Variants:
    Helige, som bor i ljuset

      Runbaeck, A.

    Sions Vekter

      Olson, D.   Steenberg, P.
      Runbaeck, A.   Winter-Hjelm, O.

    Vaken upp! en staemma bjuder
    Vakna

      Aahlen, W.   Sjoegren, A., Jr.

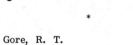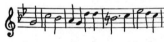

Was hilft's den Heiden (Waldis)
                                    Z 4463

    Variant:
    Om Kristus doeljes nu foer dig

        Aahlen, W.
        Runbaeck, A.

Was mein Gott will (French)   *

        Gore, R. T.   Telemann, G. P. (2)
        Stollberg, O.

    Variant:
    Vad min Gud vill

        Andersson, R.   Paulson, G.
        Lagergren, A.

Wassail (English)   *

        Ellsasser, R.
        McKinney, H. D.

We Come To You With Longing
(Vermulst)

        Vermulst, J.

We Three Kings
  See: Three Kings of Orient

We Wish You a Merry Christmas

        McKinney, H. D.

Webb   *

        McKinney, H. D.
        Young, G. E.

Weltlich Ehr und zeitlich Gut (Weisse)
                                    Z 4971a
    Gore, R. T.

Welwyn (Scott-Gatty)   *

        Copes, V. E.

Wend ab deinen Zorn   *

    Variant:
    Vaend av din vrede

        Norrman, R.
        Nyvall, J.

Wennerberg I
  See: Herren aer min herde god

Wer Gott vertraut (Calvisius)   *

    Gore, R. T.

Wer kann der Treu vergessen (Ebeling)   *

    Drischner, M.

Wer nur den lieben Gott (Neumark)   *

Albright, W.	Klenz, W.
Boehm, G.	Lagergren, A.
Bornefeld, H.	Stollberg, O.
Drischner, M.	Stout, A.
Duchow, M.	Thompson, R. (3)
Fiebig, K.	Wilson, R.
Gebhardi, L. E.	Young, G. E.

Variants:
Bremen

    Curry, W. L.

Hvo ene lader (Neumark)

Bangert, E.	Sandvold, A.
Runbaeck, A.	Winter-Hjelm, O.

Min sjael och sinne

    Edlund, L.
    Hedwall, L.

Naer ingen dager oegat skaadar

    *Rosenquist, C. E.

Neumark

    Frank, R.

Wer weiss wie nahe (Neumark)

    Telemann, G. P. (2)

Wer weiss wie nahe (Rudolfstadt)   *

    Kammeier, H.

Wer weiss wie nahe (Crasselius)
  See: Winchester New (Crasselius)

Wer weiss wie nahe (Neumark)
  See: Wer nur den lieben (Neumark)

Werde Licht, du Volk (Kocher)   *

    Variant:
    Hilf, Herr Jesu, lass gelingen
    (Kocher)

        Scheller, H.

Werde munter, mein Gemuete (Schop)   *

        Gore, R. T.   Pasquet, J.
        Johnson, D. N.   Paulson, G. (2)
        Lagergren, A. (2)   Walther, J. G.
        Manz, P.

    Variants:
    Herre, signe du och raade

        Andersson, R. (2)

    Lyft, min sjael, ur jordegruset

        Olsson, T. V.

    Som den gylne (Schop)

        Andersson, R.   Olsson, O. E.
        Bangert, E.

Were You There? (Spiritual)   *

        Brandon, G.   Smith, L.
        Lynn, G. A.   Warner, R.

West End (A. Parker)

        Parker, A.

Westminster (Turle)

        Thalben-Ball, G.

Westminster Carol
    See: Les Anges dans nos (French
    Carol)

What Is This Lovely Fragrance?
    See: Fragrance

When Christmas Morn Is Breaking
(Swedish)

        Hovdesven, E. A.

When Jesus Wept (Billings)   *

        Eliot, D.

Where He Leads Me (Norris)

    Graham, R. V.

Wie der Hirsch
  See: Freu dich sehr

Wie herrlich gibst du, Herr
  See: Psalm 8 (Geneva)

Wie lieblich ist das Haus
  See: Jervaulx Abbey

Wie nach einer Wasserquelle
  See: Freu dich sehr (Bourgeois)

Wie schoen leuchtet (Nicolai)   *

    Bach, J. C.   Klenz, W.
    Barr, J.   Lagergren, A. (2)
    Beverst, G. E.   McKinney, H. D.
    Bloch, W.   Paulson, G. (4)
    Buxtehude, D.   Schwartz, G. Von
    Gore, R. T.   Telemann, G. P. (2)
    Hoegner, F.

  Variants:
  Av hoeiheten oprunnen er

    Bangert, E.   Steenberg, P. (3)
    Haarklou, J.   Winter-Hjelm, O.
    Runbaeck, A.

  Hell morgonstjaerna, mild och ren

    Nilsson, T.

  Hoega Majestaet vi alla

    Norrman, R.
    Runbaeck, A.

  I naad och sanning bland

    Carlman, G.

  Nu segrar alla trognas hopp

    Aahlen, W.

  Saa skoen gaar morgonstjaernan fram

    Runbaeck, A. (2)

  Var haelsad, skoena morgonstund

    Andersson, R.   Melin, H.
    Haegg, G.   Olson, D.

Wie schoen leuchtet (cont.)

    Olsson, O. E.
    Runbaeck, A.

Wie soll ich dich empfangen (Crueger)   *

    Haffner, W.
    Stockmeier, W.

Wie's Gott gefaellt (Cassel)   Z 7574   

    Gore, R. T.

Wigtown (Scotch)   *

    Thalben-Ball, G.

Wilhelmus (Valerius)   *

    Variant:
    Wenn alle untreu werden

    Braeutigam, H.

Wiltshire (Smart)   *

    Thalben-Ball, G.

Winchester New (Crasselius)   *
(Wach auf, du Geist - Halle)

    Lynn, G. A.
    Paulson, G. (3)

    Variants:
    Dig skall min sjael

    Andersson, R.   Paulson, G.
    Norrman, R.

    Dir, dir, Jehova (Halle)

    Gebhardi, L. E.   Pasquet, J.
    Kammeier, H.   Pepping, E.

    Hoer, Gud, aennu sin naad (Halle)

    Aahlen, W.

    Jag nu den saekra grunden vunnit

    Runbaeck, A.

    Vaakn op og slaa

    Hovland, E.   Runbaeck, A.
    Olson, D.   Videroe, F.

Winchester New (cont.)

    Winter-Hjelm, O.

  Wer weiss wie nahe (Crasselius)

    Neubauer, H.

Winchester Old (Tye)   *

    Ore, C. W.

Windsor (Damon's)   *

    Thalben-Ball, G.

Wir beten an die Macht   *

    Schehl, J. A.

Wir Christenleut (Crueger)
  See: O Jesu Christ, dein Krippelein (Crueger)

Wir danken dir, Herr Jesu Christ,
  dass du das Laemmlein (Gesius)
              Z 479
    Gore, R. T.

Wir danken dir, Herr Jesu Christ,
  dass du fuer uns (Wittenberg)   *

    Pepping, E.   Vogt, E.
    Stockmeier, W.

Wir danken dir, Herr Jesu Christ,
  dass du vom Tod (Fischer)
  See: Erschienen ist der (Herman)

Wir glauben all an einen Gott,
  Schoepfer (Wittenberg)   *

    Bornefeld, H. (2)   Krapf, G.
    Gore, R. T.   Scheidt, S.
    Kauffmann, G. F.   Sweelinck, J. P. (2)

    Variant:
    Vi tror og troester (Walther)

      Winter-Hjelm, O.

Wir glauben an Gott den Vater (Horn)
  See: Aldrig er jeg uden vaade
  (Horn)

Wir haben schwerlich (1648)
              Z 2099
    Gore, R. T.

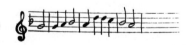

Wir wollen alle froehlich sein *
  (Spangenberg)

      Werner, F. E. H.

Wo Gott, der Herr, nicht bei uns *
  (Wittenberg)

      Bornefeld, H.   Lagergren, A.
      Dueben, A.   Schwartz, G. Von
      Gore, R. T.   Sweelinck, J. P.

    Variants:
    Jag haver en gaang varit ung

      Lindberg, O. F.

    O Jesu, naer jag haedan skall

      Andersson, R.
      Knutzen, I.

Wo Gott zum Haus (Klug) *

      Gore, R. T.   Schwartz, G. Von
      Klenz, W.

Wo soll ich fliehen hin (Regnart)
  See: Auf meinen lieben Gott
  (Regnart)

Wohl dem, der in Gottes Furcht
  (Strassburg)
                     Z 299

      Gore, R. T.

Wohlauf, die ihr hungrig seid *
  (Bohemian)

      Drischner, M.

Wolvercote (Ferguson)

      Thalben-Ball, G.

Wondrous Love (American) *

      Hustad, D.   Parker, A.
      Moyer, J. H.   Wood, D.

Woodlands (W. Greatorex)

      Thalben-Ball, G.

Woodworth (Bradbury) *

      Baumgartner, H. L.
      Johnson, D. N.

Wunderbarer Koenig (Neander)   *

    *Linke, N.   Pepping, E.
     Neubauer, H.   Wilson, R.

    Variant:
    Arnsberg

     Peek, R.

Yorkshire (Wainwright)
    See: Stockport

Zeuch ein zu deinen Toren (Crueger)   *

    Haffner, W.
    Schwartz, P.

Zion klagt mit Angst (Crueger)   *

    Schwartz, G. Von

    Variant:
    Sion klagar med stor smaerta

     Andersson, R.
     Rosenquist, C. E.

Zion's Pilgrim (Mennonite)

    Moyer, J. H.
    Wiebe, E.

Zu Bethlehem geboren   *

    Schroeder, H.

SOME COLLECTIONS OF CHORALE PRELUDES

A Child Is Born	WLSM
Advent to Whitsuntide	Hinrichsen
Album fuer Orgelspieler	C. F. Kahnt
Album Nordischer Komponisten	W. Hansen
*Anthologie (Lutheran Hymns)	Concordia
Anthology of Chorale Preludes 17th & 18th Centuries (Buszin)	Concordia
Anthology of Sacred Music (Buszin)	Concordia
*The Beginning Organist--Palme Op. 5	Hesse
Cantantibus Organis	Pustet
Cantantibus Organis	Van Rossum
Cantantibus Organis	Société Anonyme
Cantus Firmus Praeludien	B. Schott
Cantiones Gregorianae Pro Organo	B. Schott
Chorale Preludes Ancient & Modern	Peters
Chorale Preludes Old Masters (Stahl)	Steingraeber
Chorale Preludes Old Masters (Straube)	Peters
Christ Is Risen	WLSM
Das Heilige Jahr (Freylinghausen)	W. Mueller
Das Organisten Amt (Ramin)	B & H
*Der Praktische Organist (Luetzel)	Tascher'schen
Die Orgel im Kirchenjahr	Cron Luzern
Eenvoudig Koraalwerk	Ars Nova
Einfache Orgelvorspiele (Weber)	C. Kaiser
Einfache Vorspiele	Merseburger
Festal Voluntaries	Novello
First Four Centuries of Organ Music (Klein)	Assoc. Music Press
Forspil til Salmemelodier i Kirkestil	W. Hansen
Golden Treasury (Pfatteicher)	Presser
*Hering's Organ Music	Rieter-Biedermann
Hymn Preludes for the Mennonite Hymnal	Goshen College
Hymn Tune Preludes for Organ (Shanko)	Broadman
Introitus Preludier	Nordiska
*Kleemeyer's Collection, Op. 17	Siegel
Koralfoerspel (Andersson & Norrman)	Nordiska
*Laudamus Dominum (Rosel & Bangert)	Concordia
Les Maîtres Français de l'Orgue (17th & 18th Centuries)	Schola Cantorum
Liber Organi	B. Schott
L'Organiste Liturgique	Schola Cantorum

---

*Asterisks indicate titles out of print.

295

The Lutheran Organist (Reuter)	Concordia
Masterpieces of Organ Music	Liturgical Music Press
*Merk's Collection of Chorale Preludes	Leuckart
Muziek voor Kerk en Huis	Basart
Netherlands Organ Music (Hendriks)	Seyffardt
Neue Orgelvorspiele (Haag--Hennig)	Merseburger
The New Organist (1874)	J. Schuberth
Oktogon	Schwann
Old Masters of the Early Organ (A. Schering)	B & H
Old Masters of the Organ	Peters
One Faith in Song	WLSM
*Organ Fantasies on Ancient Hymns & Chorales	Lorenz
Organ Masters of the 17th & 18th Centuries	Kalmus
Organ Music for Christmas (Trevor)	Oxford
Organ Preludes, Ancient & Modern (Sumner)	Hinrichsen
*Organ Works of Modern Masters (Diebold)	O. Junne
Orgelbuch zum E. K. G. (O. Brodde)	Baerenreiter
Orgel Choraele Sammlung	Metzler
Orgel Kompositionen aus Alter & Neuer Zeit (Gauss)	Coppenrath
Orgelspiel im Kirchenjahr (Rohr)	B. Schott
Orgelvorspiele (Poppen, Reich & Strube)	Merseburger
Orgelvorspiele zu den Melodien des Choralbuchs (Grosse--Weischede)	Leuckart
Orgue et Liturgie	Schola Cantorum
*Palme, Op. 50	Hesse
Parish Organist	Concordia
Postludier (Runbaeck & Aahlen)	Nordiska
Preludes and Postludes (Held)	Augsburg
Preludes for Hymns in the Worship Supplement	Concordia
Preludes on Well-Known Hymn Tunes	Broadman
Pro Organo (Karlsen & Nielsen)	Lyche
Progressive Organist	Elkin & Co.
*Reinbrecht's Prelude Book	Vieweg
*Reinhard's "Cecilia"	B & H
*Ritter's Collection	Ries & Erler
Sacred Organ Folio	Lorenz
Seasonal Chorale Preludes (Trevor)	Oxford
*Selected Organ Compositions (Sering)	Siegel
Slaagt skal Foelge slaagters gang (Bitsch & Petersen)	W. Hansen
Te Deum Laudamus	Willemsen
*Volkmar Organ Album	Peters
Voluntaries for the Christian Year	Abingdon
Voluntaries on the Hymn of the Week	Concordia
*Zimmer, Op. 32, The Beginning Organist	Vieweg
*Zorn's Prelude Collection	Heinrichshofen
21 Orgelchoraeler Schweizerischer Komponisten	Krompholz
29 Koralforspill av Norske Organister (Sandvold)	Norsk
73 Leichte Choralpraeludien Alter & Neuer Meister (Fleischer)	Leuckart
80 Chorale Preludes by German Masters (Keller)	Peters
95 Forspil till Salmemelodier	Boesens

ADDITIONAL PUBLISHERS IN SUPPLEMENT

A R Editions--New Haven, Conn.
Basart--Amsterdam, Netherlands
Berandol--Scarborough, Ontario, Canada
Bosworth--London
Coburn Press--Sherman, Conn.
D. T. O. (Denkmaeler der Tonkunst in Oesterreich)--Oesterreichischer
    Bundesverlag, Wien
Editio Musica--Budapest, Hungary
Ed. Musicale Transatlantique--Paris, France
Electro Voice--Buchanan, Mich.
Elkan, Schildknecht, Carelius--Stockholm, Sweden
Eriks Musikhandel--Stockholm, Sweden
B. Filser--Augsburg, Germany
Fortress Press--Philadelphia, Penn.
Mark Foster Music Co. --Marquette, Mich.
R. R. Ganzevoort--Amsterdam, Netherlands
Goshen College--Goshen, Ind.
Gwynn Publ. Co. --Wales
Hirsch Foerlag--Stockholm, Sweden
Johnson Reprint Corp. --New York and London
Klecken Verlag--Germany
Koerlings Foerlag--Stockholm, Sweden
K. Littman--Breslau, Poland
Lundquists Musikfoerlag--Stockholm, Sweden
Procure de Clergé, Music Sacrée--Paris, France
Quintopus--Toronto, Ontario, Canada
Sacred Songs--Waco, Texas
Salabert--Paris, France
STIM--Manuscript Library--Stockholm, Sweden
Verbum Foerlag--Stockholm, Sweden
Verein voor Nederlandse Musiekgeschiedenis--Amsterdam, Netherlands
WESS (Wessmans Musikfoerlag)--Slite, Sweden
WORD Music--Waco, Texas

ADDITIONAL BOOKS AND HYMNALS IN SUPPLEMENT

Christian Science Hymnal. Boston, 1937.
Koralbok foer Skola och Hem (ed. O. Lindberg, H. Weman, D. Wikander).
    Stockholm: Kyrkliga Centralfoerlaget, 1968.
Liber Usualis. Tournai, Belgium: Desclée & Co., 1952.
Organ Literature: A Comprehensive Survey, by Corliss Richard Arnold.
    Metuchen, N.J.: Scarecrow Press, 1973.
Svensk Koralbok (ed. K. Peters & A. Runbaeck). Lund, Sweden: C. W. K.
    Gleerups Foerlag, 2nd Ed., 1941.
450 Noëls (M. Rouher). Paris: L. J. Biton (Schola Cantorum), 1910.

APPENDIX: REVISIONS OF ORIGINAL INDEX*

ADDED DATES AND NATIONALITIES,
VOLUME I, "COMPOSER INDEX"

Ahlberg, Verner 1896-1967
Alain, Albert 1880-1971
Albrecht, Georg von 1891-
Archer, J. Stewart 1866-
Arnold, Corliss Richard 1926-
Asma, Feike 1912-
Balogh, Louis A. 1895-1971
Bauer, Juerg German 1918-
Baumgartner, Henry Leroy 1891-1969
Berg, Gottfrid 1889-1970
Betteridge, Leslie English 1903-
Bielawa, Herbert American 1930-
Bingham, Seth 1882-1972
Black, Charles 1903-
Blatný, Joseph 1891-
Bonnal, Joseph Ermend 1880-1944
Breydert, Friedrich Matthias 1909-
Briegel, Wolfgang Carl German
Broughton, Russell 1895-1969
Buchner, Adolph E. 1826-1908
Buck, Percy Carter 1871-1947
Bunjes, Paul G. 1914-
Cellier, Alexandre 1883-1968
Claussman, Aloys French 1850-1926
Coleman, Richard H. P. 1888-1965
Commette, Edouard 1883-1967
Cummins, Richard 1936-
David, Thomas Christian German
Debois, Christian H. Danish 1882-1960
Dickinson, Peter 1934-
Dressler, John Austrian-American 1923-
Drischner, Max 1891-1971
Dupré, Marcel J. J. 1886-1971

Eberlin, Johann E. Austrian
Eder, Helmut Austrian 1916-
Edmundson, Garth 1893-1971
Erb, Marie Joseph 1858-1944
Feibel, Fred 1906-
Fletcher, Percy E. 1879-1932
Foote, Arthur 1853-1937
Frandsen, Herluf Bo Danish Contemporary
Frank, René German-American 1910-1965
Franke, Friedrich Wilhelm German 1861-1932
Gardner, John Linton 1917-
Gehrenbeck, David American
Geist, Christian Swedish ?-1711
Gibbs, Cecil Armstrong 1889-1960
Goemanne, Noel Belgian-American
Goode, Jack C. 1921-
Grabner, Hermann 1886-1969
Graham, Robert V. American 1912-
Grieb, Herbert C. 1898-
Hasse, Karl 1883-1960
Hassler, Hans Leo German 1564-1612
Healey, Derek Edward English 1936-
Hemmer, Eugene American 1929-
Hollins, Alfred 1865-1942
Hopkins, Edward J. 1818-1901
Horst, Anthon Van der 1899-1965
Huber, Paul 1918-
Huston, John 1915-
Ireland, John 1879-1962
Jacob, Dom Clément 1906-

*New material is underlined.

299

Jenkins, Joseph Wilcox American
    1928-
Keller, Hermann 1885-1967
Kinder, Ralph 1876-1952
Kint, Cor 1890-1947
Kort, Jac 1910-
Lang, Craig S. 1891-1971
Langstroth, Ivan Shed 1887-1971
Larson, Earl Roland ?-1970
Lewis, John Leo 1911-1971
Lublin, Johannes Polish 16th Century
Mader, Clarence 1904-1971
Maleingreau, Paul de 1887-1956
Marty, Adolphe 1865-1942
Mawet, Lucien Belgian 1875-1947
McClain, Charles S. Canadian
McKay, George Frederick 1899-1970
Melin, Hugo Swedish 1907-
Middleschulte, Wilhelm 1863-1943
Morén, John Teodor 1854-1932
Mulder, Ernest W. Dutch 1898-1959
Near, Gerald 1942-
Nelhybel, Vaclaw Czech 1919-
Nelson, Ronald A. American 1929-
Nieland, Herman Dutch
Nivers, Guillaume Gabriel 1632-1714
Noyon, Joseph 1888-
Olsson, Lennart 1925-
Olsson, Otto Emanuel 1879-1964
Owen, Barbara J. 1933-
Parviainen, Jarmo 1928-
Pasquet, Jean 1896-
Peloquin, C. Alexander 1918-
Perilhou, Albert French 1846-1936
Philip, Achille 1878-1959
Piedelièvre, Paul French 1902-1964
Pillney, Karl Hermann German 1896-
Planchet, D. Charles 1857-1946
Plum, P. J. M. Belgian 1899-1944
Poppen, Hermann Meinhard 1885-
    1952
Porter, Ambrose P. 1885-1971
Quehl, Hieronymous F. 18th Century
Quignard, J. René French 1887-
Raison, André circa 1650-1719
Reading, John 1677-1764
Roberts, Myron J. 1912-
Rohwer, Jens Danish
Salem, Bernhard von 16th Century
Schaffer, Robert J. American
Schehl, J. Alfred 1882-1959
Schiske, Karl 1916-1969
Schmidt, Franz Austrian
Schoof, Armin 1940-
Sinzheimer, Max 1894-
Skagerberg, Einar Swedish 1876-1969
Soederholm, Valdemar Swedish 1909-
Sowande, Fela 1905-

Speed, Robert M. 1930-
Speth, Johannes German
Stam, George Dutch 1905-
Steel, Christopher C. English 1939-
Steigleder, Johann Ulrich 1593-1635
Stout, Alan 1932-
Surzynski, M. 1866-1924
Tachezi, Herbert Austrian 1930-
Thyrestam, Gunnar Swedish 1900-
Villard, Jean Albert 1920-
Wagner, Alexander 1926-
Walton, Kenneth English-American
    1904-
Weinberger, Jaromir 1896-1967
Weitz, Guy Belgian-English 1884-
    1970
White, Louie 1921-
Williams, David Henry Welsh-
    American
Witte, Christian Friedrich 1660-1716

Aahgren, K. E. --"Vi takke dig": Insert (Swedish) after word "dig"

Ahle, J. R. --"Ich ruf' zu dir": delete (Scheidt)

Ahrens, J. --add underlined words: "Ecce Panis Angelorum (Mode 8)"
　　　　　　　　　　　　　　　　　　"Pater Noster (Liturgical)"
　　　　　　　　　　　　　　　　　　"Salve Regina (Mode 1)"
　　　　　　　　　　　　　　　　　　"Te Deum (Tone 3)"

Altrup, C. --delete; this is same as Attrup, Carl

Bach, J. C. --Parish Organist, Vol. 3: delete "Herr Gott dich loben"
　　　　　　　　and insert "Nun lob', mein Seel, den Herren"

Bach, W. F. --"Wir danken dir, Herr Jesu Christ": insert (Breslau)
　　　　　　　　after word "Christ".
　　　　　　　　Complete Organ Works (ed. Biggs)
　　　　　　　　"Christ, der du bist" should be "Christe, der du bist"
　　　　　　　　add: "Jesu, meine Freude"
　　　　　　　　　　　"Was mein Gott will"
　　　　　　　　　　　"Wir Christenleut (Fritsch)"
　　　　　　　　　　　"Wir danken dir, Herr Jesu Christ (Breslau)"

Baden, C. --12 Orgelkoraler over Norske Folkstoner: now published by
　　　　　　　　Lyche

Bangert, Emilius F. C. --add F. C. to name; publisher is W. Hansen

Barber, S. --Chorale Prelude on "Silent Night". Add: Op. 37

Barrow, Robert George--add George to name

Baeuerle, H. --enter on p. 39 and delete from p. 47

Beck, A. --76 Chorale Preludes: "Lasset uns mit Jesu": insert (Bolze)
　　　　　　　　after word "Jesu"

Benoist, F. --entry should read:
　　　　　　　　"Les Maîtres Français de l'Orgue (17 & 18 Siècles). . . .
　　　　　　　　　　　　　　　　　　Ed. Mus. de la Schola Cantorum
　　　　　　　　"Ave Maris Stella": insert (Mode 1) after "Stella"

Beyer, Michael--insert first name, Frank, before Michael

Bijster, J.--first name is Jacob

Blithman, W.--"Jesu Redemptor Omnium": insert (Sarum) after "Omnium"

Boehm, George--first name is Georg
          Chorale Preludes. . . . . B & H: should read:
          Choralbearbeitungen
          "Aus tiefer Not": insert (Phrygian) after "Not"

Bottazzi, Fra B.--L'Organiste Liturgique: insert Vol. 14

Briegel, W. C.--nationality is German, not Dutch

Bush, G.--insert Carillon before "Es ist ein Ros' "

Buxtehude, D.--Complete Works, Vol. 2: delete Chorale Preludes and
          insert Choralbearbeitungen
          Organ Works (ed. Keller), Part II: delete Chorale Preludes
          and insert Choralbearbeitungen

Cassler, G. W.--Music for Worship: insert (with easy pedals) before
          (ed. Johnson)

Claussnitzer, P.--Op. 49: 20 Preludes for Mourning and Consolation
          "Alle Menschen": insert (Mueller) after "Menschen"

Dandrieu, J. F.--delete entry of Venite Adoremus Book. See Supplement

Delestre, Chanoine R.--publisher is Schola Cantorum, not Langlais

Drakeford, R.--"Virgin Unspotted" should be: "Virgin Most Pure (English)"

Drummond, Wolff--delete entry; same as Wolff, S. Drummond

Elmore, R. H.--2 Chorale Preludes: add "Ave Maria (Arcadelt)"

Erbach, C.--"Lucis Creator Optime": insert (Sarum) after "Optime"

Fisher, N. Z.--publisher is C. Fischer, not Galaxy

Gilbert, N.--Titles should read: Pastorale on "Rockingham"; Sortie on
          "Laus Deo"

Griffiths, T. V.--Title should read: Trisagion on "Nicaea"

Harris, W. H.--Title should read: Fantasy on "Easter Hymn"

Hassler, H. L.--Entry should read: Fugue, Baroque Suite (ed. Bedell)
          "Vater Unser"

Heiller, A.--Title should read: Partita on "Freu dich sehr"

Heiss, H.--Title should read: 3 Chorale Partitas for Organ . . . B & H

Hill, L. E.--"St. Botolph": insert (Slater) after "Botolph"
          "St. Columba": insert (Irish) after "Columba"

Jimenez, M. B.--Publisher is Morelia

Johns, D.--Meditation on "St. Michael":   publisher is Doblinger, not
        Assoc. Music Press

Johnson, D. N.--Music For Worship: insert (with easy pedals) before
        (ed. Johnson)

Krapf, G.--2nd Organ Sonata: add: "Kremser" and "Nun danket alle Gott"

Kropfreiter, A. F.--Add: Partita after the following titles:
        "Ich wollt, dass ich daheime war"
        "Maria durch ein Dornwald"
        "Wenn mein Stuendlein"

Langlais, J. F.--under Suite Medievale: add:
        Meditation on "Ubi Caritas" and "Jesu Dulcis Memoria"
        Acclamation on "Christus Vincit (Gregorian)"

LeBègue, N. A.--4 Organ Pièces: entry should read:
        L'Organiste Liturgique, #8 . . . . Schola Cantorum
        4 Organ Pièces:
            Offertory on "Stabat Mater"

Ley, H. G.--"St. Columba":   insert (Irish) after "Columba"

Luebeck, V.--Insert Chaconne before "Lobt Gott, ihr Christen"

Manz, P.--10 Chorale Improvisations: Set 1 is Op. 5, Set 2 is Op. 7

Matthews, H. A.--Chorale Improvisation on "In Dulci Jubilo":
        publisher is H. W. Gray, not G. Schirmer

Merkel, G. A.--Op. 166:   "Wer nur den lieben Gott": insert (Neumark)
        after "Gott".
        Op. 137:   insert -Phrygian after word "Not".
        Seasonal Chorale Preludes (Pedals) (ed. Trevor)
            Book I: add "Ach Gott, wie manches"

Micheelsen, H. F.--change Concerto #5 to Orgelkonzert V
        change Concerto #6 to Orgelkonzert VI
        change Conzert VII to Orgelkonzert VII: Der Morgenstern
            ("Wie schoen leuchtet")
        change Orgelconcert to Orgelkonzert on "Es sungen drei
            Engel"

Miles, R. H.--3 Improvisations: add: "Something for Jesus"
        Delete "Zephyr"; add "Olive's Brow"

Nieland, H.--Fantasie: publisher is Wagenaar, not Alsbach.

Nielsen, L.--Orgelkoraler: "Jeg vil mig Herren love":   insert (Zinck)
        after word "love"

Oley, J. C.--4 Chorale Preludes: insert (ed. W. Emery)

Pach, W.--entry should read: Partita Canonica on "Vater Unser"

Pachelbel, J.--change Chorale Preludes to Choralbearbeitungen

Pasquet, J.--"Deck the Halls": publisher is H. W. Gray, not Ed. B.
            Marks

Peeters, F.--Op. 93: Entrata Festiva: add: (with trumpets, trombones
            and timpani)

Petrich, R. T.--Music For Worship: insert (with easy pedals) after the
            word "Worship"

Pillney, K. H.--Publisher is B & H, not Assoc. Music Press

Ratcliffe, D.--Entry should read: Flourish on "Wurtemburg"

Redford, J.--First Four Centuries of Music for Organ: publisher is
            Assoc. Music Press, not Crofts

Reger, M.--Op. 145:   #2: delete "Bohemian Brethren", add "Was Gott tut"
                      #3: add "Ach, was soll ich" and "Es kommt ein
                           Schiff"
                      #5: delete "O Durchbrecher (Halle)" and
                           add "Auferstanden, auferstanden"
                      #7: add "Austrian Hymn"
            Glorious Things of Thee Are Spoken: delete "Ein feste Burg"
            and add "Nun danket alle Gott"

Respighi, O.--#3 is "Ich hab' mein Sach (Cassel)"

Rogers, S. E.--Contemporary Organ Settings of Familiar Hymns: add
            "Work Song"

Rumpf, W.--Change Chorale Preludes to 15 Choralvorspiele

Salonen, S.--Koralfoerspel, Vol. 3, Op. 29: "Mae kauniin tiedaeaen" is
            correct spelling

Schroeder, H.--Op. 66 should read: Op. 11
            "In Dulci Jubilo": add: and "Vom Himmel hoch"
            "Schoenster Herr Jesu": insert (Muenster) after "Jesu"

Schwartz, G. von--Publisher is Verein Organistengilde Kiel (1937)

Schoff, A.--correct spelling is Schoof

Shroyens, R.--correct spelling is Schroyens

Slater, G. A.--Insert Canticle on before "St. Fulbert"
            Insert (Slater) after "Botolph" in "St. Botolph"

Spranger, J.--For Advent and Christmas: change the word Chorales to
            Church Songs

Stout, A.--Op. 58 now published by Augsburg

Thompson, Van Denman--under Hymn Meditations, Vol. 3, delete "Need"
            and add "Doane"

Titcomb, E. H.--Wedding Day: publisher is H. W. Gray, not Flammer

Tunder, F. --Collected Chorale Works for Organ: insert (ed. Walter)

Vaerge, A. --"Jesu, er mit liv i live":   insert (Wessnitzer) after "live"

Webber, W. S. L. --Prelude on "Helmsley":   change Prelude to Rhapsody.

White, Louie--now published by H. W. Gray

Willan, H. --6 Chorale Preludes: publisher is Concordia, not Oxford

Wikander, D. --Variations on 2 Chorales: delete "Ich dank dir, lieber
                    Herr"

Winter-Hjelm, O. --72 Chorale Preludes: change to 72 Lette Koralvorspil

Zachau, F. W. --Change Chorale Preludes to Choralbearbeitungen. . .B & H

NEW TUNE VARIANTS IN VOLUME II
"TUNE NAME INDEX"

Ach, was soll ich--add: Variant--Whither the Burden (from p. 1140)

Ach, wir armen Suender--add: Variant--Laus Tibi Christe (German)
   (p. 884)

Boenhoer mig, Gud = Variant of En syndig man (in Supplement)

Braun = Variant of Ave Maria zart (Weisse) (p. 666)

Christ Is Born = Noël - Le Messie vient de Naître (in Supplement)

Come Shepherds Awake = Noël - Allons Pasteurs (in Supplement)

Der Tag der ist so freudenreich--add: Variant--En Jungfru foedde (p. 743)

Die Sach' ist dein = Variant of Hier liegt vor deiner (Haydn) (p. 815)

Eins wuensch ich mir = Variant of Herr und Aeltster (Moravian) (p. 805)

Fountain (Early American) = Variant of Cleansing Fountain (Mason) (p. 693)

Great God = Grand Dieu = Variants of Noël - Grand Dei, ribon ribeine
   (p. 935)

Greenville (Rousseau) = Variant of Cramer (Rousseau) (p. 696)
   Delete tune on p. 788

Hit, O Jesu, samloms vi (Briegel) = Variant of Liebster Jesu (?Crueger)
   (p. 888)

Holland (Verspoet's) = Variant of Wahrer Gott, wir glauben dir (p. 1123)

Ich ruf' zu dir, Herr Jesu Christ (Klug)--add: Variant: Jeg raaber Herre
   Jesu Krist (Wittenberg) (p. 849)

Invicte Martyr Unicum (Mode 5)--add: Variant--Martyr Dei (insert on
   p. 908)

Jesus, My Heart's Delight (Pennsylvania Dutch) = Variant of Mache dich,
   mein Geist, bereit (Dresden) (p. 901)

Let Us Sing Loudly = Noël - Chantons, je vous prie (p. 935)

My Shepherd Will Supply (Early American) = Variant of Resignation (U. S.
        Southern) (p. 1025)

O du Helge Ande, kom till oss in = Variant of Veni, Sancte Spiritus (Old
        Church) (see Supplement)

O Durchbrecher alle Bande (Halle - Freylinghausen)--add: Variant:
        Auferstanden, auferstanden (p. 658 & 959)

O wie selig seid ihr doch (Crueger)--add: Variant--O huru saella aero ej
        de fromma

St. Edith (Knecht)--add: Variant: St. Hilda (Knecht) (p. 1037)

St. Edmund (Sullivan) = Variant of Fatherland (Sullivan) (p. 760)

St. Hilda--delete (Barnby); add (Knecht) and add: See: St. Edith (Knecht)
        delete tune entry

St. Mary (Hackney) = St. Mary (Pry's)

Shepherds of the Mountains = Noël - Pastre dei mountagne (Saboly) (see
        Supplement)

Sleep Holy Child (Dutch) = Dors, ma colombe (see Supplement)

Tonus Peregrinus--See also Magnificat (Tone 9) (p. 906)

Winchester Old (Tye)--add: Variant--Old 84th (insert on p. 983)

CORRECTIONS AND ADDITIONS TO TUNES, VOLUME II

Albano (Novello) For correction see Supplement.

Benton Harbor: Key signature should be 2 sharps.

Consolation (Lindeman): Last measure of tune should be:

Eola (Sellers): First note of tune should be octave lower.

Erstanden ist der Heil'ge Christ (Triller) See Supplement.
 Add this tune on p. 748 and enter under it: Walther, J. G. (3)

Es flog ein kleins Waldvoegelein
 Delete Taeublein weisse; delete Schroeder, H.

Es flog ein Taeublein weisse (15th Century) See Supplement.
 Add this tune on p. 749 and enter under it: Schroeder, H.

Evan (Havergal): Rhythm should be:

Gaudens Gaudebo (Gregorian)
 Put on p. 771

Green Hill (Stebbins) Rhythm should be:

Heart of God Last measure should be:

Heer, ik hoor See Supplement

Hic Breve Vivitur (Pettet)
 Put on p. 814

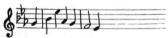

In stiller Nacht (Folk) See Supplement
 Add this tune on p. 841 and enter under it: Schroeder, H.

In the Shadow of His Wings
 Rhythm should be:

Intercessor (Parry) See Supplement

King's Majesty (George) Key signature should be 3 sharps.

Morning Star (Southern Harmony)
    Pinkham, D.
    Delete Pinkham, D. from under
    Morning Star (Harding)

Name of Jesus (E. S. Lorenz)
    Lorenz, E. J.

St. Hilda (Knecht)
    Delete (Barnby); delete tune entry; add (Knecht)

Siehe, das ist Gottes Lamm
    Put on p. 1056

Song of Symeon (Geneva) Key signature should be 2 sharps.

Surrexit Christus Hodie Delete entire entry, including tune.
    Dunn, J. P.

CORRECTIONS OF INFORMATION, VOLUME II

Ach, was soll ich   Add: Reger, M.

Auferstanden, auferstanden   Variant of O Durchbrecher (p. 959)
    Add on p. 658 and p. 959
    Delete: Reger, M. under O Durchbrecher and add under
      Auferstanden

Bohemian Brethren   Delete: Reger, M.

Breslau (Leipzig) Under Wir danken dir, Herr Jesu Christ
    add: Bach, J. S. and Bach, W. F.

Christ, der du bist der helle Tag   Delete: Bach, W. F.

Christe, der du bist Tag und Licht   Add: Bach, W. F.

Christe Redemptor Omnium (Sarum)
    Under Jesu Redemptor Omnium (Sarum) add: Blithman, W.

Christi Mutter (German) Delete: Weber, H.

Christi Mutter stand mit Schmerzen   Add: Weber, H.

Christus Vincit (Gregorian) Add: Langlais, J. F.

Copenhagen (Zinck)
    Under Jeg vil mig Herren love add: Nielsen, L.

Den signede dag med fryd (Weyse) Add: Bergh, L.

Den signade dag som vi nu haer se (Thomissoen) Delete: Bergh, L.
    (Note spelling corrections)

Doane Add: Thompson, V. D.

Es kommt ein Schiff geladen (Andernach) Add: Reger, M.

Fairest Lord Jesus (Muenster)
    Under variant Schoenster Herr Jesu (Muenster) add: Schroeder, M.

Fons Bonitans Under Pater Noster (Liturgical) add: Ahrens, J.

Greensleeves Delete: Drummond, W.

Herr Jesu Christ, wahr Mensch und Gott (Eccard)
        Under Wir danken dir, Herr Jesu Christ delete: Bach, W. F.

Hoeyr kor Kyrkjeklokka (Norse Folk Tune)
        Under Kjaerlighet er lysets kilde (Norse Folk) add: Drischner, M.

Ich hab' mein Sach Gott heimgestellt (Cassel) Add: Respighi, O.

In stiller Nacht (Latin - German) Delete: Schroeder, H.

Jesu Dulcis Memoria (Mode 1) Add: Langlais, J. F.

Jesu Redemptor Omnium Delete: Blithman, W.

Kjaerlighet er lysets kilde (Lindeman) Delete: Drischner, M.

Lucis Creator Optime (Angers) Delete: Erbach, C.

Lucis Creator Optime (Sarum - Mode 8) Add: Erbach, C.

Name of Jesus (Strom) Delete: Lorenz, E. J.

Netherlands (Valerius) Under Kremser add: Krapf, G.

Nun danket alle Gott (Crueger) Add: Krapf, G.

Olive's Brow Add: Miles, R. H.

Om nogen til ondt mig lokke vil (Haereid) Delete: Drischner, M.

Om nogen til ondt mig lokke vil (Norsk - Ehrenbord) Add: Drischner, M.

Pater Noster Delete: Ahrens, J.

Psalm 24 (Geneva - Marot)
        Under Meine Seele ist still zu Gott Delete: Kaminski, H. (See
          Supplement)

Puer Natus Est Nobis Add: Ahrens, J. and Titcomb, E. H.

Puer Nobis Nascitur (Praetorius) Dandrieu, P. (Not J. F.)
        Under Variant Puer Natus Est Nobis Delete: Ahrens, J. and
          Titcomb, E. H.

Schoenster Herr Jesu (Silesian) Delete: Schroeder, H.

Surrexit Christus Hodie   Z 287
        Under Erstanden ist der Heil'ge Christ Delete: Walther, J. G. (3)

Te Deum Laudamus (Tone 3) Add: Ahrens, J. and Nelhybel, V.

Te Deum Laudamus (Tone 8) Delete: Ahrens, J. and Nelhybel, V.

Ubi Caritas Et Amor Add: Langlais, J. F.

Vi tacke dig, O Jesu god (Swedish) Add: Aahgren, K. E.

Virgin Most Pure (English) Add: Drakeford, R.

Virgin Unspotted (American) Delete: Drakeford, R.

Vom Himmel hoch, da komm ich her Add: Schroeder, H.

Winchester Old (Tye) Add: Variant: Old 84th

Wer nur den lieben Gott Ludwig, Max (Not C. A.)

Wir danken dir, Herr Jesu Christ, dass du fuer uns (Wittenberg)
    Under Vi takka dig delete: Aahgren, K. E.

Work For the Night Is Coming (Mason)
    Under Work Song add: Rogers, S. E.

Zephyr Delete: Miles, R. H.

ADDITIONAL COPYRIGHT ACKNOWLEDGMENTS
VOLUME II (pp. 608ff.)

Song 118a (J. Roentgen) from Psalmen en Gezangen voor de Nederlandse
    Hervormde Kerk de Evangelische Gezangen

Song 182 (A. C. Schuurman) Compagnie, N. V., Amsterdam, Netherlands.
    Copyright 1938; used by permission

p. 19   under Ahle, J. R.:   "Mensch willst du leben (Walther)"
p. 28   under Arnatt, R. K.:   H. W. Gray
p. 35   under Bach, J. S.:   Catechism Preludes # 6 & 7
        "Dies sind die Heil'gen Zehn Gebot"
p. 37   under Bach, J. S.:   Orgelbuechlein #25, "Wir danken dir,
        Herr Jesu Christ (Breslau)"
p. 68   under Boellmann, L.:   Offertoire sur deux Noëls
p. 92   under Buxtehude, D.:   after Folio #17, delete (cont'd.)
p. 108 under Commette, E.:   Offertoire ("Regent Square"). . . H. W. Gray
p. 109/110   Copley, R. E.
p. 110 under Corrette, M.:   L'Organiste Liturgique, Vol. 3 . .
p. 113 under Dalm, W.:   "Nu sijt wellekomme"
p. 128 under Dragt, J.:   Variations on "Nu sijt wellekomme"
p. 128 under Draht, T.:   Op. 56 "Lobe den Herren, den"
p. 129 under Driessler, J.:   Organ Sonatas, 1. Advent "Es kommt ein
        Schiff"
p. 130 under Driessler, J.:   delete 12 Chorale Preludes on Great Hymns.
        . . J. Fischer
        "Adeste Fideles" "Veni Emmanuel"
p. 146 under Erb, M. J.:   Sorties: "Jesu, Notre Maître"
p. 151 under Fasolo, Giovanni B.:   Orgue et Liturgie, Vol. 8
p. 192 under Grieb, H. C.:   G. Schirmer
p. 233 under Hollfelder, W.:   delete O before Partita
p. 234 under Hoogewoud, H.:   "Nu sijt wellekomme"
p. 236 under Hovland, E.:   Great White Host ("Den store hvite Flok")
p. 260 under Kauder, H.:   E. C. Schirmer
p. 261 under Kauffmann, G. F.:   Seasonal Chorale Preludes (Pedal)
        (ed. Trevor) Bk. 2 . . . . Oxford
p. 261 under Kee, C.:   Cantantibus Organis
        "Nu sijt wellekomme"
        Easter Song, Jesus Lives ("Jesu, meine Zuversicht")
p. 282 under Krapf, G.:   "Quempas Carol"
p. 302/3   change ø to oe
p. 328 under Matthison-Hansen, F.:   ("Nun Botschaft kam . . .
p. 335 under Mens, L. J.:   "Nu sijt wellekomme"
p. 340 under Metzler, F.:   3 Hymns "Heut singt die liebe"
p. 344 under Michel, A.:   15 Vor- und Nachspiele . . Th. L. Verne
p. 347 under Moeller, S. O.:   change Op. 8 to Op. 5
p. 355 under Mueller-Zuerich, P.:   25 Orgelchoraele (Neue Folge) Op. 63
        "Mein schoenste Zier (In dich hab ich-Leipzig)" (2)

*Changes are underlined.

313

p. 368 under Nuenen, J. Van: "Nu sijt wellekomme"
p. 404 under Plag, J.: ("Komm Heil'ger Geist")
p. 412 Quignard, J. René is correct spelling of name
p. 418 under Ranse, M. de: Ed. Le Grand Orgue
p. 432 under Rheinberger, J.: Seasonal Chorale Preludes, add Bk. I
p. 438 under Rinck, J. C. H.: Vol. 2--"Schmuecke dich"
p. 459 under Sandvold, A.: Op. 5: delete (Freylinghausen)
p. 490 under Siedel, M.: Bk. 4--"Kommt her zu mir (Leipzig)"
p. 491/2 delete commas after Sister
p. 497 under Speuy, H. J.: publisher is Heuwekemeijer
p. 505 under Stoegbauer, I.: Op. 4--Choralfantasie on ...
p. 526 transfer "Hoeren I, vor Herre kalder" and
        "Hoer vor Helligaftens-Boen" to p. 525
p. 539 under Vermulst, J.: "Nu sijt wellekomme"
p. 540 under Verrees, L.: Prelude on O For a Closer Walk. . H. W. Gray
p. 545 "Seelenbraeutigam"
p. 549 under Volckmar, T.: Bk. I: "Ach Gott, erhoer mein Seufzen"
p. 553 under Walcha, H.: Vol. 3--24 Chorale Preludes
p. 556 under Walther, J. G.: "Erstanden ist der (Triller)"
p. 559 under Walther, J. G.: Orgelspiel im Kirchenjahr
        "Erstanden ist der (Triller)"
p. 559 under Walther, J. G.: Seasonal Chorale Preludes (Manuals) Bk. II
        "Erstanden ist der (Triller)"
p. 566 under Weegenhuise, J.: Passacaglia on "O Gloriosa Virginum"
p. 573 under Westering, P. C. van: Variations on "Nu sijt wellekomme"
p. 583 under Wikander, D.: "Kom, Helge Ande, Herre Gud" and "I denna
        ljuva sommartid"
p. 600 under Zachau, F. W.: Book II "Nun lasst uns Gott (Selnecker)"

TYPOGRAPHICAL ERRORS AND NEW SOURCES, VOL. II

p. 623 under "Christus der ist mein Leben": Scheidt, S.
p. 631 "Ack, hjaertans ve"
p. 637 "All Morgen ist ganz frisch und neu (Walther)"
p. 651 "Angel's Song"
p. 658 insert: "Auferstanden, auferstanden" See: "O Durchbrecher (Halle)"
p. 663 under "Aus tiefer Not (Strassburg)": Kuntze, C.
p. 677 under "Breslau": "Ach bleib bei uns"
p. 685 under "Christe, aller Welt Trost": Bach, J. S. (2)
p. 686 under "Christe, Qui Lux Est": See: "Christe, der du bist Tag und
        Licht"
p. 690 "Christus ist auferstanden (Cologne)"
p. 697 "Crimond (Irvine)" (Not (Scotch))
p. 719 under "Die Kirche ist ein altes Haus": Variants: "Gammal aer
        kyrkan"
p. 723 "Dig skall min sjael"
p. 762 "Foerlossningen" See: "Herr Christ, der einig Gottes Sohn"
p. 793 "Han som paa jorden bejler" See: "Hilf Gott, dass mir's gelinge
        (Thomissoen)"
p. 807 "Herre, jeg hjertelig oensker (Folk)"
p. 809 "Herzlich lieb hab' ich dich"
p. 824 "I denna ljuva sommartid (Soederblom)"
p. 831 "Ich komme vor dein Angesicht" See: "Wo Gott zum Haus nicht"
p. 846 to last entry of "Ita Missa Est" add (Gregorian)
p. 850 "Jeg vil mig Herren love (Dutch Psalm - Thomissoen)"
p. 850 "Jeg vil mig Herren love (Norse Folk)" See: Mit hjerte alltid
p. 850 "Jeg ville lova och prisa"
p. 852 & 860 "Jesu aer min haegnad" See: "Jesu, meine Freude"

p. 854   "Jesu Corona Virginum (Mode 8)"   See: "Deus Tuorum Militum
                                                   (Latin - Mode 8)"
p. 857   "Jesus fraan Nasaret (Nordquist)"
p. 864   "Jesu Redemptor Omnium (Sarum)"   See: "Christe Redemptor
                                                   (Sarum - Mode 1)"
p. 867   "Julen har engelyd (Thomissoen)"
p. 871 /2 "Kom, Helge Ande, Herre Gud"
p. 876   "Komt Zielen, dieze Dag"
p. 887   under "Liebster Jesu, wir sind hier (Ahle)" Bach, J. S. (6)
p. 912   "Mein Jesu, dem die Seraphinen (Kuehnau)" Z 5988
p. 918   "Merck toch hoe sterck (Valerius)"
p. 921   "Min sjael, du maaste, nu gloemma (Swedish Folk)"
p. 934   "Noël - A cei-ci le moître de tô l'univar" and transfer to p. 933.
p. 940 & 951 "Nu sijt wellekomme (Netherlands)"
p. 969   "O Jesu, aen de dine"
p. 971   "O Jesu Krist, du naadens brunn"
p. 981   "Ack, hjaertens ve"
p. 1020   "Uns ist gebor'n ein Kindelein"
p. 1034   "St. Columba (Irish)"
p. 1034   "St. Columba (Irons)"
p. 1038   "St. Luke (Clarke)"
p. 1059   "So geh'st du nun, mein Jesu"
p. 1060   "Sol Praeceps (Mode 3)"
p. 1086   all 4 entries: "Taenk naer en gaang"
p. 1092   "Till haerlighetens"
p. 1095   "Tunbridge (Clarke)"
p. 1099   "Ut Queant Laxis (Mode 2)"
p. 1111   "Vi tacke dig, O Jesu god (Swedish)"
p. 1119   "Vruechten"
p. 1121   "Wachet auf, ruft uns die Stimme (Nicolai)"
p. 1128   "Wassail (English)"
p. 1131   "Wenn mein Stuendlein vorhanden ist (Wolff)" Z 4482a
p. 1146   "Winchester New (Crasselius)" Z 2781
p. 1147   "Dig skall min sjael"
p. 1154   "Wo willst du hin" See: "Ach bleib bei uns"
p. 1155   "Woodbird" delete Taeublein weisse
p. 1163   Ed. Musicales de la Schola Cantorum